# BEST-SELLING
# CHAPTERS

## Introductory Level

## Chapters from 8 Books for Young People

*with Lessons for Teaching the Basic Elements of Literature*

JAMESTOWN ⛵ PUBLISHERS

*a division of* NTC/CONTEMPORARY PUBLISHING GROUP
Lincolnwood, Illinois USA

**Cover Design:** Steve Straus
**Cover Illustration:** Michael Steirnagle
**Interior Design:** Steve Straus
**Interior Illustrations:** Unit 1: Jim Buckley; Units 2, 6: Antonio Castro;
Unit 3: Holly Jones; Units 4, 5: Jim Abel; Units 7, 8: David Cunningham

ISBN: 0-89061-890-9 (hardbound)
ISBN: 0-89061-845-3 (softbound)

Published by Jamestown Publishers,
a division of NTC/Contemporary Publishing Group, Inc.
4255 West Touhy Avenue,
Lincolnwood (Chicago), Illinois 60646-1975, U.S.A.
© 1998 NTC/Contemporary Publishing Group, Inc.

890 QB 0987654321

# Acknowledgments

Acknowledgment is gratefully made to the following publishers, authors, and agents for permission to reprint these works. Every effort has been made to determine copyright owners. In the case of any omissions, the Publisher will be pleased to make suitable acknowledgments in future editions.

"The Man Who Comes to Supper" from *The Great Gilly Hopkins* by Katherine Paterson. Copyright © 1978 by Katherine Paterson. Used by permission of HarperCollins Publishers.

"Hatchet" from *Hatchet* by Gary Paulsen. Copyright © 1987 by Gary Paulsen, published by Aladdin Paperbacks.

"The Witch of Blackbird Pond" from *The Witch of Blackbird Pond* by Elizabeth George Speare. Copyright © 1958 by Elizabeth George Speare, a Yearling Book, published by Dell Publishing Co. division of Random House, Inc.

"Ghosts I Have Been" from *Ghosts I Have Been* by Richard Peck. Copyright © 1977 by Richard Peck. Used by permission of Viking Penguin, a division of Penguin Books, USA Inc.

"Shane," excerpt from *Shane* by Jack Schaefer. Copyright, 1949, © renewed 1976 by Jack Schaefer. Reprinted by permission of Houghton Mifflin Company. All rights reserved.

"In Which I Learn My Duties." Reprinted by permission of Farrar, Straus & Giroux, Inc.: Excerpt from *I, Juan de Pareja* by Elizabeth Borton de Treviño. Copyright © 1965, and copyright renewed © 1993 by Elizabeth Borton de Treviño.

"An Hour at the Races" from *Message to Hadrian* by Geoffrey Trease. Copyright © 1955 by Geoffrey Trease, published by Vanguard Press.

"The Black Thing" reprinted by permission of Farrar, Straus & Giroux, Inc.: Excerpt from *A Wrinkle in Time* by Madeleine L'Engle. Copyright © 1962, and copyright renewed © 1990 by Madeleine L'Engle Franklin.

# Contents

# To the Student

This book can help you become a better reader. Its goal is to help you enjoy and understand what you read. It teaches you how to become more involved in what you read so that books will have more meaning for you.

The reading selections in this book are chapters from eight different novels that have proved to be favorites among young people. Each selection has an introduction that provides an overview of what you will read and write about in a particular unit. The introduction also provides information about the novel and its author. Be sure to read this information carefully, since it might include details about the plot that are not included in the chapter or chapters you will be reading. This information will help "set the scene" and will help you better understand the selection, its characters, their actions, and their motivations.

The skills that you learn from this book will serve you well even beyond your school career. In the future you will read with a sharper and more critical eye. You will be alert to details and ideas that you might have missed before. The skills that you learn to become a better reader also can help you become a better speaker and thinker. For example, understanding more about the characters in novels can help you understand more about the people you know.

## Unit Format and Activities

- Each unit begins with an illustration of a scene from the unit selection. The illustration will help you make some predictions about the selection.

- The introduction begins with a summary of the selection and information about the author. It also introduces an important literary concept and gives you an opportunity to develop the concept in your own writing. Finally, it contains questions for you to consider as you read and a list of vocabulary words and their definitions.

- The full text of the selection makes up the next section.

- Following each selection are questions that test your comprehension of story events and your critical thinking skills. Answers to these questions and to other exercises in the unit should be recorded in a personal literature notebook and checked with your teacher.

- Your teacher may provide you with charts to record your progress in developing your comprehension skills: The Comprehension Skills Graph *records* your scores and the Comprehension Skills Profile *analyzes* your scores—providing you with information about the skills on which you need to focus. You can talk with your teacher about ways to work on those skills.

- The next section contains three lessons, which begin with a discussion of the literary skill upon which the unit focuses. Each lesson illustrates a technique that the author uses to develop that skill. For example, you will see how an author uses dialogue, action, and change to create and develop characters.

- Short answer exercises test your understanding of the author's techniques, as illustrated by short excerpts from the selection. You can check your answers to the exercises with your teacher and determine what you need to review.

- Each lesson also includes a writing exercise that guides you in creating an original work, using the techniques you have just studied.

- Discussion guides and a final writing activity round out each unit in the book. These activities will help sharpen your reading, thinking, speaking, and writing skills.

Reading the chapters in this book will enable you to recognize and appreciate the skills it takes to write an interesting story or novel. When you understand what makes a story or novel good, you become a better reader. The writing exercises and assignments will help you become a better writer by giving you practice in using the authors' techniques to make your own stories more interesting.

# Unit I   Character

# The Great Gilly Hopkins
by Katherine Paterson

## About the Illustration

This picture illustrates a scene from the selection you are about to read. Following are some questions that will help you begin to think about the selection. Use details from the picture as clues to answer the questions. Give reasons for your answers.

- Where do you think this story takes place?

- Who do you think the main character is?

- Look at the girl's expression. What might she be thinking and feeling?

# Unit I

## Introduction

## About the Novel

Eleven-year-old Gilly Hopkins dreams of someday meeting and moving in with her beautiful and forever-absent mother. For now, however, she must face the fact that she is a foster child in yet another foster home. Miss Ellis, her caseworker, has left Gilly at the home of Maime Trotter, whom Gilly sees as overweight and stupid. Gilly also doesn't think much of timid William Ernest, the seven-year-old boy whom Mrs. Trotter cares for along with Gilly.

Before this selection begins, readers learn that Gilly has been removed from her former foster home because of her bad behavior. Her foster mother had requested that another home be found for her. Gilly seems proud of her ability to turn people against her and is determined to make enemies in her new home to show that she doesn't belong there either.

# About the Author

Katherine Paterson was born in China, where her parents were missionaries. A few years later, she and her family relocated to the United States to escape the dangers of World War II. Like Gilly, Ms. Paterson moved often as a child, living in eighteen homes before she reached the age of eighteen. Growing up, she lived in Virginia, North Carolina, and West Virginia. She now makes her home in Vermont.

Ms. Paterson often builds her stories around sharply drawn, realistic characters who seem to take on lives of their own. In fact, she has said, "Eventually a character or characters will walk into my imagination and begin to take over my life. I'll spend the next couple of years getting to know them and telling their story."

Ms. Paterson has won awards for several of her books, including *Jacob Have I Loved, The Master Puppeteer, Bridge to Terabithia, Lyddie,* and *Flip-Flop Girl. The Great Gilly Hopkins* was named a Newbery Honor Book in 1979 and also won a number of other awards.

# About the Lessons

The lessons that follow this selection from *The Great Gilly Hopkins* focus on character. Characters are the people or animals who take part in the action of a story. Authors can let readers know what a character is like in several ways: they can describe what the character looks and acts like, what the character thinks and feels, and even what other people in the story think about the character.

# Writing: Creating Your Own Character

In the course of this unit, you will create your own interesting character and write an imaginary scene about the time you first met him or her. The following suggestions will help you get started.

- Imagine it is your first day in a new school. Think of at least three people you might meet. Write down their names.

- For each character, jot down a few notes about what he or she looks and sounds like. If you'd like, you can arrange your notes on three separate cluster maps. Write a character's name in the center of each map. Then surround each name with words or phrases that describe the character.

- Save your notes. You will use them later in the unit.

## Before Reading

The questions below will help you see how Katherine Paterson has created and described the realistic characters in *The Great Gilly Hopkins*. As you read the selection, keep these questions in mind:

- In which passages has the author described what the characters look and act like? What do you learn about the characters in these passages?

- What do you learn about the characters by what they think and feel?

- What do you learn about the characters by the ways in which others react to them?

# Vocabulary Tips

This selection includes some words that may be unfamiliar to you but that are useful for understanding the story. Below, you will find some of these words, their definitions, and sentences that show how the words are used. Look over these words before you begin to read.

**fanatic**     a person with extreme enthusiasm for a cause. My brother is such a <u>fanatic</u> for our team that he wears their colors every day.

**flatter**     to compliment, often without sincerity. Some people expect you to <u>flatter</u> them, and they don't care if you mean what you say.

**emphatically**     positively; definitely. When asked if she wanted another helping of spaghetti, she <u>emphatically</u> nodded her head up and down.

**tic**     an uncontrollable twitching of a muscle or muscles. The nervous student developed a facial <u>tic</u> before every test.

**obscenity**     offensive word or phrase. If you say an <u>obscenity</u> in the classroom, you will be sent to the principal's office.

**trifle**     to deal with something as if it were unimportant. Don't <u>trifle</u> with my feelings; this is important to me.

**seethe**     to be extremely upset or angry. John <u>seethed</u> when he saw that he had been dropped from the team in favor of a less-talented player.

**fracas**     noisy fight. The whole hockey team joined in the angry <u>fracas</u>.

# The Great Gilly Hopkins

Katherine Paterson

## The Man Who Comes to Supper

The room that Mrs. Trotter took Gilly to was about the size of the Nevinses' new station wagon. The narrow bed filled up most of the space, and even someone as skinny as Gilly had to kneel on the bed in order to pull out the drawers of the bureau opposite it. Mrs. Trotter didn't even try to come in, just stood in the doorway slightly swaying and smiling, her breath short from climbing the stairs.

"Why don't you just put your things away in the bureau and get yourself settled? Then when you feel like it, you can come on down and watch TV with William Ernest, or come talk to me while I'm fixing supper."

What an awful smile she had, Gilly thought. She didn't even have all her teeth. Gilly dropped her suitcase on the bed and sat down beside it, kicking the bureau drawers with her toes.

"You need anything, honey, just let Trotter know, OK?"

Gilly jerked her head in a nod. What she needed was to be left alone. From the bowels of the house she could hear the theme song from *Sesame Street*. Her first job would be to improve W.E.'s taste in TV. That was for sure.

"It's goin' to be OK, honey. I know it's been hard to switch around so much."

"I like moving." Gilly jerked one of the top drawers so hard it nearly came out onto her head. "It's boring to stay in one place."

"Yeah." The big woman started to turn and then hesitated. "Well—"

Gilly slid off the bed and put her left hand on the doorknob and stuck her right hand on her hip.

Mrs. Trotter glanced down at the hand on the knob. "Well, make yourself at home. You hear now?"

Gilly slammed the door after her. God! Listening to that woman was like licking melted ice cream off the carton. She tested the dust on the top of the bureau, and then, standing on the bed, wrote in huge cursive curlicues, "Ms. Galadriel Hopkins." She stared at the lovely letters she had made for a moment before slapping down her open palm in the middle of them and rubbing them all away.

The Nevinses' house had been square and white and dustless, just like every other square, white, dustless house in the treeless development where they had lived. She had been the only thing in the neighborhood out of place. Well, Hollywood Gardens was spotless once more. They'd got rid of her. No. She'd got rid of them—the whole stinking lot.

Unpacking even just the few things in her brown suitcase always seemed a waste of time to Gilly. She never knew if she'd be in a place long enough to make it worth the bother. And yet it was something to fill the time. There were two little drawers at the top and four larger ones below. She put her underwear in one of the little ones, and her shirts and jeans in one of the big ones, and then picked up the photograph from the bottom of the suitcase.

Out of the pasteboard frame and through the plastic

cover the brown eyes of the woman laughed up at her as they always did. The glossy black hair hung in gentle waves without a hair astray. She looked as though she was the star of some TV show, but she wasn't. See— right there in the corner she had written "For my beautiful Galadriel, I will always love you." She wrote that to me, Gilly told herself, as she did each time she looked at it, only to me. She turned the frame over. It was still there—the little piece of tape with the name on it. "Courtney Rutherford Hopkins."

Gilly smoothed her own straw-colored hair with one hand as she turned the picture over again. Even the teeth were gorgeous. Weren't girls supposed to look like their mothers? The word "mother" triggered something deep in her stomach. She knew the danger signal. Abruptly she shoved the picture under a T-shirt and banged the bureau drawer shut. This was not the time to start dissolving like hot Jell-O. She went downstairs.

"There you are, honey." Trotter turned away from the sink to greet her. "How about giving me a hand here with this salad?"

"No."

"Oh."

Score a point for Gilly.

"Well"—Trotter shifted her weight to her left foot, keeping her eyes on the carrots she was scraping— "William Ernest is in the living room watching *Sesame Street.*"

"My god, you must think I'm mental or something."

"Mental?" Trotter moved to the kitchen table and started chopping the carrots on a tiny round board.

"Dumb, stupid."

"Never crossed my mind."

"Then why the hell you think I'm going to watch some retard show like that?"

"Listen here, Gilly Hopkins. One thing we better get straight right now tonight. I won't have you making fun of that boy."

"I wasn't making fun of that boy." What was the woman talking about? She hadn't mentioned the boy.

"Just 'cause someone isn't quite as smart as you are, don't give you no right to look down on them."

"Who'm I looking down on?"

"You just said"—the fat woman's voice was rising, and her knife was crashing down on the carrots with vengeance —"you just said William Ernest was"—her voice dropped to a whisper—"retarded."

"I did not. I don't even know the stupid kid. I never saw him in my life before today."

Trotter's eyes were still flashing, but her hand and voice were under control. "He's had a rough time of it in this world, but he's with Trotter now, and as long as the Lord leaves him in this house, ain't anybody on earth gonna hurt him. *In any way.*"

"Good god. All I was trying to say—"

"One more thing. In this house we don't take the Lord's name in vain."

Gilly threw both her hands up in mock surrender. "All right, all right. Forget it." She started for the door.

"Supper's 'bout ready. How about going next door and getting Mr. Randolph? He eats here nights."

The word No was just about to pop out of Gilly's mouth, but one look at Trotter's eyes, and she decided to save her fights for something more important. "Which house?"

"The gray one on the right." She waved her knife vaguely uphill. "Just knock on the door. If you do it good and loud, he'll hear you. Better take your jacket. Cold out."

Gilly ignored the last. She ran out the door, through the picket gate, and onto the porch next door, stomping and jumping to keep warm. *Bam, bam, bam*. It was too cold for October. Mr. Randolph's house was smaller and more grubby-looking even than Trotter's. She repeated her knock.

Suddenly the door swung inward, revealing a tiny shrunken man. Strange whitish eyes stared out of a wrinkled, brown face.

Gilly took one look and ran back to Trotter's kitchen as fast as she could go.

"What's the matter? Where's Mr. Randolph?"

"I don't know. He's gone. He's not there."

"What d'you mean he's not there?" Trotter began wiping her hands on her apron and walking toward the door.

"He's gone. Some weird little colored man with white eyes came to the door."

"Gilly! That was Mr. Randolph. He can't see a thing. You've got to go back and bring him by the hand, so he won't fall."

Gilly backed away. "I never touched one of those people in my life."

"Well, then, it's about time, ain't it?" Trotter snapped. "Of course, if you can't manage, I can always send William Ernest."

"I can manage. Don't you worry about me."

"You probably got Mr. Randolph all confused and upset by now."

"Well, you shoulda warned me."

"Warned *you*?" Trotter banged a spoon on the table. "I shoulda warned poor Mr. Randolph. You want me to send William Ernest?"

"I said I could manage. Good god!" At this, Trotter's spoon went up in the air like a fly-swatter. "All right! I didn't say it. Hell, a person can't even talk around here."

"A smart person like you oughta be able to think of a few regular words to stick in amongst the cusses." The spoon went into the salad and stirred. "Well, hurry up, if you're going."

The little black man was still standing in the open doorway. "William Ernest?" he called gently as Gilly started up the steps.

"No," she said sharply. "Me."

"Oh." He smiled widely although his eyes did not seem to move. "You must be the new little girl." He stretched out his right hand. "Welcome to you, welcome."

Gilly carefully took the elbow instead of the hand. "Trotter said for me to get you for supper."

"Well, thank you, thank you." He reached behind, fumbling until he found the knob, and pulled the door shut. "Kind of chilly tonight, isn't it?"

"Yeah."

All she could think of was Miss Ellis. OK, so she hadn't been so great at the Nevinses', but she hadn't done anything to deserve this. A house run by a fat, fluff-brained religious fanatic with a mentally retarded seven-year-old—well, maybe he was and maybe he wasn't actually retarded, but chances were good the kid was running around with less than his full share of brains or why would Trotter make such a big deal of it? But she could've handled the two of them. It wasn't fair to throw in a blind black man who came to eat.

Or maybe Miss Ellis didn't know. Maybe Trotter kept this a secret.

The sidewalk was uneven. Mr. Randolph's toe hit a high corner, and he lurched forward.

"Watch it!" Without thinking, Gilly threw her arms around the thin shoulders and caught him before he fell.

"Thank you, thank you." Gilly dropped her arms. She thought for a horrible moment that he was going to try to grab her hand, but he didn't.

*Boy, Miss Ellis, are you ever going to be sorry you did this to me.*

"Now Mrs. Trotter did tell me your name, but I'm ashamed to say I don't seem to recall it." He tapped his head with its short, curly gray hair. "I can keep all the luxuries up here, but none of the necessities."

"Gilly," she muttered.

"I beg your pardon?"

"Gilly Hopkins."

"Oh, yes." He was shuffling painfully up Trotter's front steps. Jeez. Why didn't he get a white cane or something? "I am most pleased to make your acquaintance, Miss Gilly. I feel mighty close to all Mrs. Trotter's children. Little William Ernest is like a grandson to me. So I feel sure . . ."

"Watch the door!"

"Yes, yes, I thank you."

"Is that you Mr. Randolph?" came Trotter's voice from inside.

"Yes, indeed, Mrs. Trotter, with the sweetest little escort you'd ever hope to see."

Trotter appeared in the hallway with her hands on her hips. "How you doing in this cold weather?"

"Not my best, I'm afraid. This sweet little girl had to keep me from falling right down on my face."

"Did she now?"

*See there, Trotter? I managed.*

"I guess this old house is going to be a bit more lively now, eh, Mrs. Trotter?"

"Wouldn't be surprised," answered Trotter in a flat voice that Gilly couldn't read the meaning of.

The meal proceeded without incident. Gilly was hungry but thought it better not to seem to enjoy her supper too much. William Ernest ate silently and steadily with only an occasional glance at Gilly. She could tell that the child was scared silly of her. It was about the only thing in the last two hours that had given her any real satisfaction. Power over the boy was sure to be power over Trotter in the long run.

"I declare, Mrs. Trotter," said Mr. Randolph, "every day I think to myself, tonight's supper couldn't be as delicious as last night's. But I tell you, this is the most delicious meal I have ever had the privilege of eating."

"Mr. Randolph, you could flatter the stripe off a polecat."

Mr. Randolph let out a giggling laugh. "It isn't flattery, I assure you, Mrs. Trotter. William Ernest and Miss Gilly will bear me out in this. I may be old, but I haven't lost my sense of taste, even if some folks maintain I've lost the other four."

They went on and on like that. Mr. Randolph flattering the fat woman, and the fat woman eating it up like hot-fudge sundae with all the nuts.

What I should do, thought Gilly, as she lay that night in the narrow bed with her arms folded under her head, What I should do is write my mother. Courtney Rutherford Hopkins would probably sue county welfare if she knew what kind of place they'd forced her daughter to come to.

Miss Ellis (whose eyebrows always twitched when Gilly asked questions about Courtney) had once told her that Courtney was from Virginia. Everybody knew, didn't they, that families like Courtney's did not eat with colored people? Courtney Rutherford Hopkins was sure to go into a rage, wasn't she, when she heard that news? Perhaps the self-righteous Trotter would be put into jail for contributing to the delinquency of a minor. Miss Ellis would, of course, be fired. *Yum!*

She'll come to get me then, for sure, thought Gilly. Her mother wouldn't stand for her beautiful Galadriel to be in a dump like this for one single minute, once she knew. But how was she to know? Miss Ellis would never admit it. What kind of lies was the social worker telling Courtney to keep her from coming to fetch Gilly?

As she dropped off to sleep, Gilly promised herself for the millionth time that she would find out where Courtney Rutherford Hopkins was, write to her, and tell her to come and take her beautiful Galadriel home.

## More Unpleasant Surprises

In the tiny mirror over the bureau Gilly noted with no little satisfaction that her hair was a wreck. Yesterday before the bubble gum got into it, it had looked as though it simply needed combing. Today it looked like a lot that had been partially bulldozed—an uprooted tree here, a half wall with a crumbling chimney there. It was magnificent. It would run Trotter wild. Gilly bounced down the stairs and into the kitchen.

She held her head very straight as she sat at the kitchen table and waited for the fireworks.

"I'll take you down to the school a little after nine, hear?" Trotter said.

Of course Gilly heard. She tilted her head a little in case Trotter couldn't *see*.

"If I take you down earlier," Trotter went on, "we'll just have to sit and wait till they can take care of us. I'd as leave sit here at my own table with a cup of coffee, wouldn't you?" She put a bowl of steaming hot cereal down in front of Gilly.

Gilly nodded her head vigorously Yes.

William Ernest was staring at her, his glasses steamed up from the oatmeal. Gilly bared her teeth and shook her head violently No at him. The boy snuffled loudly and ducked his head.

"Need a tissue, William Ernest?" Trotter pulled one

from her apron pocket and gently wiped his nose. "And here's a clean one for school, honey." Trotter leaned over and tucked a tissue into his pants pocket.

Gilly craned her neck over the table as though she were trying to see the contents of W.E.'s pocket. Her head was within a couple of feet of Trotter's eyes. The woman was sure to notice.

"William Ernest got promoted to the Orange reading group yesterday. Didn't you, William Ernest, honey?"

The little boy nodded his head but kept his eyes on his bowl.

"You're gonna have to do some reading out loud and show Gilly how great you're coming along with your reading these days."

W.E. looked up for one split second with terror in his eyes. Trotter missed the look, but not Gilly, who smiled widely and shook her half-bulldozed head emphatically.

"In Orange they use hardback books," Trotter was explaining. "It's a real big step to be Orange." She leaned over Gilly to put some toast on the table. "We really worked for this."

"So old W.E.'s getting a *head*, is he?"

Trotter gave her a puzzled look. "Yeah, he's doing just fine."

"Before you know it," Gilly heard herself saying loudly, "he'll be blowing his own nose and *combing his own hair.*"

"He already does," said Trotter quietly. "Leastways most of the time." She sat down with a loud sigh at the table. "Pass me a piece of toast, will you, Gilly?"

Gilly picked up the plate, raised it to the height of her hair, and passed it across to Trotter at that level.

"Thank you, honey."

At eight thirty Trotter got William Ernest off to

school. Gilly had long since finished her breakfast, but she sat at the kitchen table, her head propped on her fists. From the doorway she could hear Old Mother Goose honking over her gosling. "OK, Big Orange, you show 'em down there today, hear?" Trotter said finally; and then the heavy door shut and she was heading back for the kitchen. As she got to the door, Gilly sat up straight and shook her head for all she was worth.

"You got a tic or something, honey?"

"No."

"I would've thought you was too young for the palsy," the huge woman murmured, sliding into her seat with the cup of coffee she'd promised herself earlier. "I see you got sneakers. That's good. You're supposed to have them for gym. Can you think of anything else you'll need for school?"

Gilly shook her head, but halfheartedly. She was beginning to feel like an oversharpened pencil.

"I think I'll go upstairs till it's time," she said.

"Oh, while you're up there, honey—"

"Yeah?" Gilly sprang to attention.

"Make the beds, will you? It does look messy to leave 'em unmade all day, and I'm not much on running up and down the stairs."

Gilly banged the door to her room for all she was worth. She spit every obscenity she'd ever heard through her teeth, but it wasn't enough. That ignorant hippopotamus! That walrus-faced imbecile! That—that—oh, the devil—Trotter wouldn't even let a drop fall from her precious William Ernest baby's nose, but she would let Gilly go to school—a new school where she didn't know anybody—looking like a scarecrow. Miss Ellis would surely hear about this. Gilly slammed her fist into her pillow. There had to be a law against foster mothers who showed such gross favoritism.

Well, she would show that lard can a thing or two. She yanked open the left top drawer, pulling out a broken comb, which she viciously jerked through the wilderness on her head, only to be defeated by a patch of bubble gum. She ran into the bathroom and rummaged through the medicine chest until she found a pair of nail scissors with which to chop out the offending hair. When despite her assault by comb and scissors a few strands refused to lie down meekly, she soaked them mercilessly into submission. She'd show the world. She'd show them who Galadriel Hopkins was— she was not to be trifled with.

"I see they call you Gilly," said Mr. Evans, the principal.

"I can't even pronounce the poor child's real name," said Trotter, chuckling in what she must believe was a friendly manner.

It didn't help Gilly's mood. She was still seething over the hair combing.

"Well, Gilly's a fine name," said Mr. Evans, which confirmed to Gilly that at school, too, she was fated to be surrounded by fools.

The principal was studying records that must have been sent over from Gilly's former school, Hollywood Gardens Elementary. He coughed several times. "Well," he said, "I think this young lady needs to be in a class that will challenge her."

"She's plenty smart, if that's what you mean."

Trotter, you dummy. How do you know how smart I am? You never laid eyes on me until yesterday.

"I'm going to put you into Miss Harris's class. We have some departmentalization in the sixth grade, but . . ."

"You got *what* in the sixth grade?"

Oh, Trotter, shut your fool mouth.

But the principal didn't seem to notice what a dope Trotter was. He explained patiently how some of the sixth-grade classes moved around for math and reading and science, but Miss Harris kept the same group all day.

What a blinking bore.

They went up three flights of ancient stairway to Miss Harris's room slowly, so that Trotter would not collapse. The corridors stank of oiled floors and cafeteria soup. Gilly had thought she hated all schools so much that they no longer could pain or disappoint her, but she felt heavier with each step—like a condemned prisoner walking an endless last mile.

They paused before the door marked "Harris–6." Mr. Evans knocked, and a tall tea-colored woman, crowned with a bush of black hair, opened the door. She smiled down on the three of them, because she was even taller than the principal.

Gilly shrank back, bumping into Trotter's huge breast, which made her jump forward again quickly. God, on top of everything else, the teacher was black.

No one seemed to take notice of her reaction, unless you counted a flash of brightness in Miss Harris's dark eyes.

Trotter patted Gilly's arm, murmured something that ended in "honey," and then she and the principal floated backward, closing Gilly into Harris–6. The teacher led her to an empty desk in the middle of the classroom, asked for Gilly's jacket, which she handed over to another girl to hang on the coatrack at the back of the room. She directed Gilly to sit down, and then went up and settled herself at the large teacher's desk to glance through the handful of papers Mr. Evans had given her.

In a moment she looked up, a warm smile lighting her face. "Galadriel Hopkins. What a beautiful name! From Tolkien, of course."

"No," muttered Gilly. "Hollywood Gardens."

Miss Harris laughed a sort of golden laugh. "No, I mean your name—Galadriel. It's the name of a great queen in a book by a man named Tolkien. But, of course, you know that."

Hell. No one had ever told her that her name came from a book. Should she pretend she knew all about it or play dumb?

"I'd like to call you Galadriel, if you don't mind. It's such a lovely name."

"No!" Everyone was looking at Gilly peculiarly. She must have yelled louder than she intended to. "I would prefer," she said tightly, "to be called Gilly."

"Yes"—Miss Harris's voice was more steel than gold now—"Yes. Gilly, it is then. Well"—she turned her smile on the rest of the class—"Where were we?"

The clamor of their answers clashed in Gilly's brain. She started to put her head down on the desk, but someone was shoving a book into her face.

It wasn't fair—nothing was fair. She had once seen a picture in an old book of a red fox on a high rock surrounded by snarling dogs. It was like that. She was smarter than all of them, but they were too many. They had her surrounded, and in their stupid ways, they were determined to wear her down.

Miss Harris was leaning over her. Gilly pulled away as far as she could.

"Did you do division with fractions at Hollywood Gardens?"

Gilly shook her head. Inside she seethed. It was bad enough having to come to this broken-down old school but to be behind—to seem dumber than the rest of the kids—to have to appear a fool in front of. . . . Almost half the class was black. And she would look dumb to *them*. A bunch of—

"Why don't you bring your chair up to my desk, and we'll work on it?"

Gilly snatched up her chair and beat Miss Harris to the front of the room. She'd show them!

At recesstime Monica Bradley, one of the other white girls in the class, was supposed to look after her on the playground. But Monica was more interested in leaning against the building and talking with her friends, which she did, keeping her back toward Gilly as she giggled and gossiped with two other sixth-grade girls, one of whom was black with millions of tiny braids all over her head. Like some African bush-woman. Not that Gilly cared. Why should she? They could giggle their stupid lives away, and she'd never let it bother her. She turned her back on them. That would show them.

Just then a ball jerked loose from the basketball game nearby and rushed toward her. She grabbed it. Balls were friends. She hugged it and ran over to the basket and threw it up, but she had been in too much of a hurry. It kissed the rim but refused to go in for her. Angrily she jumped and caught it before it bounced. She was dimly aware of a protest from the players, but they were boys and mostly shorter than she, so not worthy of notice. She shot again, this time with care. It arched and sank cleanly. She pushed someone out of the way and grabbed it just below the net.

"Hey! Who you think you are?"

One of the boys, a black as tall as she, tried to pull the ball from her hands. She spun around, knocking him to the concrete, and shot again, banking the ball off the backboard neatly into the net. She grabbed it once more.

Now all the boys were after her. She began to run across the playground laughing and clutching the ball to her chest. She could hear the boys screaming behind her, but she was too fast for them. She ran in and out of hop-scotch games and right through a jump rope, all the way back to the basketball post where she shot again, missing wildly in her glee.

The boys did not watch for the rebound. They leaped upon her. She was on her back, scratching and kicking for all she was worth. They were yelping like hurt puppies.

"Hey! Hey! What's going on here?"

Miss Harris towered above them. The fighting evaporated under her glare. She marched all seven of them to the principal's office. Gilly noted with satisfaction a long red line down the tall boy's cheek. She'd actually drawn blood in the fracas. The boys looked a lot worse than she felt. Six to one—pretty good odds even for the great Gilly Hopkins.

Mr. Evans lectured the boys about fighting on the playground and then sent them back to their home-rooms. He kept Gilly longer.

"Gilly." He said her name as though it were a whole sentence by itself. Then he just sat back in his chair, his fingertips pressed together, and looked at her.

She smoothed her hair and waited, staring him in the eye. People hated that—you staring them down as though they were the ones who had been bad. They didn't know how to deal with it. Sure enough. The principal looked away first.

"Would you like to sit down?"

She jerked her head No.

He coughed. "I would rather for us to be friends."

Gilly smirked.

"We're not going to have fighting on the playground."

He looked directly at her. "Or anywhere else around here. I think you need to understand that, Gilly."

She tilted her head sassily and kept her eyes right on his.

"You're at a new school now. You have a chance to—uh—make a new start. If you want to."

So Hollywood Gardens had warned him, eh? Well, so what? The people here would have learned soon enough. Gilly would have made sure of that.

She smiled what she knew to be her most menacing smile.

"If there's anyway I can help you—if you just feel like talking to somebody. . . ."

Not one of those understanding adults. Deliver me! She smiled so hard it stretched the muscles around her eyes. "I'm OK," she said. "I don't need any help."

"If you don't want help, there's no way I can make you accept it. But, Gilly"—he leaned forward in his chair and spoke very slowly and softly—"you're not going to be permitted to hurt other people."

She snuffled loudly. Cute. Very cute.

He leaned back; she thought she heard him sigh. "Not if I have anything to do with it."

Gilly wiped her nose on the back of her hand. She saw the principal half reach for his box of tissues and then pull his hand back.

"You may go back to your class now." She turned to go. "I hope you'll give yourself—and us—a chance, Gilly."

She ignored the remark. Nice, she thought, climbing the dark stairs. Only a half day and already the principal was yo-yoing. Give her a week, boy. A week and she'd have the whole cussed place in an uproar. But this afternoon, she'd cool it a little. Let them worry. Then tomorrow or maybe even the next day, *Wham*. She felt her old powers returning. She was no longer tired.

# Reviewing and Interpreting the Selection

Record your answers to these questions in your personal literature notebook. Follow the directions for each part.

**Reviewing**   Try to complete each of these sentences without looking back at the selection.

Recalling Facts

1. Gilly goes to Mr. Randolph's house to

    a. remind him that it is time for his favorite TV show.

    b. live there as a foster child.

    c. bring him back to Mrs. Trotter's for dinner.

    d. sell him some candy for a school drive.

Identifying Sequence

2. After Gilly takes her first look at Mr. Randolph, she

    a. runs back to Mrs. Trotter's house without him.

    b. takes his elbow and leads him out of his house.

    c. introduces herself.

    d. catches Mr. Randolph as he begins to fall.

Understanding Main Ideas

3. Gilly is glad that her hair looks messy on the first day of school because she wants to

    a. set a record for not combing her hair for the most days.

    b. start a new hairstyle trend.

    c. surprise the teacher and principal.

    d. upset Mrs. Trotter.

4. The boys on the playground are angry with Gilly because she

    a. has outplayed them.

    b. has taken their basketball.

    c. is new.

    d. calls them names.

5. A setting that is *not* featured in this selection is

    a. the welfare office.

    b. Mrs. Trotter's home.

    c. the principal's office.

    d. Miss Harris's classroom.

**Interpreting**  To complete these sentences, you may look back at the selection if you'd like.

6. Gilly recognizes a "danger signal" as she thinks about her mother. She feels she might be about to

    a. get sick.

    b. cry.

    c. tear up her mother's photograph.

    d. call her mother on the phone.

7. When Gilly catches Mr. Randolph before he falls, she proves that she

    a. is basically a nice person.

    b. will never be rude to him again.

    c. believes that she is stronger than William Ernest.

    d. is overly nervous and uptight.

8.  If Mrs. Trotter discovered that Gilly was teasing William Ernest, she probably would

    a. tell William Ernest to fight back.

    b. laugh and say it is all right for a while.

    c. punish Gilly and demand that she stop scaring William Ernest.

    d. call the welfare department and have Gilly removed from her home immediately.

9.  If you asked Gilly what she has learned in foster care, she probably would say,

    a. "If you're nice to others, they will be nice to you."

    b. "Trust no one."

    c. "Old friends are the best friends."

    d. "To have a friend, you have to be a friend."

10. The mood of this selection can be described as

    a. cheerful.

    b. peaceful.

    c. fearful.

    d. angry.

Now check your answers with your teacher. Study the questions you answered incorrectly. What types of questions were they? Talk with your teacher about ways to work on those skills.

# Character

As you read a novel like *The Great Gilly Hopkins,* you will find that its characters begin to seem like real people. Because novels can take days or even weeks to read, you might feel as if a part of you is living with the characters and getting to know them personally.

You get to know the characters in stories in much the same way you get to know your friends. First, you observe what they look like on the outside—how tall or short they are, how old they are, how they dress and wear their hair, how they talk and move. But once you spend some time with them, you see beyond those surface characteristics. You soon begin to see patterns in what they say and do. Are they usually funny or serious? Can they be counted on to think before acting, or do they often act without thinking? Then you begin to sense their moods and feelings. When you can sense how your friends are feeling, you can finally say that you know them well.

Slowly and carefully—in much the same ways as described above—the author of a novel reveals its characters. In this lesson, you will look at some of the skillful writing techniques that Katherine Paterson uses to help you get to know Gilly, Mrs. Trotter, William Ernest, Mr. Randolph, Miss Harris, and Mr. Evans:

1. Paterson describes what the characters look like.

2. She reveals what the characters do and say.

3. She reveals what the characters think and feel.

4. She reveals how others feel about the characters.

## 1 • Physical Description

When you want to make a good impression on someone new, you probably pay a lot of attention to your appearance. You pick out just the right clothes, you try to make your hair look its best, and sometimes you even practice a special way of standing or walking. Why do you go to all this trouble? It's probably because you know that many people judge you by their first impression of you—what they see and hear first.

Authors understand the importance of first impressions. When they introduce a new character, they try to give a clear picture of him or her. They try to point out physical characteristics that set that person apart from the other characters. Then, later in the story, when that character reappears, readers can more easily bring up a mental picture of the character.

Read this description of the first meeting between Gilly and her teacher, Miss Harris. See if it paints a picture in your mind. What is Gilly's first impression of her teacher?

> They paused before the door marked "Harris–6." Mr. Evans knocked, and a tall tea-colored woman, crowned with a bush of black hair, opened the door. She smiled down on the three of them, because she was even taller than the principal. . . . Miss Harris laughed a sort of golden laugh.

The first detail that strikes Gilly is that Miss Harris is not white, as Gilly had expected. She is, instead, "tea-colored," an unusual description for a woman who will later turn out to be unusual in even more ways. Miss Harris is a tall woman, even taller than the male principal, a fact that Gilly finds interesting, if not intimidating. Gilly is also struck by Miss Harris's "bush of black hair," her smile, and her "golden laugh." Altogether, Miss Harris is an impressive woman, and Gilly senses that she is in for a new and interesting experience.

In addition to judging others' appearances, Gilly also judges her own. Read this description of Gilly on the morning she is scheduled to begin school. What details create a memorable picture in your mind?

> In the tiny mirror over the bureau Gilly noted with no little satisfaction that her hair was a wreck. Yesterday before the bubble gum got into it, it had looked as though it simply needed combing. Today it looked like a lot that had been partially bulldozed—an uprooted tree here, a half wall

with a crumbling chimney there. It was magnificent. It would run Trotter wild.

Gilly's hair has bubble gum stuck in it, it needs combing badly, and it is attention-getting in the worst possible way. And the most amazing detail of all is that Gilly is overjoyed with the way she looks!

## Exercise 1

Read this passage in which Gilly examines the only photograph she has of her mother. Use what you have learned in this lesson to answer the questions that follow the passage.

> Out of the pasteboard frame and through the plastic cover the brown eyes of the woman laughed up at her as they always did. The glossy black hair hung in gentle waves without a hair astray. She looked as though she was the star of some TV show, but she wasn't. See—right there in the corner she had written "For my beautiful Galadriel, I will always love you." She wrote that to me, Gilly told herself, as she did each time she looked at it, only to me. She turned the frame over. It was still there—the little piece of tape with the name on it. "Courtney Rutherford Hopkins."
>
> Gilly smoothed her own straw-colored hair with one hand as she turned the picture over again. Even the teeth were gorgeous. Weren't girls supposed to look like their mothers?

1. Find details that describe Gilly's mother. Gilly compares her own looks with her mother's. Who does she think is more beautiful? What does this comparison tell you about how Gilly feels about herself?

2. Which details in this passage suggest that Gilly has a habit of looking at the photograph regularly? Why do you think she likes to look at it often?

Now check your answers with your teacher. Review this part of the lesson if you don't understand why an answer was incorrect.

**Writing on Your Own 1**

In this exercise you will use what you learned in this lesson to write a character description. Follow these steps:

- Review your notes for Creating Your Own Character on page 4. Choose one of the characters you imagined and make him or her the main character of your scene.

- Using your notes, write at least five sentences that describe the character. Be sure to include details that you will be able to see and hear when you meet the character for the first time in your scene.

- Let a friend read your sentences and draw a picture of your character. Then have your friend use the drawing to describe the character to you. If your friend has trouble remembering details about the character, go back and revise your sentences. Try to make the details more vivid and descriptive.

## 2 • Speech and Actions

You probably have had the experience of making a quick judgment of a person, based on what he or she looked or sounded like; then later you found out you were wrong. What made you change your mind? Most likely, that person said or did something that you did not expect. For example, an older person might have driven away from you on a motorcycle, or a tough-looking person might have pointed out a particularly beautiful flower.

You can't always trust your first impressions. They don't always turn out to be accurate. Instead, you have to pay attention to what people say and do over time. Only then will you begin to really know them.

When Gilly first goes to Mr. Randolph's house, she is surprised by his appearance. All she sees is "a tiny shrunken man" with "strange whitish eyes" and a "wrinkled, brown face." She forms a quick first impression of him, based on his appearance, and decides that he is not her kind of person. But later, when she returns to pick Mr. Randolph up, he has a chance to reveal more about himself than just his appearance. What do you learn about Mr. Randolph by what he says and does in this passage?

> The little black man was still standing in the open doorway. "William Ernest?" he called gently as Gilly started up the steps.
> "No," she said sharply. "Me."
> "Oh." He smiled widely although his eyes did not seem to move. "You must be the new little girl." He stretched out his right hand. "Welcome to you, welcome."
> Gilly carefully took the elbow instead of the hand. "Trotter said for me to get you for supper."
> "Well, thank you, thank you." He reached behind, fumbling until he found the knob, and pulled the door shut. "Kind of chilly tonight, isn't it? . . .
> " . . . Now Mrs. Trotter did tell me your name, but I'm ashamed to say I don't seem to recall it." He tapped his head with its short, curly gray hair. "I can keep all the luxuries up here, but none of the necessities."
> "Gilly," she muttered.
> "I beg your pardon?"
> "Gilly Hopkins."
> " . . . I am most pleased to make your acquaintance, Miss Gilly. . . ."

Now you know much more about Mr. Randolph, mostly because of what he said. He is gentle and soft-spoken. He is so well-mannered that he seems to have stepped out of a more civilized and slow-paced world than we live in today. He is kind and welcoming to Gilly, sincerely glad to meet her. And he has a sense of humor about his own shortcomings. His words have proven that he is definitely not the type of person you would run from, once you got to know him.

## Exercise 2

Read the passage on the next page. Use what you have learned in this lesson to answer the questions that follow the passage.

Just then a ball jerked loose from the basketball game nearby and rushed toward her. She grabbed it. Balls were friends. She hugged it and ran over to the basket and threw it up, but she had been in too much of a hurry. It kissed the rim but refused to go in for her. Angrily she jumped and caught it before it bounced. She was dimly aware of a protest from the players, but they were boys and mostly shorter than she, so not worthy of notice. She shot again, this time with care. It arched and sank cleanly. She pushed someone out of the way and grabbed it just below the net.

"Hey! Who you think you are?"

One of the boys, a black as tall as she, tried to pull the ball from her hands. She spun around, knocking him to the concrete, and shot again, banking the ball off the backboard neatly into the net. She grabbed it once more.

Now all the boys were after her. She began to run across the playground laughing and clutching the ball to her chest. She could hear the boys screaming behind her, but she was too fast for them. She ran in and out of hopscotch games and right through a jump rope, all the way back to the basketball post where she shot again, missing wildly in her glee.

1. In this passage Gilly's actions tell you much about her athletic skills and personality. Find details that suggest that Gilly is an experienced and skillful basketball player.

2. It seems that Gilly has no problem getting involved in a game that only boys are playing. Based on her actions, do you think that she usually plays only with girls, or does she participate in any games she wants to?

3. Gilly is happy that she is causing such an uproar. She steals the ball, runs around the playground with it, and shoots— partly to show that she is not afraid and is having a great time. What do all these actions suggest about Gilly and her self-confidence? How might these antics affect her fellow classmates' impressions of her?

Now check your answers with your teacher. Review this part of the lesson if you don't understand why an answer was incorrect.

**Writing on Your Own 2**

In this exercise you will write one or two paragraphs, showing your character doing or saying something that reveals more about his or her personality. Follow these steps:

- Remember that you began this unit by thinking of characters you might meet on your first day in a new school. In Writing on Your Own 1, you described what one of those characters looks and sounds like. Now write some notes about what that character might do or say to attract your attention on the first day. For example, the character might lend you some paper, steal your lunch, or act like a teacher's pet.

- Next write a paragraph describing what the character says or does. Refer to your notes as you write. Does the character do or say something surprising—something that makes you change your mind about him or her?

- Reread your paragraph. Make sure that the sentences follow a logical sequence. Make any changes that you feel are necessary.

## 3 • Thoughts and Feelings

Sometimes even two people who have known each other a long time still are not sure what the other is feeling deep inside. They can only guess. In a story or novel, however, the author often gives readers an advantage over real life. He or she can help readers "listen in" on a character's internal conversations, so readers can know with certainty what the character is thinking and feeling.

Understanding characters' thoughts and feelings sometimes helps to explain why they act as they do. A person who feels peaceful will act that way toward others. A person who feels angry will show that anger in what he or she says or does. How would you describe Gilly's feelings in the following passage?

All she could think of was Miss Ellis. OK, so she hadn't been so great at the Nevinses', but she hadn't done anything to deserve this. A house run by a fat, fluff-brained religious fanatic with a mentally retarded seven-year-old—well, maybe he was and maybe he wasn't actually retarded, but chances were good the kid was running around with less than his full share of brains or why would Trotter make such a big deal of it? But she could've handled the two of them. It wasn't fair to throw in a blind black man who came to eat.

Gilly is clearly angry and self-pitying. She shows her anger in the way she describes Mrs. Trotter—a "fat, fluff-brained religious fanatic"—and William Ernest, "a mentally retarded seven-year-old." Gilly is allowing her discomfort to erupt in resentment toward the people who are trying to help her. She is being unreasonable and she doesn't care. She feels she has gotten a bad deal in life, and she isn't going to accept it without a fight.

It wasn't fair—nothing was fair. She had once seen a picture in an old book of a red fox on a high rock surrounded by snarling dogs. It was like that. She was smarter than all of them, but they were too many. They had her surrounded, and in their stupid ways, they were determined to wear her down.

Anyone who feels as angry and mistreated as Gilly is likely to act in ways that others may find unacceptable. Gilly feels that what she does is the only dignified response to an unfair situation.

## Exercise 3

Read the following passage. Use what you have learned in this lesson to answer the questions that follow the passage.

At recesstime Monica Bradley, one of the other white girls in the class, was supposed to look after her on the playground. But Monica was more interested in leaning against the building and talking with her friends, which she did, keeping her back toward Gilly as she giggled and gossiped with two other sixth-grade girls, one of whom was black with millions of tiny braids all over her head. Like some African bushwoman. Not that Gilly cared. Why should she? They could giggle their stupid lives away, and she'd never let it bother her. She turned her back on them. That would show them.

1. How do you think Gilly feels when the girls ignore her on the playground? Which details in the passage give you clues?

2. Gilly does not stand around feeling sorry for herself and wishing the girls would notice her. Instead, she steals the boys' basketball and gets into a fight. How do you think Gilly's feelings toward the girls cause her fight with the boys?

Now check your answers with your teacher. Review this part of the lesson if you don't understand why an answer was incorrect.

## Writing on Your Own 3

In this exercise you will use what you have learned in this lesson to describe the thoughts and feelings of a character. Follow these steps:

- Imagine the thoughts and feelings of your chosen character as he or she walks into school on your first day there. Is he or she in a good mood? Has something happened to make him or her angry or excited? Write some notes about the character's thoughts and feelings on that day.

- Now look over your notes. For each idea, write a sentence. For example, if one of your notes said, "tired of the same thing every day," your sentence might say, "Today I'm going to do something really different and stir things up a bit."

- Arrange your sentences into a paragraph. Make sure the sentences follow in a logical sequence.

# Discussion Guides

1. Suppose you were a member of Miss Harris's class on Gilly's first day at school. How would you have described Gilly to your friends or family? Work with a partner or a small group to list words or phrases that you would use to describe her. Then role-play the way you would report on the "new kid in class" at the end of the day. One person should play a member of Miss Harris's class and the other should play an interested parent or friend.

2. If you were a member of a foster family that took Gilly in, would you be willing to live with her? Do you see any positive qualities in Gilly that you could encourage? How might you deal with her negative qualities? In a small group, discuss some of the things that Gilly said and did in the chapters you just read. If she had said or done these things to you and your family, how might you have handled them?

3. The setting of *The Great Gilly Hopkins* is quite realistic. Work with a group to list details about Gilly's home, her neighborhood, and her school. Then, as a group, decide how your homes, neighborhood, and school are similar to and different from Gilly's. For example, is her bedroom like yours, or is it different? Are the houses in her neighborhood like yours? Are her neighbors like yours? You can fill in a chart like the one below to explain the similarities and differences.

| | Place | Details | Alike or Different from Ours? |
|---|---|---|---|
| Gilly's Home | | | |
| Gilly's Neighborhood | | | |
| Gilly's School | | | |

# Write About a Character

Throughout this unit you have been writing about an interesting character. Now is the time to describe that character in a scene about your first day in a new school.

If you have any questions about the writing process, refer to Using the Writing Process beginning on page 295.

- Assemble the work you did for all the writing exercises in this unit. You should have four pieces of writing: *a*) rough notes about at least three characters, *b*) five sentences describing one of those characters, *c*) a paragraph that reveals something about that character by describing his or her speech or actions, and *d*) a paragraph that reveals that character's thoughts and feelings. Reread these pieces of writing now to get ideas for the description you are about to write.

- Write a description of your first day at a new school. Write from the first-person point of view, using the words *I* and *me*. Begin by explaining that it is your first day there. Describe your feelings. Then briefly describe each new person you meet. Be sure to describe your one chosen character thoroughly. Describe the way he or she looks, acts, and speaks. Also describe what he or she thinks and feels, as well as your reaction to him or her.

- Reread your description. Did you include details that paint a picture of at least one important character? Did you describe some of that character's actions, words, and thoughts? Did you describe your own reactions to him or her?

- Proofread to find any grammar, spelling, capitalization, and punctuation errors. Then make a clean, final copy to share in a class book or to store in your writing portfolio.

# Unit 2 Setting

# Hatchet
by Gary Paulsen

## About the Illustration

This picture illustrates a scene from the selection you are about to read. Following are some questions that will help you begin to think about the selection. Use details from the picture as clues to answer the questions. Give reasons for your answers.

- Where does this story take place?

- What do you think the boy is doing here?

- How do you think the boy feels?

# Unit 2

| | |
|---|---|
| **Introduction** | About the Novel |
| | About the Author |
| | About the Lessons |
| | Writing: Creating a Setting |
| **Selection** | Hatchet |
| | *by* Gary Paulsen |
| **Unit Focus** | Setting |
| **Activities** | Reviewing and Interpreting the |
| | Selection |
| | Discussion Guides |
| | Write a Story Introduction |

## Introduction

### About the Novel

Thirteen-year-old Brian Robeson is on his way to Canada to visit his father for the first time since his parents' divorce. He and the pilot are the only passengers in their small, single-engine plane. Brian is still upset about his parents' divorce and thinks often of what he calls the Secret that destroyed their marriage. Even when the pilot allows him to try his hand at the plane's controls for a few minutes, Brian still feels depressed and gloomy.

Somewhere over the Canadian wilderness, the pilot suddenly doubles over in pain. He suffers a severe heart attack and quickly falls unconscious. In terror, Brian soon realizes that the pilot is dead and that his own survival depends on his ability to land the plane safely. Brian attempts to radio for help but fails. The only thing he can do is wait for the plane to run out of fuel. He hopes that when that time comes, the plane will crash into a lake rather than trees, so he'll stand a better chance of survival.

As these chapters begin, the plane has finally run out of fuel, and Brian is about to panic. Read the selection to see how he copes with his problems, both in the air and in the wilderness below.

# About the Author

Besides making a living as a writer, Gary Paulsen has had jobs as a teacher, an electronic field engineer, a singer, an actor, a director, a rancher, a soldier, a farmer, a truck driver, a trapper, and a sailor. As a hobby, Paulsen runs dogsleds and has even competed in the grueling Iditarod race that runs from Anchorage to Nome, Alaska. An avid sailor, Paulsen also survived a storm in the Pacific Ocean in a fiberglass sailboat.

Paulsen has written and published two plays, many short stories, several hundred magazine articles, and a variety of fiction and nonfiction books. He draws on his diverse experiences to write the exciting adventure stories for which he is best known. A number of his books have been named Newbery Honor books, including *The Winter Room, Dogsong,* and *Hatchet,* the source of this selection.

Paulsen is devoted to his writing career. Once when giving advice to an aspiring writer, he said, "What matters is writing. What matters is baring your soul on paper. What matters is fighting with your fears and struggling with the honesty of looking at who you really are." This struggle of facing fears and discovering one's strengths and weaknesses are themes in many of Paulsen's books.

# About the Lessons

The lessons that follow this selection focus on the element of setting. Setting is when and where a story takes place. Writers often describe a story's setting in great detail to make readers feel as if they are there with the characters. The setting often helps determine what happens in a story. It also can affect the feelings, or mood, of both the characters and the readers.

# Writing: Creating a Setting

The wilderness setting of *Hatchet* affects everything that the main character, Brian, does. Author Gary Paulsen has worked hard to make the setting seem real to his readers. In the course of this unit, you will create and describe a setting of your own, and you will write a story introduction using that setting. The suggestions below will help you get started.

- Think about books you have read or movies you have seen. What kinds of settings are most exciting or interesting to you? List a few of your favorite settings.

- Think about places you have been or places you would like to visit. Some places might be close by—your home, your school, a park. Other places might be far away—Africa, the moon. List a few of these places.

- Make a chart like the one below. In the first column, choose some of the settings or places you just listed and that you might want to describe in a story introduction. In the other columns, try to fill in a few details for each sense. If you can't think of at least one detail for each sense, you probably won't be able to make that setting believable. Examples of details for the setting of a city street might be as follows: flashing stoplights (sight), honking cars (hearing), exhaust fumes (smell), hard sidewalks (touch), and hot dogs from a street vendor (taste).

|  | **Sight** | **Hearing** | **Smell** | **Touch** | **Taste** |
|---|---|---|---|---|---|
| Setting 1 |  |  |  |  |  |
| Setting 2 |  |  |  |  |  |

After you have finished your chart, choose the setting for which you have listed the most details. You will write about that setting later in the unit, so save your chart.

# Before Reading

The questions below will help you appreciate the settings that Gary Paulsen has created in *Hatchet*. As you read, try to answer the questions.

- The settings change quickly in the beginning of this selection. Which details tell you about how each setting looks, sounds, and feels?

- How does each setting determine how Brian acts?

- How does each setting make you feel?

## Vocabulary Tips

This selection contains some words that may be unfamiliar to you but that are important for understanding the story. Below, you will find some of these words, their definitions, and sentences that show how the words are used. Look them over before you begin to read. If there are any other words that you do not know and cannot figure out from the way they are used, be sure to look them up in a dictionary.

| | |
|---|---|
| altitude | height above the earth. The airplane traveled at an <u>altitude</u> of 10,000 feet. |
| horizon | line where the sky seems to meet the earth or sea. We watched the sun slowly dip below the <u>horizon</u>. |
| wrenching | a violent twisting or pulling. A sudden wind caused a <u>wrenching</u> of the bicycle, and the boy lost his balance and fell off. |
| raked | scraped or scratched. The wolf <u>raked</u> at the sides of its cage with its claws. |
| muck | wet, sticky soil. I ruined my shoes when I stepped into the <u>muck</u>. |
| coarse | rough. Sandpaper has a <u>coarse</u> surface. |
| stand | a group of plants or trees. The farmer looked proudly at his <u>stand</u> of corn. |

# Hatchet

Gary Paulsen

Going to die, Brian thought. Going to die, gonna die, gonna die—his whole brain screamed it in the sudden silence.

Gonna die.

He wiped his mouth with the back of his arm and held the nose down. The plane went into a glide, a very fast glide that ate altitude, and suddenly there weren't any lakes. All he'd seen since they started flying over the forest was lakes and now they were gone. Gone. Out in front, far away at the horizon, he could see lots of them, off to the right and left more of them, glittering blue in the late afternoon sun.

But he needed one right in front. He desperately needed a lake right in front of the plane and all he saw through the windshield were trees, green death trees. If he had to turn—if he had to turn he didn't think he could keep the plane flying. His stomach tightened into a series of rolling knots and his breath came in short bursts . . .

There!

Not quite in front but slightly to the right he saw a lake. L-shaped, with rounded corners, and the plane was nearly aimed at the long part of the L, coming from the bottom and heading to the top. Just a tiny bit to the right. He pushed the right rudder pedal gently and the nose moved over.

But the turn cost him speed and now the lake was

above the nose. He pulled back on the wheel slightly and the nose came up. This caused the plane to slow dramatically and almost seem to stop and wallow in the air. The controls became very loose-feeling and frightened Brian, making him push the wheel back in. This increased the speed a bit but filled the windshield once more with nothing but trees, and put the lake well above the nose and out of reach.

For a space of three or four seconds things seemed to hang, almost to stop. The plane was flying, but so slowly, so slowly . . . it would never reach the lake. Brian looked out to the side and saw a small pond and at the edge of the pond some large animal—he thought a moose—standing out in the water. All so still looking, so stopped, the pond and the moose and the trees, as he slid over them now only three or four hundred feet off the ground—all like a picture.

Then everything happened at once. Trees suddenly took on detail, filled his whole field of vision with green, and he knew he would hit and die, would die, but his luck held and just as he was to hit he came into an open lane, a channel of fallen trees, a wide place leading to the lake.

The plane, committed now to landing, to crashing, fell into the wide place like a stone, and Brian eased back on the wheel and braced himself for the crash. But there was a tiny bit of speed left and when he pulled on the wheel the nose came up and he saw in front the blue of the lake and at that instant the plane hit the trees.

There was a great wrenching as the wings caught the pines at the side of the clearing and broke back, ripping back just outside the main braces. Dust and dirt blew off the floor into his face so hard he thought there must have been some kind of explosion. He was momentarily blinded and slammed forward in the seat, smashing his head on the wheel.

Then a wild crashing sound, ripping of metal, and the plane rolled to the right and blew through the trees, out over the water and down, down to slam into the lake, skip once on water as hard as concrete, water that tore the windshield out and shattered the side windows, water that drove him back into the seat. Somebody was screaming, screaming as the plane drove down into the water. Someone screamed tight animal screams of fear and pain and he did not know that it was his sound, that he roared against the water that took him and the plane still deeper, down in the water. He saw nothing but sensed blue, cold blue-green, and he raked at the seatbelt catch, tore his nails loose on one hand. He ripped at it until it released and somehow—the water trying to kill him, to end him—somehow he pulled himself out of the shattered front window and clawed up into the blue, felt something hold him back, felt his windbreaker tear and he was free. Tearing free. Ripping free.

But so far! So far to the surface and his lungs could not do this thing, could not hold and were through, and he sucked water, took a great pull of water that would—finally—win, finally take him, and his head broke into light and he vomited and swam, pulling without knowing what he was, what he was doing. Without knowing anything. Pulling until his hands caught at weeds and muck, pulling and screaming until his hands caught at last in grass and brush and he felt his chest on land, felt his face in the coarse blades of grass and he stopped, everything stopped. A color came that he had never seen before, a color that exploded in his mind with the pain and he was gone,

gone from it all, spiraling out into the world, spiraling out into nothing.

Nothing.

The memory was like a knife cutting into him. Slicing deep into him with hate.

The Secret.

He had been riding his ten-speed with a friend named Terry. They had been taking a run on a bike trail and decided to come back a different way, a way that took them past the Amber Mall. Brian remembered everything in incredible detail. Remembered the time on the bank clock in the mall, flashing 3:31, then the temperature, 82, and the date. All the numbers were part of the memory, all of his life was part of the memory.

Terry had just turned to smile at him about something and Brian looked over Terry's head and saw her.

His mother.

She was sitting in a station wagon, a strange wagon. He saw her and she did not see him. Brian was going to wave or call out, but something stopped him. There was a man in the car.

Short blond hair, the man had. Wearing some kind of white pullover tennis shirt.

Brian saw this and more, saw the Secret and saw more later, but the memory came in pieces, came in scenes like this—Terry smiling, Brian looking over his head to see the station wagon and his mother sitting with the man, the time and temperature clock, the front wheel of his bike, the short blond hair of the man, the white shirt of the man, the hot-hate slices of the memory were exact.

The Secret.

Brian opened his eyes and screamed.

For seconds he did not know where he was, only that the crash was still happening and he was going to die, and he screamed until his breath was gone.

Then silence, filled with sobs as he pulled in air, half crying. How could it be so quiet? Moments ago there was nothing but noise, crashing and tearing, screaming, now quiet.

Some birds were singing.

How could birds be singing?

His legs felt wet and he raised up on his hands and looked back down at them. They were in the lake. Strange. They went down into the water. He tried to move, but pain hammered into him and made his breath shorten into gasps and he stopped, his legs still in the water.

Pain.

Memory.

He turned again and sun came across the water, late sun, cut into his eyes and made him turn away.

It was over then. The crash.

He was alive.

The crash is over and I am alive, he thought. Then his eyes closed and he lowered his head for minutes that seemed longer. When he opened them again it was evening and some of the sharp pain had abated—there were many dull aches—and the crash came back to him fully.

Into the trees and out onto the lake. The plane had crashed and sunk in the lake and he had somehow pulled free.

He raised himself and crawled out of the water, grunting with the pain of movement. His legs were on fire, and his forehead felt as if somebody had been pounding on it with a hammer, but he could move. He pulled his legs out of the lake and crawled on his hands and knees until he was away from the wet-soft shore and near a small stand of brush of some kind.

Then he went down, only this time to rest, to save something of himself. He lay on his side and put his head on his arm and closed his eyes because that was all he could do now, all he could think of being able to do. He closed his eyes and slept, dreamless, deep and down.

There was almost no light when he opened his eyes again. The darkness of night was thick and for a moment he began to panic again. To see, he thought. To see is everything. And he could not see. But he turned his head without moving his body and saw that across the lake the sky was a light gray, that the sun was starting to come up, and he remembered that it had been evening when he went to sleep.

"Must be morning now . . . " He mumbled it, almost in a hoarse whisper. As the thickness of sleep left him the world came back.

He was still in pain, all-over pain. His legs were cramped and drawn up, tight and aching, and his back hurt when he tried to move. Worst was a keening throb in his head that pulsed with every beat of his heart. It seemed that the whole crash had happened to his head.

He rolled on his back and felt his sides and his legs, moving things slowly. He rubbed his arms; nothing seemed to be shattered or even sprained all that badly. When he was nine he had plowed his small dirt bike into a parked car and broken his ankle, had to wear a cast for eight weeks, and there was nothing now like that. Nothing broken. Just battered around a bit.

His forehead felt massively swollen to the touch, almost like a mound out over his eyes, and it was so tender that when his fingers grazed it he nearly cried. But there was nothing he could do about it and, like the rest of him, it seemed to be bruised more than broken.

I'm alive, he thought. I'm alive. It could have been different. There could have been death. I could have been done.

Like the pilot, he thought suddenly. The pilot in the plane, down into the water, down into the blue water strapped in the seat . . .

He sat up—or tried to. The first time he fell back. But on the second attempt, grunting with the effort, he managed to come to a sitting position and scrunched sideways until his back was against a small tree where he sat facing the lake, watching the sky get lighter and lighter with the coming dawn.

His clothes were wet and clammy and there was a faint chill. He pulled the torn remnants of his windbreaker, pieces really, around his shoulders and tried to hold what heat his body could find. He could not think, could not make thought patterns work right. Things seemed to go back and forth between reality and imagination—except that it was all reality. One second he seemed only to have imagined that there was a plane crash, that he had fought out of the sinking plane and swum to shore; that it had all happened to some other person or in a movie playing in his mind. Then he would feel his clothes, wet and cold, and his forehead would slash a pain through his thoughts and he would know it was real, that it had really happened. But all in a haze, all in a haze-world. So he sat and stared at the lake, felt the pain come and go in waves, and watched the sun come over the end of the lake.

It took an hour, perhaps two—he could not measure time yet and didn't care—for the sun to get halfway up.

With it came some warmth, small bits of it at first, and with the heat came clouds of insects—thick, swarming hordes of mosquitos that flocked to his body, made a living coat on his exposed skin, clogged his nostrils when he inhaled, poured into his mouth when he opened it to take a breath.

It was not possibly believable. Not this. He had come through the crash, but the insects were not possible. He coughed them up, spat them out, sneezed them out, closed his eyes and kept brushing his face, slapping and crushing them by the dozens, by the hundreds. But as soon as he cleared a place, as soon as he killed them, more came, thick, whining, buzzing masses of them. Mosquitos and some small black flies he had never seen before. All biting, chewing, taking from him.

In moments his eyes were swollen shut and his face puffy and round to match his battered forehead. He pulled the torn pieces of his windbreaker over his head and tried to shelter in it but the jacket was full of rips and it didn't work. In desperation he pulled his T-shirt up to cover his face, but that exposed the skin of his lower back and the mosquitos and flies attacked the new soft flesh of his back so viciously that he pulled the shirt down.

In the end he sat with the windbreaker pulled up, brushed with his hands and took it, almost crying in frustration and agony. There was nothing left to do. And when the sun was fully up and heating him directly, bringing steam off of his wet clothes and bathing him with warmth, the mosquitos and flies disappeared. Almost that suddenly. One minute he was sitting in the middle of a swarm; the next, they were gone and the sun was on him.

Vampires, he thought. Apparently they didn't like

the deep of night, perhaps because it was too cool, and they couldn't take the direct sunlight. But in that gray time in the morning when it began to get warm and before the sun was full up and hot—he couldn't believe them. Never, in all the reading, in the movies he had watched on television about the outdoors, never once had they mentioned the mosquitos or flies. All they ever showed on the naturalist shows was beautiful scenery or animals jumping around having a good time. Nobody ever mentioned mosquitos and flies.

"Unnnhhh." He pulled himself up to stand against the tree and stretched, bringing new aches and pains. His back muscles must have been hurt as well—they almost seemed to tear when he stretched—and while the pain in his forehead seemed to be abating somewhat, just trying to stand made him weak enough to nearly collapse.

The backs of his hands were puffy and his eyes were almost swollen shut from the mosquitos, and he saw everything through a narrow squint.

Not that there was much to see, he thought, scratching the bites. In front of him lay the lake, blue and deep. He had a sudden picture of the plane, sunk in the lake, down and down in the blue with the pilot's body still strapped in the seat, his hair waving . . .

He shook his head. More pain. That wasn't something to think about.

He looked at his surroundings again. The lake stretched out slightly below him. He was at the base of the L, looking up the long part with the short part out to his right. In the morning light and calm the water was absolutely, perfectly still. He could see the reflections of the trees at the other end of the lake. Upside down in the water they seemed almost like another forest, an upside-down forest to match the real one. As he watched, a large bird—he thought it looked like a crow but it seemed larger—flew from the top, real forest, and the reflection-bird matched it, both flying out over the water.

Everything was green, so green it went into him. The forest was largely made up of pines and spruce, with stands of some low brush smeared here and there and thick grass and some other kind of very small brush all over. He couldn't identify most of it—except the evergreens—and some leafy trees he thought might be aspen. He'd seen pictures of aspens in the mountains on television. The country around the lake was moderately hilly, but the hills were small—almost hummocks—and there were very few rocks except to his left. There lay a rocky ridge that stuck out overlooking the lake, about twenty feet high.

If the plane had come down a little to the left it would have hit the rocks and never made the lake. He would have been smashed.

Destroyed.

The word came. I would have been destroyed and torn and smashed. Driven into the rocks and destroyed.

Luck, he thought. I have luck, I had good luck there. But he knew that was wrong. If he had had good luck his parents wouldn't have divorced because of the Secret and he wouldn't have been flying with a pilot who had a heart attack and he wouldn't be here where he had to have good luck to keep from being destroyed.

If you keep walking back from good luck, he thought, you'll come to bad luck.

He shook his head again—wincing. Another thing not to think about.

The rocky ridge was rounded and seemed to be of

some kind of sandstone with bits of darker stone layered and stuck into it. Directly across the lake from it, at the inside corner of the L, was a mound of sticks and mud rising up out of the water a good eight or ten feet. At first Brian couldn't place it but knew that he somehow knew what it was—had seen it in films. Then a small brown head popped to the surface of the water near the mound and began swimming off down the short leg of the L leaving a V of ripples behind and he remembered where he'd seen it. It was a beaver house, called a beaver lodge in a special he'd seen on the public channel.

A fish jumped. Not a large fish, but it made a big splash near the beaver, and as if by a signal there were suddenly little splops all over the sides of the lake— along the shore—as fish began jumping. Hundreds of them, jumping and slapping the water. Brian watched them for a time, still in the half-daze, still not thinking well. The scenery was very pretty, he thought, and there were new things to look at, but it was all a green and blue blur and he was used to the gray and black of the city, the sounds of the city. Traffic, people talking, sounds all the time—the hum and whine of the city.

Here, at first, it was silent, or he thought it was silent, but when he started to listen, really listen, he heard thousands of things. Hisses and blurks, small sounds, birds singing, hum of insects, splashes from the fish jumping—there was great noise here, but a noise he did not know, and the colors were new to him, and the colors and noise mixed in his mind to make a green-blue blur that he could hear, hear as a hissing pulse-sound and he was still tired.

So tired.

So awfully tired, and standing had taken a lot of

energy somehow, had drained him. He supposed he was still in some kind of shock from the crash and there was still the pain, the dizziness, the strange feeling.

He found another tree, a tall pine with no branches until the top, and sat with his back against it looking down on the lake with the sun warming him, and in a few moments he scrunched down and was asleep again.

# Reviewing and Interpreting the Selection

Record your answers to these questions in your personal literature notebook. Follow the directions for each part.

**Reviewing**   Try to complete each of these sentences without looking back at the selection.

Identifying
Cause and Effect

1. Brian wants the plane to land in a lake because he

    a. does not want to hit the moose standing in the pond.

    b. has missed the airport.

    c. knows that landing in the trees will tear the plane apart.

    d. wants to be near food.

Identifying
Sequence

2. The first thing that Brian does after the plane crashes is

    a. grab his suitcase.

    b. call for help on the radio.

    c. swim out the broken front window.

    d. think about his mother and the Secret.

Recalling
Facts

3. In the morning, Brian is attacked by a

    a. snake.

    b. swarm of mosquitos.

    c. hungry bear.

    d. hungry wolf.

4. The biggest problem Brian faces is that

    a. his parents are divorced.

    b. he can't get to the plane anymore.

    c. there are black flies in the area.

    d. he is all alone.

5. All of these are settings in this selection *except*

    a. the cockpit of a falling plane.

    b. underwater in a lake.

    c. a forest.

    d. an airport.

**Interpreting**   To complete these sentences, you may look back at the selection if you'd like.

6. Thinking about seeing his mother in a car with a man makes Brian angry because

    a. the man is not his father.

    b. his mother had promised to take Brian shopping.

    c. his mother ignored him.

    d. his mother was late picking him up.

7. Now that Brian is alone in the wilderness, he probably will

    a. try to walk to the closest town.

    b. look for food, water, and shelter.

    c. do nothing and hope he will be rescued.

    d. make friends with the animals.

8. Brian would say he is a lucky boy because

    a. he gets to spend a summer in the Canadian wilderness.

    b. he likes animals.

    c. his plane landed in the lake instead of on the rocks.

    d. he likes to be alone.

9. From the description of Brian's surroundings, you can tell that

    a. it is winter.

    b. he is close to a number of big cities.

    c. it will be easy to live there.

    d. it is summer.

10. You know that Brian is a good problem-solver because he

    a. manages to land the plane.

    b. brings supplies from the plane.

    c. knows all about wilderness animals.

    d. is impressed by the beauty of the scenery.

Now check your answers with your teacher. Study the questions you answered incorrectly. What types of questions were they? Talk with your teacher about ways to work on those skills.

# Setting

Every story takes place in a certain place and at a certain time. The time and place of a story is its setting. In some stories, the setting is not described in much detail because it is not that important. The events in the story could happen in just about any place and at any time. In other stories, however, the setting plays as important a part in the story as the characters do. In order for the story to work, it could happen only in a specific place and at a specific time.

In some stories, the setting is very realistic. In other stories, such as science fiction or fairy tales, the setting is fantastic and imaginary. Whether the setting is realistic or fantastic, the author provides details that make the setting believable. The details let you see, hear, smell, taste, and feel what the characters are experiencing, and the whole story becomes more real.

The setting of a story is like the scenery in a play. As the curtain opens on a play and you see that the setting is a New York City classroom, you can be fairly certain that the characters will not be dressed as knights in armor and will not be fighting dragons.

In a way, the setting can determine what happens in a story. For example, if an author sets a story in colonial America, the characters would not be able to watch television. An author must be careful to include details that could really happen in a certain time and place, or the story won't be believable.

Authors also use the details of a setting to create the mood of a story. Reading about a character walking through a dark forest with huge trees that reach out and grab anyone who passes by creates a mood that can make readers feel as nervous as the character.

Setting, like character and plot, is an important element of a story. Thinking about the setting and how the author is using it will increase your understanding of the story. In these lessons, we will look at these ways in which author Gary Paulsen uses setting to help tell the story:

1. He uses a variety of details to make you feel that you are in the setting along with the character.

2. He uses the setting to determine what happens in the story.

3. He shows how the setting affects the character's mood.

4. He uses the setting and mood to influence readers' feelings.

## 1 • Setting and Details

Have you ever played a game called twenty questions? In it, you have twenty chances to guess the person, place, or thing your opponent has in mind. Although the game is fun, writers do not want their readers to have to play twenty questions when reading their books. They want important details to be immediately clear to their readers. They don't want their readers to have to guess where the characters are, what they are experiencing, and why. So authors include plenty of details to help readers sense (see, hear, smell, taste, and feel) what the characters sense.

Read this passage from *Hatchet* to see how Gary Paulsen introduces us to the world Brian discovers after his plane crashes.

A fish jumped. Not a large fish, but it made a big splash near the beaver, and as if by a signal there were suddenly little splops all over the sides of the lake—along the shore—as fish began jumping. Hundreds of them, jumping and slapping the water. Brian watched them for a time, still in the half-daze, still not thinking well. The scenery was very pretty, he thought, and there were new things to look at, but it was all a green and blue blur and he was used to the gray and black of the city, the sounds of the city. Traffic, people talking, sounds all the time—the hum and whine of the city.

Here, at first, it was silent, or he thought it was silent, but when he started to listen, really listen, he heard thousands of things. Hisses and blurks, small sounds, birds singing, hum of insects, splashes from the fish jumping—there was great noise here. . . .

This is not just a description of the setting, it is a discovery process. Brian is using his senses of sight and hearing to learn about his surroundings. We readers "see" what Brian sees, bit by bit, detail by detail. We see and are surprised by the fish. We hear the sounds that the fish, birds, and insects make. When Brian first saw the lake from the plane, it was just a scene, like a still-life painting. Now, however, it is no longer a painting. It is an area brimming with life, movement, and sound.

All of the details that Gary Paulsen includes—the splashes of the fish, the blue and green colors, the hisses and hums of the insects—make the setting come alive. We are there with Brian, seeing and hearing and feeling what he is experiencing.

## Exercise 1

Read this passage, which details the action of the plane crashing into the lake. Then use what you have learned in this lesson to answer the questions that follow the passage.

> There was a great wrenching as the wings caught the pines at the side of the clearing and broke back, ripping back just outside the main braces. Dust and dirt blew off the floor into his face so hard he thought there must have been some kind of explosion. He was momentarily blinded and slammed forward in the seat, smashing his head on the wheel.
>
> Then a wild crashing sound, ripping of metal, and the plane rolled to the right and blew through the trees, out over the water and down, down to slam into the lake, skip once on water as hard as concrete, water that tore the windshield out and shattered the side windows, water that drove him back into the seat. Somebody was screaming, screaming as the plane drove down into the water.

1. Which details describe what Brian is seeing? Which details describe what he is hearing?

2. There are details in this passage that appeal to the sense of touch. Is the wheel soft or hard? How do you know? Which

details let you know how the water feels? Which other details appeal to the sense of touch?

Now check your answers with your teacher. Review this part of the lesson if you don't understand why an answer was incorrect.

## Writing on Your Own 1

In this exercise you will use what you have learned in this lesson to write a paragraph that describes a setting. Follow these steps:

- Review the details of the setting you chose in Creating a Setting on pages 42–43. If you think of any more details, add them to the chart.

- Write a sentence for each detail. For example, a sentence about a city street might be, "The smell of exhaust from the passing buses made me sick to my stomach." If you'd like, you can include more than one detail in the same sentence.

- Combine all your detail sentences into a paragraph that describes your chosen setting. Begin with a topic sentence, such as, "The forest at midday was alive with sights and sounds," or "When I stepped into the classroom, some familiar items caught my eye." The topic sentence should identify the setting's place or time. The rest of the sentences should add details to make the setting seem real.

- Reread your paragraph. Make sure that the order in which you described the setting makes sense. Make any changes that you feel would improve the paragraph.

## 2 • Setting and Actions

You have just climbed into a school bus. You ride it every day, so by now you know just what to expect: You will find a friend to sit with, you two will talk about homework or teachers or other students, and then you will say goodbye to your friend and step down off the bus.

The minute you enter the bus, you know that you will not have to fight a grizzly bear or climb a mountain during the next half hour. The setting you are in makes those actions unlikely or impossible.

In the same way that the place you're in determines your actions, the setting of a story or novel determines a character's actions. The author creates a setting to give characters a logical place in which to act out the story. In this passage from *Hatchet*, the author has placed Brian in an exciting setting. He is the only survivor in a tiny plane that is flying out of control over a remote wilderness. Brian doesn't have much choice in what he can do. His actions are controlled by the setting and the situation, as you will see in the following passage.

> But he needed one [a lake] right in front. He desperately needed a lake right in front of the plane and all he saw through the windshield were trees, green death trees. If he had to turn—if he had to turn he didn't think he could keep the plane flying. His stomach tightened into a series of rolling knots and his breath came in short bursts . . .
>
> There!
>
> Not quite in front but slightly to the right he saw a lake. L-shaped, with rounded corners, and the plane was nearly aimed at the long part of the L, coming from the bottom and heading to the top. Just a tiny bit to the right. He pushed the right rudder pedal gently and the nose moved over.
>
> But the turn cost him speed and now the lake was above the nose. He pulled back on the wheel slightly and the nose came up. This caused the plane to slow dramatically and almost seem to stop and wallow in the air. The controls became very loose-feeling and frightened Brian, making him push the wheel back in. This increased the speed a bit but filled the windshield once more with nothing but trees, and put the lake well above the nose and out of reach.

Brian is in a small plane above a remote wilderness, and the pilot of the plane is dead. Brian very easily could panic in this situation, but he acts on instinct instead. His desperation and fear have triggered his will to survive. So he tries to crash-land the plane in a lake in order to soften the landing. Brian's immediate world consists of the inside of the tiny plane and the fearsome world outside, full of threatening trees and water. Because these settings are so extreme, Brian can't stop to worry whether his decisions are the best ones. He has time only to think and act as quickly as possible.

## Exercise 2

Read the following passage. Then use what you have learned in this lesson to answer the questions that follow the passage.

It took an hour, perhaps two—he could not measure time yet and didn't care—for the sun to get halfway up. With it came some warmth, small bits of it at first, and with the heat came clouds of insects—thick, swarming hordes of mosquitos that flocked to his body, made a living coat on his exposed skin, clogged his nostrils when he inhaled, poured into his mouth when he opened it to take a breath.

It was not possibly believable. Not this. He had come through the crash, but the insects were not possible. He coughed them up, spat them out, sneezed them out, closed his eyes and kept brushing his face, slapping and crushing them by the dozens, by the hundreds. But as soon as he cleared a place, as soon as he killed them, more came, thick, whining, buzzing masses of them. Mosquitos and some small black flies he had never seen before. All biting, chewing, taking from him.

In moments his eyes were swollen shut and his face puffy and round to match his battered forehead. He pulled the torn pieces of his windbreaker over his head and tried to shelter in it but the jacket was full of rips and it didn't work. In desperation he pulled his T-shirt up to cover his face, but that exposed the skin of his lower back and the mosquitos and flies attacked the new soft flesh of his back so viciously that he pulled the shirt down.

In the end he sat with the windbreaker pulled up, brushed with his hands and took it, almost crying in frustration and agony. There was nothing left to do.

1. What in this setting determines Brian's actions? How does he react to the problem the setting presents?

2. Is Brian able to overcome the problem that this passage describes? How do you know? What might Brian's future plans include if he doesn't want to experience another mosquito attack?

Now check your answers with your teacher. Review this part of the lesson if you don't understand why an answer was incorrect.

## Writing on Your Own 2

In this exercise you will write about a conflict that could take place in your chosen setting. Follow these steps:

- Reread the description of the setting that you wrote for Writing on Your Own 1. Think about what might logically happen to a character in that setting. What kind of problems, or conflicts, might a character face? List some possible conflicts that could happen in that setting.

- Choose one of the conflicts on your list. Write at least three sentences to explain why it would be logical for that conflict to happen in your chosen setting.

## 3 • Setting and Feelings

If someone told you that you were going to an amusement park all day today, how would you feel? If you like amusement parks, you probably would feel excited. You have fun at amusement parks, and you usually feel happy at them. The place where you are has a strong influence on how you feel.

In a novel, the characters' moods, or feelings, are influenced by their surroundings too. In *Hatchet*, the different settings—and what happens in them—greatly influence Brian's moods and feelings. Author Gary Paulsen describes each setting in such a way that when you read about it, your feelings change right along with Brian's.

Read this passage from *Hatchet* to see how Brian feels right after his plane crashes into the lake.

. . . He saw nothing but sensed blue, cold blue-green, and he raked at the seatbelt catch, tore his nails loose on one hand. He ripped at it until it released and somehow—the water trying to kill him, to end him—somehow he pulled himself out of the shattered front window and clawed up into the blue, felt something hold him back, felt his windbreaker tear and he was free. Tearing free. Ripping free.

But so far! So far to the surface and his lungs could not do this thing, could not hold and were through, and he sucked water, took a great pull of water that would—finally—win, finally take him, and his head broke into light and he vomited and swam, pulling without knowing what he was, what he was doing. Without knowing anything. Pulling until his hands caught at weeds and muck, pulling and screaming until his hands caught at last in grass and brush and he felt his chest on land, felt his face in the coarse blades of grass and he stopped, everything stopped. A color came that he had never seen before, a color that exploded in his mind with the pain and he was gone, gone from it all, spiraling out into the world, spiraling out into nothing.

Brian is frantic. He feels that the water is trying to kill him, and he wants to escape it. He is terrified that the plane will be his grave, and he is determined to get out as quickly as possible. He becomes reckless, tearing and pulling without caring that he is hurting himself. When he reaches the shore, he is still wild and screaming as he claws his way out of the water. As you read this exciting passage, you probably became excited and nervous about whether Brian would live or die. You might have even felt tired when he finally reached the shore. All the details that Paulsen provides about the setting helped you share in Brian's experiences and feelings.

## Exercise 3

Read this passage. Use what you have learned in this lesson to answer the questions that follow the passage.

He looked at his surroundings again. The lake stretched out slightly below him. He was at the base of the L, looking up the long part with the short part out to his right. In the morning light and calm the water was absolutely, perfectly still. He could see the reflections of the trees at the other end of the lake. Upside down in the water they seemed almost like another forest, an upside-down forest to match the real one. As he watched, a large bird—he thought it looked like a crow but it seemed larger—flew from the top, real forest, and the reflection-bird matched it, both flying out over the water.

Everything was green, so green it went into him. . . .

1. How is Brian's mood in this passage different from his mood in the first passage in this lesson?

2. Which details show that Brian has time to appreciate his surroundings now?

Now check your answers with your teacher. Review this part of the lesson if you don't understand why an answer was incorrect.

## Writing on Your Own 3

Use what you have learned in this lesson to write about a setting in two different ways. Follow these steps:

- Choose a setting that you can picture easily. You can use the same setting that you used in the first two writing exercises, or you may choose a different one.

- Write two separate descriptions of that setting. In the first description, make the place seem calm, peaceful, and happy. Use details to create a pleasant mood.

- In the second description, use the same setting—only this time, make the place seem frightening or sad. Choose your words carefully to help create the appropriate mood.

# Discussion Guides

1. Stories like *Hatchet* are often called survival stories. Together with the rest of your class, make a list of stories you have read, or movies or television programs you have seen, in which a character or characters must fight for their survival. Use the following questions to help you compare the titles on your list to *Hatchet*.

   • How are the settings like or unlike the settings in *Hatchet*?

   • How are the main characters like or unlike Brian?

   • How do the characters' survival techniques compare to Brian's?

2. Many people enjoy vacationing in settings like the one in which Brian crashes. With a small group of classmates, talk about what is appealing about such a setting, from a vacationer's point of view. Then create a poster or brochure describing the area and listing its most appealing features.

3. Imagine you are in Brian's place, stranded in the wilderness. The only difference is that you have a backpack full of equipment with you. What is in your backpack? Work with a small group to decide which items would be most useful to have in the backpack. Remember to consider the size and weight of each object. You probably wouldn't be able to carry more than about thirty pounds, so choose only the most useful objects—the ones that would keep you alive the longest. After your group has decided on its items, compare them with those of other groups to see which items they thought were most important.

# Write a Story Introduction

You have been working on ideas for interesting settings throughout this unit. Your final writing project will be to write an introduction to a short story. The introduction should be about one or two paragraphs long. It should introduce readers to the setting and the main character or characters. It also should set the mood and get readers ready for the conflict.

If you have any questions about the writing process, refer to Using the Writing Process, beginning on page 295.

- Assemble the work you did for all the writing exercises in this unit. You should have four pieces of writing: *a*) your chart with details about several settings; *b*) your paragraph that describes one of those settings and makes it seem real; *c*) your three sentences explaining why a particular conflict would be likely to take place in that setting; and *d*) two descriptions of a single setting, each one creating a different feeling, or mood. Reread your pieces of writing now to get ideas for the story introduction you are about to write.

- Before you begin writing, ask yourself these questions:

    Where and when will my story take place?

    Will it be told from the first-person point of view, using the pronouns *I* and *me*? Or will it be told from the third-person point of view, using the pronouns *he, she,* and *they*?

    Who will be the main character or characters?

    What mood do I wish to create?

- After you have answered the questions above, begin writing your first draft. Start with a sentence that will pull readers into the story and make them wonder what will happen next. Here is an example: "The cave explorer thought he had seen it all, but even he was shocked as he examined his most recent discovery." Continue by describing the setting and the main character briefly. Use specific details to make the setting seem as real as possible to your readers. Choose your words carefully to create a particular mood. Include hints about the conflict that will come next in the story.

- Put your writing away for a while, then return to it later to reread it. After a brief "cooling-off period," you may find details that are out of order or that are not specific enough. Make any changes that are necessary to improve your writing, including correcting any spelling, capitalization, punctuation, and grammar errors.

- Share your final piece of writing with others by posting it on a bulletin board or adding it to a class book. Also save a copy in your writing portfolio.

# Unit 3   Conflict

# The Witch of Blackbird Pond
by Elizabeth George Speare

## About the Illustration

This picture illustrates a scene from the chapter you are about to read. Following are some questions that will help you begin to think about the chapter. Use details from the picture as clues to answer the questions. Give reasons for your answers.

- Where do you think this scene is taking place?

- What is happening?

- When is it happening? How do you know?

- Look at the women's facial expressions? What do they tell you about how the women are feeling?

# Unit 3

## Introduction

## About the Novel

The American coastline looks dark and foreboding to Katherine Tyler when she first sees it from the deck of the sailing ship, the *Dolphin*. The year is 1687. Kit, as she is known, is a passenger on her way to the town of Wethersfield, in the Connecticut colony. The spirited sixteen-year-old is going there to live with her only living relatives—her Aunt Rachel, Uncle Matthew, and cousins Judith and Mercy.

Kit grew up on the sunny island of Barbados, with her wealthy and loving grandfather. He has just died, and Kit has decided that the only place she will be welcome is with these relatives she has never met. While on board the ship, Kit becomes friends with a young sailor named Nat Eaton. Nat, whose family lives near Wethersfield, is a bit of a rebel who often ignores the strict rules of the Puritan colonies.

When Kit first arrives in Connecticut, she is disappointed at the coldness of both the place and its people. She fears that she, with her informal island ways, will never fit in. But she soon comes to love her adopted family. She also becomes friends with an old Quaker woman named Hannah. Because Hannah does not share the religion of the rest of the community, and because she lives alone in a little cabin near Blackbird Pond, people believe that she is a witch. Kit doesn't care what others say; she knows that Hannah is a good, kind woman who would never harm anyone. Hannah has suffered much at the hands of the Puritans, and she misses her dead husband Thomas. Even so, she is kind to Kit and to others who come to her home in peace.

## About the Author

Elizabeth George Speare was born in 1908 in Melrose, Massachusetts. After graduating from Boston University, she taught high school English. She married in 1936, moved to Connecticut, and had two children. Initially she wrote short stories, articles, and one-act plays—mostly about her family's experiences—which she sold to magazines.

One day, Speare stumbled onto a true story about a woman from New England. The woman seemed an ideal heroine for a historical novel. Speare began to write about the young woman's adventures, filling in the unknown parts with characters and events from her own imagination. The result was Speare's first novel, *Calico Captive*.

For her second book, Speare visited Wethersfield, Connecticut, and thought about what it must have been like 300 years before. An imaginary girl began to walk and talk in Speare's mind—the girl who became the heroine of *The Witch of Blackbird Pond*. The book won the Newbery Medal in 1959. Speare's next book, *The Bronze Bow*, won the Newbery Medal in 1962.

Among Speare's other books are *Life in Colonial America* and *The Sign of the Beaver*, another historical novel for young adults, which was a Newbery Honor Book.

In order to make the characters in historical fiction seem real, Speare had to do a great deal of research. She compared doing research to going on a scavenger hunt, during which she spent much of her time searching for information in libraries, museums, historic houses, and old letters. Her discoveries of the past filled her with a renewed appreciation and understanding of the present world.

In 1989, Speare received the Laura Ingalls Wilder Award for her contributions to children's literature. Speare was honored for producing work that was filled not only with authentic historical details but also with exciting conflicts and strong, memorable characters. Speare died in 1994, in Tucson, Arizona.

## About the Lessons

The lessons that follow this chapter from *The Witch of Blackbird Pond* focus on conflict. Every good story has at least one conflict. A *conflict* is a problem or struggle of some kind that is important to the plot of a story. A conflict can be either external or internal. There are four kinds of *external conflict* in stories: 1) between two characters, 2) between a character and society, 3) between two groups, and 4) between a character and a force of nature. There is one kind of *internal conflict*: the struggle that takes place in a person's own mind. Much of the enjoyment of reading a story comes from seeing how the conflict or conflicts are resolved.

## Writing: Developing a Conflict

Authors need to develop conflicts that will keep readers reading. Conflicts can occur within a character's mind, or they can occur between a character and the people or forces around him or her. In this unit, you will practice developing exciting conflicts. The suggestions below will help you get started.

- Every conflict takes place in a certain setting. In what kind of setting would you like to write about a conflict—in the desert? the ocean? a classroom? When might the conflict take place—in the past? the future? the present? Make a list of a few possible settings.

- Then think about what kinds of conflicts are most likely to happen in each setting. Next to each setting on your list, jot down notes about a possible conflict that could occur there.

- Decide on the characters who might be involved in the conflict. What are they doing in this setting? What are they like? How might they react to problems? Make a third column on your list, and next to each setting and conflict, write a description of the character or characters involved. Save your list. You will use it later in this unit.

# Before Reading

The questions below will help you see how Elizabeth George Speare has developed the conflicts in *The Witch of Blackbird Pond.* As you read the selection, think about the answers to the following questions:

- What different kinds of conflicts do the characters face?

- What can you learn about the characters from the way they handle these conflicts?

- How do the conflicts and the actions they provoke help to advance the plot?

# Vocabulary Tips

This selection includes some words that may be unfamiliar to you but that are useful for understanding the story. Below, you will find some of these words and their definitions, as well as sentences that show how the words are used. Look them over before you begin to read.

**delirious**  mentally confused, often as the result of a high fever or a shock. This patient is <u>delirious</u>, so someone should watch over her constantly.

**poultice**  moist substance that is spread on a cloth, heated, and placed over a painful or inflamed part of the body. The doctor placed a <u>poultice</u> of healing herbs over the patient's shoulder.

**consternation**  paralyzing terror. The cab driver had a look of <u>consternation</u> when his cab hit a large patch of ice.

**hysterical**  feeling uncontrollable fear. The mother became <u>hysterical</u> when she thought her baby was missing.

**dumfounded**  amazed to the point of speechlessness; more commonly spelled <u>dumbfounded</u>. I was absolutely dumbfounded that the mayor was reelected, considering his past performance.

**serenity**  peace. Some people want excitement on vacation, but others want <u>serenity</u>.

**obstinate**  stubborn; inflexible. The <u>obstinate</u> toddler refused to give back his sister's toy.

**sodden**  soaked with water. If I want to go swimming again right away, I guess I'll have to wear this <u>sodden</u> swimsuit.

# The Witch of Blackbird Pond

Elizabeth George Speare

Five days after John Holbrook's departure Judith fell ill. Her mother, inclined at first to attribute her complaints to moping, took a second look at her flushed cheeks and put her to bed. Within two more days alarm had spread to every corner of Wethersfield. Sixteen children and young people were stricken with the mysterious fever, and none of the familiar remedies seemed to be of any benefit. For days Judith tossed on the cot they had spread for her in front of the hearth, burning with fever, fretful with pain, and often too delirious to recognize the three women who hovered about her. A young surgeon was summoned from Hartford to bleed her, and a nauseous brew of ground roasted toads was forced between her cracked lips, to no avail. The fever simply had to run its course.

On the fourth day Kit felt chilly and lightheaded, and by twilight she was thankful to sink down on the mat they dragged to the fireside near her cousin. Her bout with the malady was short, however. Her wiry young body, nourished by Barbados fruits and sunshine, had an elastic vitality, and she was back on her feet while Judith was still barely sitting up to sip her gruel. Dressing rather shakily, Kit was compelled to ask Mercy's assistance with the buttons down her back, and was shocked when her older cousin suddenly bent double in a violent fit of coughing. Kit whirled round on her.

"How long have you been coughing like that?" she demanded. "Let me feel your hand! Aunt Rachel, for heaven's sakes, get Mercy to bed quick! Here she's trying to wait on us!"

Tears of weakness and protest ran down Mercy's cheeks as Rachel stooped to take off her oldest daughter's shoes. Kit heated the warming pan to take the chill off Mercy's bed in the corner, and Mercy buried her face in the pillows as though it were a shame past bearing that she should cause so much trouble.

Mercy was seriously ill. Twice the young doctor rode out from Hartford to bleed her. The third time he stood looking soberly down at her. "I dare not bleed her further," he said helplessly.

Rachel raised timid eyes to her husband. "Matthew— do you think—that perhaps Gershom Bulkeley might know something to help her? He is so skilled."

Matthew's lips tightened. "I have said that man does not come into my house," he reminded her. "We will hear no more about it."

Rachel, already worn from the long vigil with Judith, was near the breaking point. Matthew, after working in the fields all day, forced his wife against her will to get some rest while he sat by his daughter's bedside at night. Judith watched helplessly, still too weak even to comb her own hair. The meals fell to Kit, and she did the best she could with them, measuring out the corn meal, stirring up the pudding, spooning it into a bag to boil, and cursing the clumsiness that she had never taken the pains to overcome. She built up the fire, heated kettles of water for the washing, so that Mercy might have fresh linen under her restless body. She fetched water, and strained a special gruel for Judith, and spread her uncle's wet clothes to dry before the fire. At night she dozed off, exhausted, and woke with a start sure that something was left undone.

Mercy lay on some remote borderland between sleeping and waking. Nothing could rouse her, and every breath was such a painful struggle that the slow rasp of it filled the whole house. Fear seeped in at the corners of the room. The family dared not speak above a whisper, though certainly Mercy was beyond hearing. On the fourth morning of Mercy's illness Matthew did not go to work at all, but sat heavily at the table, turning the pages of the Bible, searching in vain for some hope to cling to, or shut himself in the company room where they heard his heavy tread back and forth, back and forth, the length of the room. Toward noontime he took down his coat from the peg. "I am going out for a time," he said hoarsely.

He had one sleeve in the coat when a knock sounded at the door, and as he drew back the bolt a man's voice grated harshly through the silent room.

"Let me in, man. I've something to say."

Matthew Wood stepped back from the door, and the Reverend Bulkeley loomed on the kitchen threshold.

"Matthew," he said, "you're a stubborn mule and a rebel. But this is no time for politics. Time was your Mercy was like my own daughter. Let me see her, Matthew. Let me do what I can, with God's help, to save her."

Matthew's voice was almost a sob. "Come in, Gershom," he choked. "God bless you! I was coming to fetch you."

Dr. Bulkeley's solid presence brought to them all new hope. "I have a theory," he told them. "I've read something like it, and 'twill do no harm to try. Cook me some onions in a kettle."

For four long hours Kit labored at Dr. Bulkeley's

bidding. She sliced onions, blinking her eyes against the stinging tears. She kept the fire blazing under the iron kettle. When the onions were cooked to just the right softness, Dr. Bulkeley piled them in a mass on a linen napkin and applied the blistering poultice to Mercy's chest. As soon as the poultice cooled a new one must be ready.

Late in the afternoon the doctor rose to his feet. "There are others I must tend to," he muttered. "Keep her warm. I'll be back before midnight."

Kit busied herself to prepare a meal which none of them could eat. With fingers so heavy from fatigue and fear that she could scarcely force them to move, she cleared the table and put away the untouched food. She wondered if ever again she would escape from the sound of that dreadful breathing. Her own lungs ached with every sighing breath that Mercy drew.

Then without warning a new fear came rushing in upon her. From without the house there was an approaching sound of stamping feet and murmuring voices, gathering volume in the roadway outside. There was a crashing knock on the outer door. The three women's eyes met in consternation. Matthew Wood reached the door in one stride and flung it open.

"How dare you?" he demanded in low-voiced anger. "Know you not there is illness here?"

"Aye, we know right enough," a voice replied. "There's illness everywhere. We need your help to put a stop to it."

"What do you want?"

"We want you to come along with us. We're going for the witch."

"Get away from my house at once," ordered Matthew.

"You'll listen to us first," shouted another voice, "if you know what's good for your daughter."

"Keep your voices down, then, and be quick," warned Matthew. "I've no time to listen to foolishness."

"Is it foolishness that there's scarce a house in this town but has a sick child in it? You'd do well to heed what we say, Matthew Wood. John Wetherell's boy died today. That makes three dead, and it's the witch's doing!"

"Whose doing? What are you driving at, man?"

"The Quaker woman's. Down by Blackbird Pond. She's been a curse on this town for years with her witchcraft!"

The voices sounded hysterical. "We should have run her out long ago."

"Time and again she's been seen consorting with the devil down in that meadow!"

"Now she's put a curse on our children. God knows how many more will be dead before morning!"

"This is nonsense," scoffed Matthew Wood impatiently. "There's no old woman, and no witchcraft either could bring on a plague like this."

"What is it then?" shrilled a woman's voice.

Matthew passed a hand over his forehead. "The will of God—" he began helplessly.

"The curse of God, you mean!" another voice screamed. "His judgment on us for harboring an infidel and a Quaker."

"You'd better come with us, Matthew. Your own daughter's like to die. You can't deny it."

"I'll have naught to do with it," said Matthew firmly. "I'll hold with no witch hunt."

"You'd better hold with it!" the woman's voice shrilled suddenly. "You'd better look to the witch in your own household!"

"Ask that high and mighty niece of yours where she spends her time!" another woman shouted from the darkness. "Ask her what she knows about your Mercy's sickness!"

The weariness dropped suddenly from Matthew Wood. With his shoulders thrown back he seemed to tower in the doorway.

"Begone from my house!" he roared, his caution drowned in anger. "How dare you speak the name of a good, God-fearing girl? Any man who slanders one of my family has me to reckon with!"

There was a silence. "No harm meant," a man's voice said uneasily. " 'Tis only woman's talk."

"If you won't come there's plenty more in the town who will," said another. "What are we wasting our time for?"

The voices receded down the pathway, rising again in the darkness beyond. Matthew bolted the door and turned back to the dumfounded women.

"Did they wake her?" he asked dully.

"No," sighed Rachel. "Even that could not disturb her, poor child."

For a moment there was no sound but that tortured breathing. Kit had risen to her feet and stood clinging to the table's edge. Now the new fear that was stifling her broke from her lips in an anguished whisper.

"What will they do to her?"

Her aunt looked up in alarm. Matthew's black brows drew together darkly. "What concern is that of yours?"

"I know her!" she cried. "She's just a poor helpless old woman! Oh, please tell me! Will they harm her?"

"This is Connecticut," answered Matthew sternly. "They will abide by the law. They will bring her to trial, I suppose. If she can prove herself innocent she is safe enough."

"But what will they do with her now—tonight—before the trial?"

"How do I know? Leave off your questions, girl. Is there not trouble enough in our own house tonight?" He lowered himself into a chair and sunk his head in his hands.

"Go and get some sleep, Kit," urged Rachel, dreading any more disturbance. "We may need you later on."

Kit stared from one to the other, half frantic with helplessness. They were not going to do anything. Unable to stop herself she burst into tears and ran from the room.

Upstairs, in her own room, she stood leaning against the door, trying to collect her wits. She would have to get to Hannah. No matter what happened, she could not stay here and leave Hannah to face that mob alone. If she could get there in time to warn her—that was as far as she could see just now.

She snatched her cloak from the peg and, carrying her leather boots in her hand, crept down the stairs. She dared not try to unbolt the great front door but instead tiptoed cautiously through the cold company room into the back chamber and let herself out the shed door into the garden. She could hear shouts in the distance, and slipping hurriedly into her boots she fled along the roadway.

In Meeting House Square she leaned against a tree for an instant to get her bearing. The crowd was gathering, a good twenty men and boys and a few women, carrying flaring pine torches. In the hoarse shouting and the heedless screaming of the women there was a mounting violence, and a terror she had never known before closed over Kit's mind like fog. For a moment her knees sagged and she caught at the tree for support. Then her mind cleared again, and skirting the square, darting from tree to tree like a savage, she made her way down Broad Street and out onto South Road.

She had never before seen the Meadows by moonlight. They lay serene and still, wrapped in thin veils of drifting mist. She found the path easily, passed the dark clump of willows, and saw ahead the deep shining pool that was Blackbird Pond and a faint reddish glow that must be Hannah's window.

Hannah's door was not even bolted. Inside, by the still-flickering embers of the hearth, Hannah sat nodding in her chair, fast asleep. Kit touched the woman's shoulder gently.

"Hannah dear," she said, struggling to control her panting breath. "Wake up! 'Tis Kit. You've got to come with me, quickly."

"What is it?" Hannah jerked instantly awake. "Is it a flood?"

"Don't talk, Hannah. Just get into this cloak. Where are your shoes? Here, hold out your foot, quick! Now—"

There was not a moment to spare. As they stepped into the darkness the clamor of voices struck against them. The torches looked very near.

"Not that way! Down the path to the river!"

In the shelter of the dark bushes Hannah faltered, clutching at Kit's arms. She could not be budged. "Kit! Why are those people coming?"

"Hush! Hannah, dear, please—"

"I know that sound. I've heard it before. They're coming for the Quakers."

"No, Hannah, come—I"

"Shame on thee, Kit. Thee knows a Quaker does not run away. Thomas will take care of us."

Desperately Kit shook the old woman's shoulders. "Oh, Hannah! What shall I do with you?" Of all times for Hannah to turn vague!

But Hannah's brief resolution suddenly gave way, and all at once she clung to Kit, sobbing like a child.

"Don't let them take me again," she pleaded. "Where is Thomas? I can't face it again without Thomas."

This time Kit succeeded in half dragging the sobbing woman through the underbrush. They made a terrible rustling and snapping of twigs as they went, but the noise behind them was still louder. The crowd had reached the cottage now. There was a crashing, as though the furniture were being hurled to splinters against the walls.

"She was here! The fire is still burning!"

"Look behind the woodpile. She can't have got far."

"There's the cat!" screeched a woman in terror. "Look out!"

There was a shot, then two more.

"It got away. Disappeared into thin air."

"There's no bullet could kill that cat."

"Here's the goats. Get rid of them too!"

"Hold on there! I'll take the goats. Witched or no, goats is worth twenty shillings apiece."

"Scotch the witch out!"

"Fire the house! Give us a light to search by!"

Desperately the two women pushed on, over a marshy bog that dragged at their feet, through a cornfield where the neglected shocks hid their scurrying figures, past a brambly tangle, to the shelter of the poplar trees and the broad moonlit stretch of the river. There they had to halt, crouching against a fallen log.

Behind them a flare of light, redder than the moonlight, lit up the meadows. There was a hissing and crackling.

"My house!" cried out Hannah, so heedlessly that Kit clapped a hand over her mouth. "Our own house that Thomas built!" With the tears running down her own cheeks, Kit flung both arms around the trembling woman, and together they huddled against the log and watched till the red glow lessened and died away.

For a long time the thrashing in the woods continued. Once voices came very close, and the search party went thwacking through the cornfield. Two men came out on the beach, not twenty feet from where they hid.

"Could she swim the river, think you?"

"Not likely. No use going on like this all night, Jem. I've had enough. There's another day coming." The men climbed back up the river bank.

When the voices died away it was very still. Serenity flowed back over the meadows. The veil of mist was again unbroken. After a long time, Kit dared to stretch her aching muscles. It was bitterly cold and damp here by the river's edge. She drew Hannah's slight figure closer against her, like a child's, and presently the woman's shuddering ceased, and Hannah drifted into the shallow napping of the very old.

There was no such escape for Kit. Her first surge of relief soon died away, and her thoughts, numbed by the sheer terror of pursuit, began to stir again in hopeless circles. What chance did they have when morning came? Should she rouse Hannah now and push on down the river? But where could they go? Hannah was exhausted; all her strength seemed to have died with the dying flames of her house. She could take Hannah home with her, where at least there would be warm clothes and hot food. But her uncle was a selectman. It would be his bounden duty to turn Hannah over to the law. And once they had her locked up in jail, what then? What use would a trial be with no one to speak in her defence but a foolish girl who was suspected of being a witch herself? Hannah could not even be trusted to answer the questioning straight. Like as not her mind would wander and she would talk about her Thomas.

Yet as the long hours wore away Kit could find no better solution. Whatever might happen, Hannah needed immediate care. Even the jail would be better than this unprotected place. As the first gray light slanted along the river, Kit made up her mind. They would not risk the main roads. They would pick their way along the shore of the river and cut through the meadows back to her uncle's house.

Then, unbelievably, out of the mist came the miracle. First two points of mast, then sails, transparent and wraithlike in the fog, then, as Kit strained her eyes, the looming hull, the prow, and the curved tail of a fish. The *Dolphin*! Glory be to heaven! The most beautiful sight in the world! The *Dolphin*, moving down toward Wright's Island on a steady breeze.

Kit leaped to her feet. "Hannah! Wake up! Look—look there!" Her stiff lips could scarcely babble. She flung her arms into the air, waving wildly. She could hear a man's voice across the water, but the fog rolled tantalizingly between her and the ship. She tore off her petticoat and waved it hysterically. But she dared not shout, and if she could not attract their notice the *Dolphin* would sail past down the river and their chance would be gone.

Kicking off her shoes, Kit waded into the water, plunged in and struck out toward the ship. It was a very short swim, but she had overdrawn her strength for days past. She was panting when the black hull loomed over her head, and at first she could barely raise her voice above the wash of the ship. She drew a careful breath and tried again.

There was a cry above her and a sound of running feet. "Ahoy! All hands! Man overboard!"

" 'Tis a woman!"

"Hold on there, ma'am, we're coming!"

She heard shouted orders; a thumping and creaking of ropes. Then the lifeboat swung out over her head and lowered with a smack into the water. Nat and the redheaded sailor were inside, and she had never before been so happy to see anyone.

"I knew it," groaned the redheaded one, as she clung, gasping, to the side of the boat.

"Kit! What kind of a game is this?"

"Hannah—she's in terrible trouble, Nat. They burned her house. Please—can you take her on the *Dolphin*?"

They dragged her over the side of the boat. "Where is she?" Nat demanded. "Tell the captain to heave to!" he yelled up toward the deck. "We're going ashore."

"There," pointed Kit, "by that pile of logs. We've been there all night. I didn't know what to do, and when I saw the ship—" All at once she was sobbing and babbling like a three-year-old, about the witch hunt, and the chase through the cornfield, and the man who had come so close. Nat's hands closed over hers hard and steady.

" 'Tis all right, Kit," he said, over and over. "We'll take you both on and get you some dry clothes. Just hold on a few minutes more till we get Hannah." The boat scraped the shore.

Still dazed, Hannah accepted the miracle and the prospect of a journey like a docile child. Then after two shaky steps she turned obstinate. She would not set foot in the boat without her cat.

"I can't go off without her," she insisted. "I just can't, and thee ought to know that, Nat. She'd just grieve her heart out with no home to go to and me gone off on a ship."

"Then I'll get her," said Nat. "You wait here, and keep quiet, both of you."

Kit was outraged. If she had been Nat she would have picked Hannah up and carried her off in the boat with no more nonsense. As he strode up the bank, she scrambled after him through the wet underbrush. "You're crazy, Nat!" she protested, her teeth chattering with cold. "No cat is worth it. You've got to get her out of here. If you could have heard those people—"

"If she's set on that cat she's going to have it. They've taken everything else." Nat stood in the midst of the charred cinders that had been the little house. "Damn them!" he choked. "Curse all of them!" He kicked a smoldering log viciously.

They searched the trampled garden and presently they heard a cautious miaow. The yellow cat inched warily from beneath a pumpkin vine. She did not take to the idea of capture. They had to stalk her, one on each side of the garden, and Nat finally dived full length under a bush, dragged the cat out, and wrapped it tightly in his own shirt. Back at the shore Hannah received the writhing bundle with joy and climbed obediently into the rowboat.

"Where are we going, Nat?" she asked trustfully.

"I'm taking you to Saybrook for a visit with my grandmother. You'll be good company for her, Hannah. Come on, Kit. Father will go on without us."

"I'm not going, Nat. All I wanted was to see Hannah safe."

Nat straightened up. "I think you'd better, Kit," he said quietly. " 'Till this thing blows over, at least. This is our last trip before winter. We'll find a place for you in Saybrook and bring you back first trip next spring."

Kit shook her head.

"Or you can go on to the West Indies with us."

Barbados! The tears sprang to her eyes. "I can't, Nat. I have to stay here."

The concern in his eyes hardened to awareness. "Of course," he said courteously. "I forgot. You're going to be married."

" 'Tis Mercy," she stammered. "She's terribly ill. I couldn't go, I just couldn't, not knowing—"

Nat looked intently at her, and took one step nearer. The blue eyes were very close. "Kit—"

"Ahoy, there!" There was a bellow from the *Dolphin*. "What's keeping you?"

"Nat, quick! They'll hear the shouting!"

Nat jumped into the boat. "You'll be all right? You need to get warm—"

"I'll go home now. Only hurry—"

She stood watching as the boat pulled away from the sand. Halfway to the ship Nat turned to stare back at her. Then he raised an arm silently. Kit raised her own arm to wave back, and then she turned and started back along the shore. She dared not wait to see them reach the *Dolphin*. In another moment she would lose every shred of commonsense and pride and fling herself into the water after the rowboat and plead with them not to leave her behind.

Though it was long past daybreak now, her luck still held. She met no one in the north field. Once she dodged behind a brushpile as the town herder came by with some cows to pasture. She reached the house without further danger. The shed door was still unbolted, and she let herself in and crept noiselessly through the house. She heard a murmur of voices, and as she reached the hallway the door to the kitchen opened.

"Is that you, Kit?" Aunt Rachel peered at her. "We decided to let you sleep, poor child. Dr. Bulkeley has been here all night. Praise God—he says the fever is broken!"

In her joy and weariness, Aunt Rachel did not even notice the sodden dress and hair under Kit's woolen cloak.

# Reviewing and Interpreting the Selection

Record your answers to these questions in your personal literature notebook. Follow the directions for each part.

**Reviewing**   Try to complete each of these sentences without looking back at the selection.

Recalling Facts

1. When Matthew Wood hears the accusations against Hannah, he says,

    a. "This is nonsense."
    b. "We should have run her out long ago."
    c. "She's been consorting with the devil."
    d. "God bless you!"

Identifying Cause and Effect

2. When the angry mob leaves her uncle's house, Kit is frustrated because

    a. her uncle forbids her to help Hannah.
    b. Mercy isn't feeling any better yet.
    c. she realizes that her family isn't going to help Hannah.
    d. she realizes there is nothing she can do to help Hannah.

Understanding Main Ideas

3. The townspeople plan to capture Hannah to stop her from

    a. being a Quaker.
    b. living alone near Blackbird Pond.
    c. teaching their children how to read.
    d. putting a curse on their children.

4.  Just after Nat offers to take Hannah
    aboard the *Dolphin,*

    a. Kit waves goodbye to them.

    b. Hannah takes a short nap.

    c. Hannah demands that her cat be
    brought to her.

    d. the mob burns Hannah's home.

Recognizing
Literary Elements
(Setting)

5. Much of this chapter takes place

    a. aboard the ship *Dolphin.*

    b. on the meadow near Blackbird Pond.

    c. on the river near the Connecticut colony.

    d. in the Wethersfield jail.

**Interpreting**  To complete these sentences, you may look back at
the selection if you'd like.

Making
Inferences

6.  Considering Hannah's reaction to Kit, it
    seems that Hannah

    a. trusts Kit.

    b. doesn't recognize Kit because it is so dark.

    c. is afraid of Kit.

    d. can't tell her friends from her enemies.

Analyzing

7.  Because Kit decides not to go with Nat and
    Hannah, it means that she

    a. doesn't really like or trust Nat.

    b. feels a sense of responsibility to her
    family.

    c. loves the town of Wethersfield too much
    to leave.

    d. is afraid that people in the new town
    won't like her.

8. If the townspeople find out Kit has helped
   Hannah escape, they probably will

   a. ask her to find Hannah and bring her
      back.

   b. ignore the whole incident.

   c. accuse her of being a witch too.

   d. thank her for stopping them from mak-
      ing a big mistake.

Making
Generalizations

9. The general truth about human nature
   that this chapter proves best is

   a. frightened people find strength in group
      action even when what the group does
      is wrong.

   b. all people love their children.

   c. visitors from other places usually don't
      understand the people they are visiting.

   d. old people always need help to cope
      with daily life.

Understanding
Literary
Elements
(Character)

10. Kit is a brave person because she

    a. follows her uncle's advice.

    b. goes to rescue Hannah alone.

    c. hides from the angry mob.

    d. talks Hannah into coming with her.

Now check your answers with your teacher. Study the questions
you answered incorrectly. What types of questions were they? Talk
with your teacher about ways to work on those skills.

# Conflict

Some people like to keep diaries in which they record each day's memorable events. In addition, they may write some of their secret thoughts and feelings. Imagine poking through an attic one day and finding an old diary. You begin to read this entry, made many years ago.

November 1: I went to school. Then I came home.

Not exactly riveting, is it? But add a little conflict and see how much more exciting the story becomes:

November 1: I can't understand why my best friend wouldn't talk to me at school today. She totally ignored me when I saw her in the hall, and she wouldn't sit next to me at lunch. I feel terrible. When I got home, I was so upset that I yelled at my little brother for no reason at all.

Now you probably want to read the following days' entries to find out what happened next. Did the diary's owner ever find out why her friend was ignoring her? If so, how did she deal with the problem? You'll probably keep reading until you find the answer to these questions and the solution to the problem.

As you can see, without conflict, a story is just a listing of events, like the first diary entry. In the second entry, conflict gives you a reason to read on—to find out how the friend deals with her problem.

When actual people or story characters face a conflict, they usually have three basic choices. Depending on the specifics involved, they can: 1) run away from the problem, 2) figure out how to live with the problem, or 3) face the problem and overcome it. Usually, in stories, facing and overcoming the problem is the most interesting response. The way in which a character overcomes a difficulty reveals much about him or her. And the actions the character takes to overcome the problem can make for an exciting plot.

In these lessons, you will look at ways in which Elizabeth George Speare develops conflict in *The Witch of Blackbird Pond*:

1. She develops different kinds of conflicts.

2. She reveals what the characters are like by showing how they deal with the conflicts.

3. She uses the conflicts to advance the plot of the story.

## 1 • Kinds of Conflict

As you may recall, conflict can be either external or internal. An *external conflict* refers to a conflict between one character and another character, between a character and a force of nature— such as a tornado or extreme temperatures, between a character and society, or between two groups of people. An *internal conflict* is a struggle that takes place within a character's own mind.

External conflicts are the ones you usually see in action shows on television. For example, some cowboys are having an argument in a saloon. Pretty soon the argument builds to a roaring fight in which people are breaking bottles and chairs over each other's heads. Clearly, this is an example of an external conflict among characters or groups—the "good guys" and the "bad guys."

When the cowboys leave the saloon, they are faced with a dust storm that threatens to destroy their ranches unless they can find a way to fight and survive it. This is an example of an external conflict between characters and a force of nature. Soon, a federal judge rides into town and tells the cowboys they'll be punished if they keep having fights in the saloon. The cowboys then face an external conflict that society has created.

When a character struggles to decide what to do or what to believe, he or she is experiencing internal conflict. A cowboy's internal conflict might be the struggle he goes through in deciding whether to save his money or spend it all in town on payday.

Read the following passage from *The Witch of Blackbird Pond* and decide which kind or kinds of conflict are taking place.

> . . . There was a crashing knock on the outer door. The three women's eyes met in consternation. Matthew Wood reached the door in one stride and flung it open.
>
> "How dare you?" he demanded in low-voiced anger. "Know you not there is illness here?"
>
> "Aye, we know right enough," a voice replied. "There's illness everywhere. We need your help to put a stop to it."
>
> "What do you want?"
>
> "We want you to come along with us. We're going for the witch."
>
> "Get away from my house at once," ordered Matthew.
>
> "You'll listen to us first," shouted another voice, "if you know what's good for your daughter."
>
> "Keep your voices down, then, and be quick," warned Matthew. "I've no time to listen to foolishness."
>
> "Is it foolishness that there's scarce a house in this town but has a sick child in it? You'd do well to heed what we say, Matthew Wood. John Wetherell's boy died today. That makes three dead, and it's the witch's doing! . . . "
>
> "This is nonsense," scoffed Matthew Wood impatiently. "There's no old woman, and no witchcraft either could bring on a plague like this."

You can find two kinds of external conflict in this passage. At first, Matthew Wood is angry at his neighbors because they have disturbed his sick daughter (conflict between characters). But soon the conflict becomes a clash between Matthew and the society in which he lives. His neighbors believe that an old woman is a witch who is making their children sick, but Matthew thinks that such talk is nonsense. His neighbors want him to join in the witch hunt, but he refuses.

## Exercise 1

Read the following passage from the chapter. Nat has just urged Kit to escape the angry mob with him and Hannah. With regret,

Kit replies that she must stay in Wethersfield to care for her sick cousin, Mercy. Use what you have learned in this lesson to answer the questions that follow the passage.

> She [Kit] stood watching as the boat pulled away from the sand. Halfway to the ship Nat turned to stare back at her. Then he raised an arm silently. Kit raised her own arm to wave back, and then she turned and started back along the shore. She dared not wait to see them reach the *Dolphin*. In another moment she would lose every shred of commonsense and pride and fling herself into the water after the rowboat and plead with them not to leave her behind.

1. What kind of conflict is Kit dealing with in this passage, internal or external?

2. What two forces or desires are in conflict?

Now check your answers with your teacher. Review this part of the lesson if you don't understand why an answer was incorrect.

## Writing on Your Own 1

In this exercise, you will use what you learned in this lesson to write two conflicts that your character will face. Follow these steps:

- Review the notes you took for Developing a Conflict on pages 77–78. Choose the character and setting for which you have the most ideas.

- Choose two conflicts that your character will face. One conflict should be external, and one should be internal. The external conflict can be one that your character has with another character, a force of nature, or society. The internal conflict should be a question or issue with which your character is struggling. Try to make the conflicts work together.

- Write a few sentences that describe what each conflict is about.

## 2 • Conflict and Character

You know that there are several ways in which an author can reveal a character. One way is by showing how the character reacts to conflict. Does the character get angry? Does he or she fall apart under pressure or find the strength to face and overcome problems?

You learn a great deal about Kit from the way she reacts to the news that her elderly friend Hannah is in danger. Just before the following passage from *The Witch of Blackbird Pond*, an angry mob has come to the Wood home asking for Matthew Wood to participate in their witch hunt. Although Matthew has refused to join the mob, the family has decided not to get involved in the accused witch's problems.

> Kit stared from one to the other, half frantic with helplessness. They were not going to do anything. Unable to stop herself she burst into tears and ran from the room.
>
> Upstairs, in her own room, she stood leaning against the door, trying to collect her wits. She would have to get to Hannah. No matter what happened, she could not stay here and leave Hannah to face that mob alone. If she could get there in time to warn her—that was as far as she could see just now.
>
> She snatched her cloak from the peg and, carrying her leather boots in her hand, crept down the stairs. She dared not try to unbolt the great front door but instead tiptoed cautiously through the cold company room into the back chamber and let herself out the shed door into the garden. She could hear shouts in the distance, and slipping hurriedly into her boots she fled along the roadway.

At first, Kit bursts into tears because she feels her frustration so deeply. But then she turns her frustration into action and makes a quick decision to help Hannah. She quietly gets dressed and slips out of the house. Although she can hear the shouts of the mob, she doesn't even consider turning back. Kit understands that she is putting herself in danger, but she willingly accepts that danger to help her friend.

## Exercise 2

Read this passage, in which Kit arrives at Hannah's home just ahead of the mob. Then use what you have learned in this lesson to answer the questions that follow the passage.

"Hannah dear," she said, struggling to control her panting breath. "Wake up! 'Tis Kit. You've got to come with me, quickly."

"What is it?" Hannah jerked instantly awake. "Is it a flood?"

"Don't talk, Hannah. Just get into this cloak. Where are your shoes? Here, hold out your foot, quick! Now—"

There was not a moment to spare. As they stepped into the darkness the clamor of voices struck against them. The torches looked very near.

"Not that way! Down the path to the river!"

In the shelter of the dark bushes Hannah faltered, clutching at Kit's arms. She could not be budged. "Kit! Why are those people coming?"

"Hush! Hannah, dear, please—"

"I know that sound. I've heard it before. They're coming for the Quakers."

"No, Hannah, come—I"

"Shame on thee, Kit. Thee knows a Quaker does not run away. Thomas will take care of us."

Desperately Kit shook the old woman's shoulders. "Oh, Hannah! What shall I do with you?" Of all times for Hannah to turn vague!

But Hannah's brief resolution suddenly gave way, and all at once she clung to Kit, sobbing like a child.

"Don't let them take me again," she pleaded. "Where is Thomas? I can't face it again without Thomas."

1. Hannah is an old woman who has seen trouble before in her life. From what she says about how Quakers respond to danger,

how do you think she would have reacted to conflict when she was a young woman?

2. How does Hannah react to conflict now? What might she have done if she had been alone when the mob came to her home?

Now check your answers with your teacher. Review this part of the lesson if you don't understand why an answer was incorrect.

## Writing on Your Own 2

In this exercise you will write a paragraph giving a description of your character, as well as several sentences about how your character will respond to conflicts. Follow these steps:

- Review the notes you have made about your character. Then write a short paragraph describing the character.

- Try to picture your character's responses to the conflicts you described in the first Writing on Your Own exercise. Write a few sentences describing the way you think he or she would react.

## 3 • Conflict and Plot

Conflict by itself does not make a good story. You don't read a story simply to find out what problems a character is facing. You also read to discover the character's response to the problems. Conflicts bring responses in the form of plot events. As the conflicts become more and more intense, action by the characters always follows.

Think about *The Witch of Blackbird Pond*. Note how each conflict in the story leads to an action, which leads to another conflict, and so on. Before this chapter begins, a tension develops between Hannah and the Puritan community in which she lives (conflict with society). Then an epidemic sweeps Wethersfield (conflict with nature), causing the community to look for a scapegoat to blame their problems on. Hannah, being different from the rest of the people in the town, is the natural target of their fear and desperation. But as Matthew Wood proves, not all community members are in agreement about Hannah (conflict between characters). When the citizens turn on Hannah, Kit feels she must sneak away and rescue Hannah from the mob (internal conflict). Then, when the mob is disappointed at not finding Hannah at home, they burn her house down.

Each conflict generates an action, which in turn creates an additional conflict. Each conflict feeds on the one that came before, building the tension until the eventual climax, when a decision will be made that will change the course of the plot.

## Exercise 3

Read the following passage, in which Kit and Hannah are still hiding near Hannah's burned-out cabin. Then use what you have learned in this lesson to answer the questions.

> There was no such escape for Kit. Her first surge of relief soon died away, and her thoughts, numbed by the sheer terror of pursuit, began to stir again in hopeless circles. What chance did they have when morning came? Should she rouse Hannah now and push on down the river? But where could they go? Hannah was exhausted; all her strength seemed to have died with the dying flames of her house. She could take Hannah home with her, where at least there would be warm clothes and hot food. But her uncle was a selectman. It would be his bounden duty to turn Hannah over to the law. And once they had her locked up in jail, what then? What use would a trial be with no one to speak in her defence but a foolish girl who was suspected of being a witch herself? Hannah could not even be trusted to answer the questioning straight. Like as not her mind would wander and she would talk about her Thomas.

1. How do the previous conflicts between Kit and Hannah and the people of Wethersfield lead Kit into this difficult situation?

2. What other options does Kit see for Hannah at this time? What other problems will each option lead to?

Now check your answers with your teacher. Review this part of the lesson if you don't understand why an answer was incorrect.

## Writing on Your Own 3

In this exercise you will explain how earlier conflicts lead to a major conflict. Follow these steps:

- Review your notes from the previous Writing on Your Own exercises. Think about the conflicts you have chosen. Now, work backwards to set your plot in motion. Think of other, smaller conflicts that might lead to these major conflicts.

- Write a few sentences explaining how earlier conflicts build on one another to lead to a major conflict. For example, suppose two hikers have an argument about which one will carry the snakebite kit. Neither one wants the extra weight in the backpack, so the kit is left behind. Later, when one of the hikers is bitten by a snake, the small disagreement earlier creates a major conflict.

# Discussion Guides

1. How much do you know about the historical period in which this novel is set? In the villages and towns of colonial New England, the belief that witches lived in the neighborhood was common. In Salem, Massachusetts, the fear of witches reached its peak in 1692. Research this strange time in American history and present your findings to the rest of the class in an oral report.

2. The people of colonial America were no different from people today who fear what they don't understand or are not used to. The citizens of Wethersfield imagined the worst of Hannah because she was different from them. Think about the way that people in your community, the nation, or the world react to differences among people. Work with a small group to find examples of people in the modern world who are treated with suspicion or cruelty because they are different. Share your examples with other groups.

3. This novel includes many details about life in the 1600s. Work with a group to list all the details that unmistakably set this story during that time period. For example, when Judith becomes ill at the beginning of the chapter, her concerned family tries to help her by setting her cot in front of the hearth and then bleeding her. When possible, compare the practices, objects, or beliefs with those of today. For example, Judith would not undergo bleeding today; she would most likely be prescribed antibiotics instead.

# Write a Scene Using Conflict

You have been working with conflict in a number of ways in this unit's writing exercises. Now it is time to combine those ideas in a scene that highlights conflict.

If you have questions about the writing process, refer to Using the Writing Process (page 295).

- Assemble the writing you did for all the exercises in this unit. You should have four pieces of writing: *a*) your notes about the setting and the characters in your conflict, *b*) your choice of an external and an internal conflict, *c*) your description of your character and your explanation of how he or she will react to the conflicts you have chosen, *d*) your explanation of how minor conflicts lead to major ones.

- Write a scene showing how at least two major conflicts develop, using your notes as guides. Use the characters and setting that you developed in earlier exercises. Describe both an external and an internal conflict. Include both dialogue and action. Let the conflicts build to a climax—a point of highest tension.

- Read your scene aloud to several classmates. Ask each listener to predict how the main character will resolve the conflict. You may want to use some of your classmates' ideas to complete the story later. For now, as you read the scene, listen for any places that need revising. Ask your listeners if they can suggest improvements. Make any revisions you agree with.

- Proofread your scene to find spelling, grammar, punctuation, and capitalization errors. Make a final copy and save it in your writing portfolio. Later, you may want to use the scene as part of a complete short story to share with the class.

# Unit 4    The Narrator

# Ghosts I Have Been
by Richard Peck

## About the Illustration

This illustration gives you clues about what will happen in the selection you are about to read. Describe who is in the scene and discuss what they might be doing. Use details from the illustration to help explain your ideas. Then use the following questions to help you begin to think about the selection:

- When do you think this scene takes place—in the present, the past, or the future? About what year might it be?

- What do you suppose the girls are doing?

- Which of the girls appears to be the center of attention at the moment?

# Unit 4

## Introduction

## About the Novel

*Ghosts I Have Been* is the second book in a series about Blossom Culp, a girl living in a small Midwestern town during the early 1900s. Blossom's mother, proud of her gypsy blood, makes a meager living by telling fortunes and cooking up herbal medicines.

As the story begins, Blossom discovers that her friend Alexander Armsworth plans to celebrate Halloween by joining some rougher boys in tipping over privies (outhouses). Blossom's efforts to scare the boys away from her neighbor's privy result in the neighbor shooting the gang leader, Les Dawson, in the behind with rock salt. When she gets caught, Blossom tells the neighbor that her name is Letty, and Les hears the neighbor call her by that name. So Les blames his troubles on Letty Shambaugh, the richest and bossiest girl in Blossom's class.

At school the next day, Les begins to beat Letty. Blossom, feeling guilty, intervenes to save her. The principal, Miss Spaulding, intervenes to save Blossom. As the two girls recuperate in Miss

Spaulding's office, Blossom happens to see marked test papers on the principal's desk.

Letty's mother comes for her daughter, bringing along Letty's little brother Newton. After Mrs. Shambaugh learns how Blossom helped her girl, she rewards Blossom by sending her new clothes. When she insists that Letty also show some gratitude, Mrs. Shambaugh sets off a string of surprising events.

## About the Author

Richard Peck was born in 1934 in Decatur, Illinois, the model for Bluff City in this selection. From the time his mother read to him as a child, he wanted to be a writer. He attended college in Indiana and England and served in the Army as a chaplain's assistant before becoming an English teacher. In 1971 he left the classroom to become a full-time writer. Peck now lives in New York City but spends a great deal of his time traveling and visiting schools to stay close to his audience.

Peck has written over 20 novels for middle graders and young adults, several of which have been made into films. He has won many awards, including the 1990 Margaret A. Edwards Award from the American Library Association and the *School Library Journal,* the 1990 National Council of Teachers of English/ALAN Award for outstanding contributions to young adult literature, and the Edgar Allan Poe Award from the Mystery Writers of America (twice). *Ghosts I Have Been* was an ALA Best Book for Young Adults, a *School Library Journal* Best Book of the Year, and a *New York Times* Outstanding Book of the Year.

## About the Lessons

The lessons that follow this selection from *Ghosts I Have Been* focus on the narrator—the person telling the story. The lessons examine the point of view of the narrator and the roles he or she plays in a story. They also look at how the narrator sets a tone for the story. Finally, they examine the mood, or feeling, that the narrator inspires in the audience.

# Writing: Developing a Narrator

Sometimes the narrator of a story tells about events in which he or she takes part. At other times the events are described by someone outside the action. The person telling the story determines which facts are mentioned. A writer, therefore, considers several possible narrators before settling on the one who will tell the story best.

As you complete the lessons in this unit, you will learn more about how to choose a narrator and how to bring both your narrator and your writing to life. Later you will write an anecdote—a brief story—as it would be told by the narrator you have chosen. Prepare for writing your anecdote by trying these suggestions:

- Imagine taking a trip with several other people in a vehicle such as a bus, a train, or a plane. The passengers should include both friends and strangers. Where is the vehicle? Where is it headed?

- Briefly describe three of the people on the vehicle. Note whether they know each other or you. Focus on their attitudes and how they behave, rather than on how they look.

- What might happen along the way to make the trip funny, thrilling, dangerous, or otherwise memorable? How would each of your three passengers be likely to react? How would you react? List at least three events that you might use in an anecdote about this trip.

- Save your notes. You will use them later on in the unit.

# Before Reading

The following questions will help you see how author Richard Peck has developed the narrator in *Ghosts I Have Been*. As you read the selection, think about the answers to these questions:

- Who is the narrator of this story? Is he or she one of the characters or someone outside the action?

- What information does the narrator give about himself or herself?
- What feeling do you get as you read this selection? How does what the narrator says affect how you feel?

## Vocabulary Tips

This selection uses some words that may be unfamiliar to you but that are important for understanding the story. Below, you will find some of these words, their definitions, and sentences that show how the words are used. Look them over before you begin to read.

| | |
|---|---|
| **clique** | a small circle of people who look down on everyone outside the circle. The club was dominated by a <u>clique</u> of snobs. |
| **languish** | droop; become weak. During the days without rain, the garden <u>languished</u>. |
| **dredge** | to gather up, as from the bottom of a river, with a tool made of a net on a frame, or as if using such a tool. At the party, I <u>dredged</u> my memory for the names of the other guests. |
| **simpering** | characterized by a silly, faked smile. The <u>simpering</u> tattletale loved to get others into trouble. |
| **sever** | cut off. Doctors can sometimes reattach <u>severed</u> fingers. |
| **shrouded** | wrapped; covered. The mountains were <u>shrouded</u> in a thick fog. |
| **pandemonium** | a scene of wild disorder. When Lizzy's pet snake got out of its box, <u>pandemonium</u> broke out in the classroom. |
| **retribution** | well-deserved punishment. The youth was ordered to do community service as <u>retribution</u> for his crime. |

# Ghosts I Have Been

Richard Peck

In earlier times I would have hastened to trap Alexander Armsworth in some out-of-the-way spot and there told him I'd save him from a sure thrashing at Miss Spaulding's hand. She'd got the names of Champ Ferguson and Bub Timmons out of me with no trouble. She'd already dealt with Les Dawson. And she'd called him "Leslie" as she walloped him, adding insult to injury.

But my new refined appearance made me refine my methods as well. Alexander would put two and two together. Even he would figure that I was the Ghost in the Privy and that I'd had a private word with Miss Spaulding. Let him learn in his own time, and let him stew in his own juice. It would dawn on him that he owed me a favor, and I could wait. He knows I collect my debts.

At school next day I caused some comment but nothing direct. Though I was dressed better than most and entirely unlike myself, nobody came near. They were in the habit of paying me no mind. Still, many looked. I expect Letty Shambaugh explained to all and sundry that my outfit was her mother's gift. But it didn't seem to dawn on her just how her fate and mine had entwined themselves.

Somewhere in my travels I'd come by a length of plaid taffeta ribbon. I tied my unruly hair back with it as best I could. And this was the crowning touch to my new appearance. I've already said I am not vain, but I was not far from it that day. Alexander seemed not to know me at all.

At lunch I laid out a nickel for a cup of milk and was having that with an apple when Letty Shambaugh came up, dragging her feet. There were purple marks on both our necks, souvenirs of the departed Les Dawson.

"Say, listen, Blossom," she said in a loud voice right in my face, "Mama says I should . . . well, anyway, you want to come over to my house after school today?" She eyed my new Select Dry Goods, and I could hear the ring of the cash register in her head. Her mama was clearly leaning on her to show me some friendship, and I enjoyed the pain Letty was having.

"I don't mind," I replied.

"You mean you won't come?" she said, brightening.

"I mean I will." And I did.


None of the Sunny Thoughts and Busy Fingers would walk me to Letty's house after school, not even Letty. I figured out my own way along Fairview Avenue, turning up late. As I climbed the porch steps, I knew I'd sooner face Les Dawson in a rage than a clique of stuck-up snips. But it's not my way to turn back.

Though the Shambaugh place is nowhere near as large as the Armsworth mansion, it surpassed all my experience. There were rugs upon rugs, a profusion of overstuffed furniture, and of course electric lights. I walked in, supposing no one would answer if I knocked.

There in the front parlor all flopped on the floor with their skirts daintily tucked under their ankles were the club members: Letty, along with Nola Nirider and Ione Williams and Maisie Markham and Harriet Hochhuth and the Beasley twins, Tess and Bess, who are identical.

Now several of these were the very same girls who'd

done me an injury back in fourth grade when I was new in town. And none of them had spoken a civil word to me since. Still, they were trying to act grown up. Harriet Hochhuth let out a strangled gasp and clutched her forehead when she saw me enter. Evidently nobody remembered to tell her I was included. But Tess and Bess leaned her way and whispered her into the picture.

Luckily for me Mrs. Shambaugh was passing among the group with refreshments. She had what Miss Spaulding would call "a civilizing influence" on them. "Why here is Blossom!" she cried. "Make room for her in your little circle, girls!" Letty's tongue shot out of her rosebud lips at her mother's blind side.

"How grateful we *all* are that Blossom was the one girl who stood up for Letty when she needed a *friend* the *most*!" boomed Mrs. Shambaugh. "I do *wonder* where the *rest* of her friends were in her *hour* of *need*!"

All the rest of her friends stared down into their little glass cups of apple juice.

There was a plate of finger sandwiches on the floor. And as conversation languished when Mrs. Shambaugh was near, everybody chewed on them quietly. Though I was starved, I only had two. Maisie Markham wolfed down six, but she was soon to be sorry.

Finally Mrs. Shambaugh left us, and I wondered how a club worked. Nobody said much at first, though everybody shot everybody else looks full of meaning. At last Letty opened the meeting by putting down her cup and saying, "Oooo, I just hate apple juice, don't you?" And everybody agreed.

After more silence Letty sucked in her cheeks, saying, "Well, Blossom, you can't be here at the meeting without being a club member. And you can only belong for this one meeting." And everybody agreed.

This suited me well enough, since I didn't see much

to it beyond the eats. "But you can't belong even for today without an initiation." And everybody agreed to this too. You never saw a group of girls more agreeable.

Letty could tell I didn't know what an initiation was. She twitched her shoulders importantly and explained. "You must entertain the group by showing off some talent such as singing or playing a piece on the piano. Or you can tell a story that is either very scary or about boys. Since you don't have any talents, you can start telling the story now. But keep your voice down, and if Mother comes back in the room suddenly, shut up."

I thought it was not wise to tell anything I knew about boys to a bunch who might know more. They were only waiting to laugh at me anyhow. So I tried to dredge up something scary to tell them. With such a simpering group, I thought this might not be to hard. At once I recollected an experience my mama had, one of several similar and stranger than fiction.

I cleared my throat and began. "My mama has the Gift of Second Sight."

"Oh, Heaven help us," Ione Williams said, "she's going to tell whoppers about her awful mother."

"Do you want to hear this story or not?" I inquired.

"Shut up, girls, and let's just see what she has to say," Letty remarked in her position as president.

Well, I told the story, which was an entirely true event. Mere white truth in simple nakedness, as the poet says. But I added little touches and extras to it. The bare bones of the story are these. When we lived down at Sikeston, my mama commanded respect for her powers and could sometimes help out the law when she felt like it. Sikeston is in many ways backward and largely lawless.

Now and again dead bodies turn up and lie unclaimed in the morgue, a tramp of either sex found in a ditch or bodies washed up on the riverbank. As I say, it is not an up-and-coming town, so there was no system of fingerprinting or the like for identification.

If a body hung around unspoken for in the morgue till it like to get ripe, the sheriff cut off its head and put it in a jar of alcohol for future reference. Anybody missing a relative could apply for a look through the jar collection. Certain people looked just for thrills. The rest of the body below the neck was buried at County expense.

One such a body turned up in a plowed field and excited comment, though the sheriff kept the details quiet. This was no ordinary corpse. It was a young woman of gentle birth and some beauty, now fading, wearing dressmaker clothes. And nobody claimed her, though a general notice went out.

Her severed head was in a jar on the sheriff's shelf before my mama got drawn in. The face on the head kept its beauty, even in death and alcohol. It bobbed in its jar before the sheriff's gaze. At last the mystery of it preyed on his thoughts until he called on my mama to identify the head with her powers.

She was brought into the room where the head reposed. By then the sheriff had pulled a croaker sack over the jar for his own peace of mind. Of course I was not along when my mama was sent for, but I can picture her in that chamber of death, dressed for the occasion. When she was about her business, she always threw a long shawl over her head. With her black eyes and dark lips and the gold crosses in her ears, she made an impression on all who saw her. Many would cross the street.

She stood before the shrouded jar and began to sway. Several witnesses were brought in and looked on. Mama told the sheriff not to show her the head until her Inner Sight had its chance. So they waited while she went into one of her trances.

After some moments a voice within Mama began to chant, "I see a young woman of breeding with hands unused to rough work. I see her too sheltered from the wickedness of this world to be proof against its dangers. I see her face before me, not in death, but as it was in life and is no more. She is past her first youth now, easy prey to any scoundrel who might cross her path and whisper lies into her ears.

"Her ears!" my mama moaned. "Oh, her pore ears, for some beast of a man has jerked the emerald eardrops from her lobes, and left them ragged! And her eyes! Her eyes stare into mine, and they are her only natural imperfection. For one eye is robin's egg blue and t'other is hazel."

My mama fell silent then. And several in the room were unsure if she was playacting or not. But the sheriff reached over and pulled the sack off the jar. Pandemonium broke out then, and one man fainted. There were no ladies present, of course, except for Mama and the head.

Days before, when the sheriff had covered the jar with the sack, the eyes on the lady's head were closed. But when he whipped the sack off, the eyes on the severed head were wide open, staring into Mama's. And one of the dead eyes was robin's egg blue, and the other was hazel.

Some witnesses made for the door. But others stayed behind to see that the lobes on the staring head's pierced ears were torn indeed, just like Mama said.

She continued, still half in her trance, but addressed the dead head directly: "Yore people will find you now, for there is another feature which they will know you by. You have had a gold tooth in yore head since you was a girl. It's on the left side of yore mouth and chipped somewhat. What with that and them eyes, you will be reunited with yore loved ones, but naturally you won't know it, you pore cut-up thing."

At that, Mama seemed to come to herself and look around. She always knows exactly what she's said in any of her fits and swoons. Somebody urged the sheriff to lift out the head from the alcohol and check around in the clenched mouth to see if there was a chipped gold tooth anywhere in there. "And while you are about it," my mama mentioned, "you will find a knot the size of two walnuts at the base of the skull beneath her back hair where she was knocked in the head with a bottle and killed by a tall man with a squint and a limp wearing a ring in the shape of a serpent."

The sheriff got the lid off the jar and reached down into the alcohol. He drew the ghastly head up; it hung by the hair in the air, dripping from the neck. All but the stoutest hearted turned aside while the sheriff explored in the head's mouth, drawing up one side. The mouth fell open, as if obedient. Sure enough, there was the gold tooth, slightly chipped in a mouth that seemed half to grin beneath them piercing eyes. The lump was on the back of the skull too.

A detail description of the head went out to all the towns on the river. Shortly thereafter some well-to-do people of Stuttgart, Arkansas, answered the call. They were the dead woman's folks and come north for a view of her head. Not knowing she was dead, they'd never reported her missing.

She'd eloped with an implement salesman who'd killed her on her wedding night for the emeralds in her ears and the money in her purse. He'd spirited the body as far as Sikeston, where he'd dumped it. Then the crafty devil sent telegrams to the dead woman's kin from various places, signed with her name. Come to find out, he'd done this with many women and made a living at it.

He was a monster, and he was caught. For Mama seen him with her Second Sight: snake ring, limp, squint, and all. A man answering that description was rounded up in Texarkana. He was hanged there on the tree in Spring Lake Park they keep for that purpose. Mama got very little credit and no reward. Still, a public demonstration of her skills brought people to her for advice and vision, though few could pay and fewer did. She was later hounded out of town by a more progressive element.

That's the sum and substance of the story I entertained the Sunny Thoughts and Busy Fingers girls with. They were an interested audience in spite of themselves. Though when I come to where the sheriff holds up the severed head and pokes into her green mouth for the gold tooth, it was too much for Maisie Markham.

I paused there because Maisie jumped up and made a run for the porch. We all watched from the window as she hung over the railing and threw up into the forsythia. Directly that interruption was over, Tess and Bess urged me to go on. They were so encouraging that Letty made a nasty gesture at them with one of her fingers. Maisie came back and stretched out on the couch to hear how the story ended.

When I finished up, they fidgeted but were speechless, except for Harriet Hochhuth, who said, "How do you suppose the head happened to open its eyes?"

But Letty said, "Oooo, that was *repulsive*. I wish I hadn't heard it."

"Well, you *said* it was to be scary," said Tess or Bess,

"and it *was.*" This was brave of her, but she soon fell back. Letty was sending her a silent message. It may have been that if everybody liked the story, I'd have to be made a life member of the club.

"It wasn't a story," Letty explained. "It was just a lot of Blossom's lies. She couldn't tell the truth if she tried." She waited then till everybody had to agree. This might not have got my dander up, but the next thing Letty said did. "There is no such thing as Second Sight as everybody knows. And if there was, *Blossom's* family wouldn't have any. Heaven knows, they don't have anything else."

"That's a lie right there," I said. And then before I thought: "I have the Second Sight, my own self."

"Aha! I saw this coming!" crowed Letty, jumping up. "If you have the Second Sight, Blossom Culp, let's see it. Haul off and do something spooky. Talk is *cheap,* Blossom, particularly yours. Prove it!"

"That's right. You'd better prove it, Blossom," all agreed. I liked to have fainted with the strain of the moment, because they looked ready to act on me and ruin my new outfit if I didn't deliver. Even Maisie was recovering fast and raising up from the couch. Her little pig eyes looked mean.

I didn't truly think they'd cut me up for bait. Not with Mrs. Shambaugh somewhere in the house. But I had to satisfy them or slink off in disgrace. Pride is a terrible thing sometimes. I racked my brains and played for time.

"We have to be in a dim room," I remarked. "It's too bright in here. After dark would be better."

"*Now*, Blossom," Letty said, and her little dimpled hands were on her hips, and her little dimpled elbows were fanning the air. "We can go into the room where Daddy smokes and pull the blind."

Everybody made a rush for this room, under the back

stairs. Letty yanked heavy curtains across the window. "*Now* what do you need, Blossom, a crystal ball?" She poked the girls nearest her in the gloom to remind them to laugh. I did just notice, though, that being in a darker place with me had quieted them down some. One more point in my favor and they might desert Letty completely, if only long enough to cover my retreat. Then I got a sudden inspiration, more secondhand than Second Sight. It was in regard to something I'd spied in the principal's office.

I pulled out a straight chair and sat down with my back to the door. As there weren't enough chairs to go around, the rest had to settle at my feet. So far so good, I thought. "It takes me a while to warm up," I mentioned.

"Don't be too long," Letty warned, "or we'll give you a broom, and you can fly home on it, ha ha."

I began to sway in my chair then, starting up slow. I always have been able to roll my eyes up into my head so only the whites show. As a kid I practiced that by the hour. "Oh, look what's happening to her eyes, isn't that sickening!" somebody said.

I moaned low in my throat, wishing I'd thought to ask for a candle. Candlelight always adds a touch. But I proceeded without it. In a far-off voice I began to moan a poem, working up from a whisper:

> *The . . . ghost . . . am . . . I*
> *Of . . . winds . . . that . . . die*
> *Alike . . . on . . . land . . . and . . . sea*
> *O Second Sight! O Second Sight!*
> *Send one small glimpse to me!*

Commencing with a real poem I have by heart, I added an ending to suit the occasion. By then my eyes were rolled so far back in my head I was looking at my brains. But you could hear a pin drop in the room.

"What is this vision I see before my inner eyes?" I asked, and waited as if for an answer. "A crime. A crime has been committed. A crime that will be punished with fearful retribution!"

"Oh dear," came Harriet Hochhuth's voice, "I don't really care too much for this sort of thing."

"And the criminal is not far off!" I continued. "No wait! Two outlaws . . . and in this very room!"

"Make her stop," someone said in small voice.

There was stirring on the floor as, I suppose, everybody shifted around on the lookout for floating initials.

"I see the initials of one of the crooks. The letters are floating in the air before me."

"N. N. are two of the initials," I continued. "And the others are . . I. and let me see . . . W.! Oh, what have these two been up to that will only lead them to a thrashing from a heavy hand?"

Whispers came from the floor around me as several came to their own conclusions about the owners of the initials. "They are cheats, these two," I moaned on, completely warmed up. "They've passed the answers on the United States geography test back and forth. But their crime has come to light."

There was a general intake of breath from the floor as I got more specific. Miss Spaulding had wound up our United States geography on Monday with a stiff test. I'd seen the papers on her desk, and I knew she'd caught Nola Nirider and Ione Williams red-handed. All their wrong answers were the same, and there were plenty of them. Miss Spaulding is not to be trifled with.

"Sacramento is the capital of California, not San Diego as these two culprits both put down. And Robert E.

Lee hails from Virginia, not Kentucky. There is more evidence before my eyes, but my powers grow dimmmmmm. I only see two more letters—a couple of Fs. But those are grades.

"But I can hear the sounds of bottoms being smacked and shrieks of pure pain!"

The curtain rings clattered as Letty swept the drapes back. Light flooded the room. I let my eyeballs roll forward to see Ione and Nola shrinking on the carpet in the midst of the rest.

"Did you two cheat on the test?" Letty barked, taking charge again with her usual bossiness.

"Certainly not," said Nola.

"What if we did?" said Ione, who is more brazen.

"Well, if that doesn't just about make me sick!" spat out Letty. "While all the rest of us beat our brains out studying, you two went off by yourselves and cheated! Then you had no more sense than to get caught."

"Just how do you know that?" said Ione, very sassy. "We don't even have the tests back yet, so how do you know?"

"Because Blossom said so," Letty snapped. Then she caught her breath. She'd given me credit and could not take it back. She shot me a look guiltier than Nola and Ione combined. For I had told—or foretold—something no living soul could know, except for Miss Spaulding. And I'd been believed. I had Letty in a cleft stick then, with no time to think. Both Ione and Nola looked plain scared, both of me and Miss Spaulding. Nola commenced to sob, anticipating pain.

But then something happened that even I could not explain. My eyes did not roll back, yet I seemed to go blind for a second. There was a peal of thunder that nobody else seemed to hear. Then a strange flash, like lightning at night—jagged and blue. The room and the girls flickered and faded from me, and I spoke without conscious thought:

"Oh dear," I said, "Newton just fell off the back of the trolley and was run over by Miss Dabney's electric auto."

Then I blinked and saw the room clear and all the girls' eyes staring at me. But only for a moment. The next second was split by a powerful shriek from Mrs. Shambaugh. Evidently she'd been eavesdropping behind the door the entire time. When I remarked that her little boy had just been run over—several blocks away— the shock of it nearly carried her off.

It was a confused hour later before it dawned on me. The blood had not run too thin. I had the Gift of Second Sight and the Power to See the Unseen. And maybe more.

# Reviewing and Interpreting the Story

Record your answers to these questions in your personal literature notebook. Follow the directions for each part.

**Reviewing**  Try to complete each of these sentences without looking back at the story.

Recalling Facts

1. The story that Blossom tells is

   a. one that she makes up.

   b. one that she has read in a book but changes a bit to make it sound original.

   c. about something that happened to Blossom herself.

   d. about something that happened to her mother.

Identifying
Cause and Effect

2. Letty invites Blossom to a meeting of her Sunny Thoughts and Busy Fingers club because

   a. her mother told her to do so.

   b. she wants to hear a scary story.

   c. she is grateful to Blossom.

   d. she thinks Blossom's family has nothing of value.

Understanding
Main Ideas

3. Letty's behavior toward her mother shows that she

   a. loves and respects her mother.

   b. obeys her mother unwillingly.

   c. is terrified of her mother.

   d. feels sorry for her mother.

4. All of these features help establish the setting *except*

   a. the listing of wrong answers on the geography test.

   b. Blossom's use of such old-fashioned words as *wallop, languished, reposed,* and *swoon.*

   c. the description of the rooms in the Shambaugh home.

   d. references to a privy, a trolley, and an electric auto.

5. Blossom's mother describes the murderer

   a. as soon as the local sheriff asks her for information.

   b. before the murderer can leave town

   c. after she goes into a trance in the sheriff's office.

   d. during the meeting of the Sunny Thoughts and Busy Fingers club.

**Interpreting** To complete these sentences, you may look back at the selection if you'd like.

6. When describing how the other girls at the club meeting supported everything Letty said, Blossom notes, "You never saw a group of girls more agreeable." Her comment is intended to

   a. praise the club members.

   b. make fun of the club members.

   c. praise Letty's management skills.

   d. win favor with Letty.

Making Inferences

7. Mrs. Shambaugh says, "How grateful we *all* are that Blossom was the *one* girl who stood up for Letty when she needed a *friend* the *most*!" Letty's guests correctly infer, or conclude, that Mrs. Shambaugh

   a. wants Blossom to take more refreshments than the others.

   b. is speaking for everyone present.

   c. wants the other girls to feel ashamed of themselves for not helping Letty.

   d. doesn't know as much as they do about friendship.

Predicting Outcomes

8. By the end of this excerpt, the reader expects that later in the story

   a. Nola and Ione will cheat on another test but will get away with it with Blossom's help.

   b. the people of Sikeston will invite Blossom and her mother to use their gifts of Second Sight to solve more crimes.

   c. Blossom and Letty will become best friends.

   d. Blossom will experience Second Sight again.

Understanding Literary Elements (Character)

9. Blossom's mother is remarkable for her

   a. beauty.

   b. elegant speech.

   c. knowledge of things not knowable by normal means.

   d. dedication to Truth.

10. Which of these statements is one that
    Blossom would agree with but Letty would
    disagree with?

    a. Children should always model them-
       selves after their parents.

    b. You should judge people by their
       actions, not by how much money they
       have.

    c. It's more important for a person to be
       loyal to his or her group than it is to be
       kind to others.

    d. Some things that happen cannot be
       explained scientifically.

Now check your answers with your teacher. Study the questions
you answered incorrectly. What types of questions were they? Talk
with your teacher about ways to work on those skills.

# The Narrator

Tornadoes, hurricanes, and floods are frightening to live through but fascinating to watch from a distance. When one of these natural disasters occurs, every news program is full of interviews with weather forecasters, survivors, disaster relief workers, even ham radio volunteers who relay messages from victims to their distant friends and relatives. Why do newscasters and audiences want to hear from so many different people? Because each one of these narrators sees a different part of the event. Each one can give a unique view of what is happening. Each one tells a slightly different story about the same happening.

In the same way, the story of what happens in a work of fiction depends on the person telling it, that is, the narrator. The narrator is not the same person as the writer. Instead, the narrator is a person created by the writer. Sometimes that person knows everything that happens to all of the characters. At other times the person knows only what he or she sees, hears, and feels during a certain event or period of time.

The author chooses a narrator just as a newscaster chooses which person to interview. However, the author of a novel lets the narrator talk much longer than a news interview lasts, so readers learn a great deal about the narrator as well as about the events. We discover the narrator's attitude toward what happens. Also, depending on what the narrator says and the way he or she says it, we react emotionally.

In the following lessons, we will look at these ways in which author Richard Peck develops and uses the narrator in *Ghosts I Have Been*:

1.  Peck selects the narrator's point of view.

2.  He lets readers know something about the narrator.

3.  He uses the narrator's words to establish a tone and create a mood.

## 1 • Point of View

The perspective from which a story is told is called the story's *point of view*. There are two main points of view: first person and third person. In a story told from the *first-person* point of view, the narrator is a main character in the story. He or she uses the personal pronouns *I* and *me*. In a story told from the *third-person* point of view, the narrator is someone outside the story and uses the pronouns *he, she,* and *they*. A third-person narrator does not take part in the action.

It is clear from its title that *Ghosts I Have Been* is told in the first person. Notice how many times *I, me,* and *my* appear in the first two paragraphs of the excerpt:

> In earlier times I would have hastened to trap Alexander Armsworth in some out-of-the-way spot and there told him I'd saved him from a sure thrashing at Miss Spaulding's hand. She'd got the names of Champ Ferguson and Bub Timmons out of me with no trouble. She'd already dealt with Les Dawson. And she'd called him "Leslie" as she walloped him, adding insult to injury.
>
> But my new refined appearance made me refine my methods as well. Alexander would put two and two together. Even he would figure that I was the Ghost in the Privy and that I'd had a private word with Miss Spaulding. Let him learn in his own time, and let him stew in his own juice. It would dawn on him that he owed me a favor, and I could wait. He knows I collect my debts.

When a story is told from the first-person point of view, the narrator has a limited knowledge of events and knows only what he or she can reasonably know as a character in the story. This character tells what he or she sees, hears, does, thinks, and feels.

When a story is told from the third-person point of view, the narrator is not a character in the story. Sometimes the narrator focuses on one character and tells only what that character does and thinks. At other times, the narrator knows everything that happens in the story and tells what several or all of the characters do, think, and feel.

This excerpt from *Ghosts I Have Been* includes an anecdote—a story within a story. As you read this passage from that anecdote, look for clues that tell whether the narrator is telling the anecdote from a first-person or a third-person point of view.

My mama fell silent then. And several in the room were unsure if she was playacting or not. But the sheriff reached over and pulled the sack off the jar. Pandemonium broke out then, and one man fainted. There were no ladies present, of course, except for Mama and the head.

Days before, when the sheriff had covered the jar with the sack, the eyes on the lady's head were closed. But when he whipped the sack off, the eyes on the severed head were wide open, staring into Mama's. And one of the dead eyes was robin's egg blue, and the other was hazel.

Some witnesses made for the door. But others stayed behind to see that the lobes on the staring head's pierced ears were torn indeed, just like Mama said.

Blossom is not taking part in the story herself. She is describing how her mother is helping a sheriff with a murder investigation. Her story is in the third person. We learn not only what Mrs. Culp says and does, but what onlookers think about her actions.

## Exercise 1

Read the following passage, in which Blossom goes to Letty's house for a club meeting. Use what you have learned in this lesson to answer the questions that follow the passage.

There was a plate of finger sandwiches on the floor. And as conversation languished when Mrs. Shambaugh was near, everybody chewed on them quietly. Though I was starved, I only had two. Maisie Markham wolfed down six, but she was soon to be sorry.

Finally Mrs. Shambaugh left us, and I wondered how a club worked. Nobody said much at first, though everybody shot everybody else looks full of meaning. At last Letty opened the meeting by putting down her cup and saying, "Oooo, I just hate apple juice, don't you?" And everybody agreed.

After more silence Letty sucked in her cheeks, saying, "Well, Blossom, you can't be here at the meeting without being a club member. And you can only belong for this one meeting." And everybody agreed.

This suited me well enough, since I didn't see much to it beyond the eats. "But you can't belong even for today without an initiation." And everybody agreed to this too. You never saw a group of girls more agreeable.

1. Locate phrases that tell about the following: something the narrator does, something she observes, something she hears, something she thinks, and something she has questions about.

2. What does the narrator say about Maisie Markham to arouse the reader's curiosity about coming events?

Now check your answers with your teacher. Review this part of the lesson if you don't understand why an answer was incorrect.


## Writing on Your Own 1

In this exercise you will use what you have learned in this lesson to decide on an anecdote, a narrator, and the point of view. Follow these steps:

- Review your answers to the questions in Developing a Narrator on page 113. Decide what memorable event will happen to your group of travelers. Write a sentence or two describing it.

- Review your characters. In telling your anecdote, do you want to focus on one of them or tell about all equally? If you focus on one character, will that character tell the story? Decide on the narrator and the point of view you will use in your anecdote. Add this information to your notes.

## 2 • Getting to Know the Narrator

When a story is told in the first person, readers are usually given a great deal of information about the narrator. They learn what the narrator does and why. They learn what events happen and how the narrator feels about those events.

As you read this passage, be aware of what Blossom tells about herself—her appearance, attitude, and interests. How does she look now? How has she looked in the past? What is her attitude toward her appearance? Does she expect that her change in appearance will cause a change in others' attitudes toward her?

> At school next day I caused some comment but nothing direct. Though I was dressed better than most and entirely unlike myself, nobody came near. They were in the habit of paying me no mind. Still, many looked. I expect Letty Shambaugh explained to all and sundry that my outfit was her mother's gift. But it didn't seem to dawn on her just how her fate and mine had entwined themselves.
>
> Somewhere in my travels I'd come by a length of plaid taffeta ribbon. I tied my unruly hair back with it as best I could. And this was the crowning touch to my new appearance. I've already said I am not vain, but I was not far from it that day. Alexander seemed not to know me at all.

Blossom doesn't seem to mind that everyone knows her new outfit is a gift. She doesn't seem to mind that the majority of the students are unconcerned with her change in appearance. Nevertheless, the fact that Blossom adds her taffeta ribbon to her new outfit suggests that, although she never had the chance to be vain before, she is concerned about her appearance. The final sentence hints that she had hoped for a different effect on Alexander.

When a story is told in the third person, readers must make more of an effort to find out information about the speaker. Nevertheless, the narrator's choice of words and details hint at his or her character.

Notice how Blossom describes her mother in her third-person account of the episode with the head:

When we lived down at Sikeston, my mama commanded respect for her powers and could sometimes help out the law when she felt like it. . . .

She was brought into the room where the head reposed. By then the sheriff had pulled a croaker sack over the jar for his own peace of mind. Of course I was not along when my mama was sent for, but I can picture her in that chamber of death, dressed for the occasion. When she was about her business, she always threw a long shawl over her head. With her black eyes and dark lips and the gold crosses in her ears, she made an impression on all who saw her. Many would cross the street.

Blossom notes that her mother gave help "when she felt like it" and that she had a special way of dressing when she was "about her business." She also notes that this gave her mother a frightening appearance, causing many people to cross the street upon seeing her.

## Exercise 2

Read the following passage in which Blossom prepares to use her Second Sight to scare the club members. Use what you have learned in this lesson to answer the questions that follow the passage.

I began to sway in my chair then, starting up slow. I always have been able to roll my eyes up into my head so only the whites show. As a kid I practiced that by the hour. "Oh, look what's happening to her eyes, isn't that sickening!" somebody said.

I moaned low in my throat, wishing I'd thought to ask for a candle. Candlelight always adds a touch. But I proceeded without it. In a far-off voice I began to moan a poem, working up from a whisper:

> *The . . . ghost . . . am . . . I*
> *Of . . . winds . . . that . . . die*
> *Alike . . . on . . . land . . . and . . . sea*
> *O Second Sight! O Second Sight!*
> *Send one small glimpse to me!*

Commencing with a real poem I have by heart, I added an ending to suit the occasion. By then my eyes were rolled so far back in my head I was looking at my brains. But you could hear a pin drop in the room.

1. What does the narrator say or do that shows she possesses each of these qualities?

   intelligence     showmanship     sense of humor

2. Does she indicate that she feels any guilt about her actions? Locate support for your answers in the passage.

Now check your answers with your teacher. Review this part of the lesson if you don't understand why an answer was incorrect.

## Writing on Your Own 2

In this exercise you will write a biography of your narrator and choose the language that he or she will use. Follow these steps:

- Review your description and notes from Writing on Your Own 1. Write a brief biography for your narrator. Mention important events in the past that could influence his or her actions or comments. In addition, list several of the narrator's qualities that should be brought out in your anecdote.

- What sort of language will your narrator use? A narrator who is well educated in the English language will speak differently from one who is poorly educated or one who normally uses a different language or a dialect. An older person will not use the same words—especially slang—as a teenager. Write a one-paragraph summary of the anecdote in your narrator's voice, as he or she would talk.

- Read your paragraph to a partner and ask for feedback. What can your partner tell about the narrator from that paragraph?

## 3 • Tone and Mood

Suppose your sister gives you money to buy tickets to a concert and you lose the money. What tone of voice will you use when you tell her what happened? What if, instead of losing the money, you stand in a long line and manage to get the last two tickets to the concert? How will your tone of voice differ when you give your sister this news?

Just as your tone will be different in each case, so will your mood, or feelings. The words you use will show how you are feeling, or what your mood is. If you lose the money, your mood will be gloomy or embarrassed. You will use words such as *sorry* or *careless* when you tell your sister what happened. If you get the last two tickets, however, your mood will be happy or proud. You'll use words such as *lucky* or *terrific*.

Your tone and mood will also affect the way your sister reacts to what you are saying. She will be angry or disappointed to hear you lost the money, pleased or excited to hear that you got the tickets.

Writers use tone and mood to keep their readers interested. A writer's tone expresses how he or she feels about a subject. Mood is the feeling that readers get from a story or poem. A writer's tone might be humorous, disapproving, or sympathetic. The mood of a story might be suspenseful, thoughtful, or gloomy.

Listening to the words of a narrator will help readers understand the tone and mood of a story. The writer carefully chooses the narrator's words and describes his or her feelings in a way that affects readers' feelings. Over the course of a novel, the tone and mood will change from episode to episode.

Read this passage from *Ghosts I Have Been*. In Blossom's account of how her mother helped investigate a murder, the sheriff is checking out the information Mrs. Culp gave in her trance. Is the tone one of fear or of great discomfort? What details does the narrator include to lead readers to share that feeling?

The sheriff got the lid off the jar and reached down into the alcohol. He drew the ghastly head up; it hung by the hair in the air, dripping from the neck. All but the stoutest hearted turned aside while the sheriff explored in the head's mouth, drawing up one side. The mouth fell open, as if obedient. Sure enough, there was the gold tooth, slightly chipped in a mouth that seemed half to grin beneath them piercing eyes. The lump was on the back of the skull too.

Unlike a ghost story—which would surprise listeners with the sudden appearance of a floating head—this description has a realistic, logical background. So there is no fear in the narrator's tone. Yet, a strong sense of discomfort is brought out by the use of words such as *ghastly* and *dripping*. Even more effective are the details about the mouth falling open obediently and yet grinning, and the dead eyes piercing the onlookers. The mood is far from cheerful.

## Exercise 3

Read the following passage, which describes what happens after Blossom claims she has Second Sight. Then use what you have learned in this lesson to answer the questions after the passage.

"Aha! I saw this coming!" crowed Letty, jumping up. "If you have the Second Sight, Blossom Culp, let's see it. Haul off and do something spooky. Talk is *cheap*, Blossom, particularly yours. Prove it!"

"That's right. You'd better prove it, Blossom," all agreed. I liked to have fainted with the strain of the moment, because they looked ready to set on me and ruin my new outfit if I didn't deliver. Even Maisie was recovering fast and raising up from the couch. Her little pig eyes looked mean.

I didn't truly think they'd cut me up for bait. Not with Mrs. Shambaugh somewhere in the house. But I had to satisfy them or slink off in disgrace. Pride is a terrible thing sometimes. I racked my brains and played for time.

"We have to be in a dim room," I remarked. "It's too bright in here. After dark would be better."

"*Now*, Blossom," Letty said, and her little dimpled hands were on her hips, and her little dimpled elbows were fanning the air. "We can go into the room where Daddy smokes and pull the blind."

Everybody made a rush for this room, under the back stairs. Letty yanked heavy curtains across the window. "*Now* what do you need, Blossom, a crystal ball?" She poked the girls nearest her in the gloom to remind them to laugh. I did just notice, though, that being in a darker place with me had quieted them down some.

1. What details about Letty and the other girls establish a tense tone at the beginning of this passage? Is Blossom's attitude fearful? Why or why not? How would you label it?

2. The tone changes slightly as the setting changes. What words make the tone a bit more serious and the mood more spooky?

Now check your answers with your teacher. Review this part of the lesson if you don't understand why an answer was incorrect.

## Writing on Your Own 3

In this exercise you will use what you learned in this lesson to set a tone and create a mood for your anecdote. Follow these steps:

- Review your answer for Writing on Your Own 2. Then choose a single scene from your anecdote. Write a paragraph or outline to summarize what has happened to lead up to this scene.

- Next, write a few paragraphs about the scene. If you are using a third-person narrator who knows what many characters think and do, put in all the detail that you think is needed to create the right tone. If you are using a first-person narrator who is telling about one character, remember to tell only what the chosen character would be aware of. Use words and details that set a tone and create a mood.

- Read your account of the scene to one or more classmates. Discuss the scene with them. Who was the narrator? What was the narrator's tone, or attitude? What mood did your writing create? Your classmates can suggest changes and improvements to make the narrator, tone, and mood clearer.

# Discussion Guides

1. Have you encountered cliques like Letty Shambaugh's club? Why are such groups formed? What do their members get out of them? In what ways are such groups harmful to their members and to nonmembers? What can be done to end or survive a clique? Discuss this issue with your class or a small group. Together, develop a set of recommendations for a young person moving into a small town like Bluff City where the school has cliques like Letty's.

2. How do you suppose a newscast might have covered Mrs. Culp's visit to the sheriff's office to use her Second Sight in a murder investigation? Prepare a news feature a few minutes long concerning this event and present it to your class. You could work alone to develop a radio report. Or a small group of students could act out the scene as Blossom related it, adding a reporter who interviews people on the scene.

3. From what you have learned about Mrs. Shambaugh and Mrs. Culp in this chapter, which mother would you be happier with? Why? Discuss this question with your classmates. Make a list of reasons offered in favor of each woman.

4. Should law enforcement officials regularly call on people who believe they have Second Sight or some other mysterious ability to discover facts? Join one or more students to debate this question. Before the debate, group members must do some research. Find instances in which people with ESP (extra-sensory perception) have provided clues that helped in solving murders, thefts, or other cases—or tried to provide such clues.

   Immediately before holding the debate for your class, ask for a show of hands to see which side of the question your listeners favor. After the debate, ask for a second show of hands to discover whether your arguments changed any listeners' opinions.

# Write an Anecdote

You have been developing the narrator, tone, and mood of an anecdote about some events that happened on a journey. You have already outlined at least part of your story and have written one scene. Now you will add to these elements to complete your anecdote.

If you have questions about the writing process, refer to Using the Writing Process (page 295).

- Assemble the writing you did for the exercises in this unit. You should have these pieces of writing: *a)* notes on three people traveling together and on several events that will happen on that journey, *b)* a statement about your choice of a narrator, *c)* a biography of your narrator and a summary of the anecdote in your narrator's voice, and *d)* a single scene from the anecdote.

- Make additional notes about your characters or about events that you want to include in your anecdote. Then write a rough draft.

- Read your anecdote to a partner or to a group who can provide feedback. Ask them to point out passages that should be improved. Make any revisions you agree with.

- Proofread to find spelling, grammar, punctuation, and capitalization errors. Make a corrected copy and save it in a portfolio of your writing.

# Unit 5 Theme

# Shane
by Jack Schaefer

## About the Illustration

Describe what you think is happening in this scene. Use details from the drawing to give reasons for your answers. Then use the following questions to begin thinking about the selection:

- Where and when do you think this scene is taking place?

- What are the two men trying to do?

- What clues in the illustration suggest how they are feeling?

- How do you think the boy feels about the men and what they are doing? What clues in the illustration suggest how he feels?

# Unit 5

## Introduction

## About the Novel

*Shane* is a classic story of the American West. In the summer of 1889, a quiet, mysterious stranger named Shane rides onto the Wyoming ranch of Joe Starrett, his wife Marian, and their young son Bob. The Starretts immediately like the gentle but oddly dangerous stranger. They invite Shane to stay on and help them on their ranch as long as he wants to. On a tour of the ranch, Joe points out a huge, ugly tree stump in the yard near his house. He describes his frustration at not being able to get rid of the stump. He says it is too strong.

Just before the chapter presented in this unit begins, a local peddler comes onto the ranch. He and Shane have a disagreement, and Joe takes Shane's side against the greedy peddler. To show Joe his gratitude, Shane picks up an axe and starts chopping away at the huge tree stump. Joe picks up his own axe and together, without speaking, the two men work on the old stump.

After you read this chapter of *Shane*, read the rest of the novel to find out how Shane and the homesteaders fight an evil cattle baron named Fletcher, who has his eye on their land and plans to run them off, legally or illegally.

## About the Author

Jack Schaefer (1907–1991) was born in Cleveland, Ohio, and was educated at Oberlin College and Columbia University. He began his career as a reporter for United Press and worked as an editor and a writer for several newspapers before he started his free-lance writing career. Although Schaefer had never been west of Ohio when he wrote *Shane*—his first novel—it is often considered one of the finest examples of Old West fiction ever written. *Shane* was such a popular novel that in 1953 it was made into a successful movie.

Schaefer wrote several other novels, including *The Canyon, Company of Cowards,* and *Monte Walsh.* He also wrote collections of short stories, including *The Big Range, The Pioneers,* and *The Kean Lands.* In 1961, his novel *Old Ramon* was named a Newbery Honor Book and an American Library Association Notable Book. In 1975, Schaefer received the Distinguished Achievement Award from the Western Literature Association.

## About the Lessons

Everyone has certain beliefs and values that they live by. When writers write, they often express their own beliefs through the characters and events in their stories. These beliefs and attitudes are referred to as *themes*. Themes express messages, or lessons, about life and human nature. Often, the main theme of a story is expressed through a lesson that the main character learns. For example, in the classic novel *A Christmas Carol*, the main lesson that Ebenezer Scrooge learns is that it is never too late to change one's behavior.

Authors rarely state a story's theme directly. Instead, they leave it up to their readers to figure out the theme. Sometimes a story can have more than one theme. Readers will recognize these themes, based on their own knowledge and experiences. So, a theme that is important to one reader may not be important—or even apparent—to another reader.

Writers use specific techniques to develop their themes. You will learn more about these techniques in the lessons that follow.

## Writing: Developing Themes

Some writing is meant simply to entertain. Much of the time, however, beneath the action and descriptions, writers have themes or messages that they want to share with their readers. What message about life could you share in your writing? At the end of this unit, you will write a dialogue that expresses a message, or theme. In the dialogue, you will have a chance to share some of your own beliefs, feelings, and values through what your characters say and do. Use the suggestions below to start thinking about what you want to say in your dialogue.

- Think of some important lessons that you have already learned in life. How did you learn those lessons? Why are they important to you? Did you learn them on your own, or did someone help you learn them? Write down a few lessons that you could later turn into themes.

- Next to each lesson that you just listed, write a brief description of how you learned it.

- If there are other lessons that you did not learn personally but that you feel you might want to write about, add them to the list. Then save your list in your writing portfolio. You will be using it later in the unit.

## Before Reading

The questions below will help you see how author Jack Schaefer develops the theme in this chapter from *Shane*. As you read the chapter, keep these questions in mind:

- What main theme, or lesson, do the characters learn?

- How do the characters' words and actions support that theme?

- Which symbols help illustrate the theme?

# Vocabulary Tips

This selection uses some words that may be unfamiliar to you but that are important for understanding the story. Below, you will find some of these words, their definitions, and sentences that show how the words are used. Look them over before you begin reading the selection.

**splendid**    worthy of praise; impressive. The audience members were treated to a <u>splendid</u> performance.

**fascination**    irresistible attraction. The idea of visitors from other worlds has a strong <u>fascination</u> for many people.

**taproot**    the main root of a plant, usually stronger than the others and going straight down. It is important to kill the <u>taproot</u> if you want to get rid of a dandelion.

**exasperation**    extreme anger or irritation. The dog owner's <u>exasperation</u> was obvious as he once again searched for his runaway pet.

**ungainly**    clumsy; awkward. A colt appears <u>ungainly</u> when it is first born, but it eventually becomes a graceful horse.

**sheepish**    embarrassed. The pitcher had a <u>sheepish</u> grin on his face after he threw his fastball over the backstop.

**quizzical**    teasing. When I saw the <u>quizzical</u> look on her face, I knew I was in for one of her little jokes.

# Shane

Jack Schaefer

It was exciting at first watching them. They were hitting a fast pace, making the chips dance. I thought maybe each one would cut through a root now and stop. But Shane finished his and looked over at father working steadily away and with a grim little smile pulling at his mouth he moved on to another root. A few moments later father smashed through his with a blow that sent the axe head into the ground beneath. He wrestled with the handle to yank the head loose and he too tackled another root without even waiting to wipe off the dirt. This began to look like a long session, so I started to wander away. Just as I headed around the corner of the barn, mother came past the corner.

She was the freshest, prettiest thing I had ever seen. She had taken her hat and stripped the old ribbon from it and fixed it as Shane had told her. Some of the flowers by the house were in a small bouquet in front. She had cut slits in the brim and the sash from her best dress came around the crown and through the slits and was tied in a perky bow under her chin. She was stepping along daintily, mighty proud of herself.

She went up close to the stump. Those two choppers were so busy and intent that even if they were aware she was there they did not really notice her.

"Well," she said, "aren't you going to look at me?"

They both stopped and they both stared at her.

"Have I got it right?" she asked Shane. "Is this the way they do it?"

"Yes, ma'am," he said. "About like that. Only their brims are wider." And he swung back to his root.

"Joe Starrett," said mother, "aren't you at least going to tell me whether you like me in this hat?"

"Lookahere, Marian," said father, "you know darned well that whether you have a hat on or whether you don't have a hat on, you're the nicest thing to me that ever happened on God's green earth. Now stop bothering us. Can't you see we're busy?" And he swung back to his root.

Mother's face was a deep pink. She pulled the bow out and the hat from her head. She held it swinging from her hand by the sash ends. Her hair was mussed and she was really mad.

"Humph," she said. "This is a funny kind of resting you're doing today."

Father set the axe head on the ground and leaned on the handle. "Maybe it seems funny to you, Marian. But this is the best resting I've had for about as long as I can remember."

"Humph," said mother again. "You'll have to quit your resting for a while anyhow and do what I suppose you'll call work. Dinner's hot on the stove and waiting to be served."

She flounced around and went straight back to the house. We all tagged her in and to an uncomfortable meal. Mother always believed you should be decent and polite at mealtime, particularly with company. She was polite enough now. She was being special sweet, talking enough for the whole table of us without once saying a word about her hat lying where she had thrown it on the chair by the stove. The trouble was that she was too polite. She was trying too hard to be sweet.

As far as you could tell, though, the two men were not worried by her at all. They listened absently to her talk, chiming in when she asked them direct questions, but otherwise keeping quiet. Their minds were on that old stump and whatever it was that old stump had come to mean to them and they were in a hurry to get at it again.

After they had gone out and I had been helping mother with the dishes awhile, she began humming low under her breath and I knew she was not mad any more. She was too curious and puzzled to have room for anything else.

"What went on out there, Bob?" she asked me. "What got into those two?"

I did not rightly know. All I could do was try to tell her about Ledyard and how our visitor had called him on the cultivator. I must have used the wrong words, because, when I told her about Ledyard talking mean and the way Shane acted, she got all flushed and excited.

"What do you say, Bob? You were afraid of him? He frightened you? Your father would never let him do that."

"I wasn't frightened of him," I said, struggling to make her see the difference. "I was—well, I was just frightened. I was scared of whatever it was that might happen."

She reached out and rumpled my hair. "I think I understand," she said softly. "He's made me feel a little that way too." She went to the window and stared toward the barn. The steady rhythm of double blows, so together they sounded almost as one, was faint yet clear in the kitchen. "I hope Joe knows what he's doing," she murmured to herself. Then she turned to me. "Skip along out, Bob. I'll finish myself."

It was no fun watching them now. They had eased down to a slow, dogged pace. Father sent me once for the hone, so they could sharpen the blades, and again for a spade so he could clear the dirt away from the lowest roots, and I realized he might keep me running as long as I was handy. I slipped off by myself to see how mother's garden was doing after the rain and maybe add to the population in the box of worms I was collecting for when I would go fishing with the boys in town.

I took my time about it. I played pretty far afield. But no matter where I went, always I could hear that chopping in the distance. You could not help beginning to feel tired just to hear it, to think how they were working and staying at it.

Along the middle of the afternoon, I wandered into the barn. There was mother by the rear stall, up on a box peering through the little window above it. She hopped down as soon as she heard me and put a finger to her lips.

"I declare," she whispered. "In some ways those two aren't even as old as you are, Bob. Just the same—." She frowned at me in such a funny, confiding manner that I felt all warm inside. "Don't you dare tell them I said so. But there's something splendid in the battle they're giving that old monster." She went past me and toward the house with such a brisk air that I followed to see what she was going to do.

She whisked about the kitchen and in almost no time at all she had a pan of biscuits in the oven. While they were baking, she took her hat and carefully sewed the old ribbon into its old place. "Humph," she said, more to herself than to me. "You'd think I'd learn. This isn't Dodge City. This isn't even a whistle stop. It's Joe Starrett's farm. It's where I'm proud to be."

Out came the biscuits. She piled as many as she could on a plate, popping one of the leftovers into her mouth and giving me the rest. She picked up the plate and marched with it out behind the barn. She stepped over the cut roots and set the plate on a fairly smooth spot on top of the stump. She looked at the two men, first one and then the other. "You're a pair of fools," she said. "But there's no law against me being a fool too." Without looking at either of them again, she marched away, her head high, back toward the house.

The two of them stared after her till she was out of sight. They turned to stare at the biscuits. Father gave a deep sigh, so deep it seemed to come all the way from his heavy work shoes. There was nothing sad or sorrowful about it. There was just something in him too big to be held tight in comfort. He let his axe fall to the ground. He leaned forward and separated the biscuits into two piles beside the plate, counting them even. One was left on the plate. He set this by itself on the stump. He took up his axe and reached it out and let it drop gently on the lone biscuit exactly in the middle. He rested the axe against the stump and took the two halves of the biscuit and put one on each pile.

He did not say a word to Shane. He pitched into one pile and Shane did into the other, and the two of them faced each other over the last uncut roots, munching at those biscuits as if eating them was the most serious business they had ever done.

Father finished his pile and dabbled his fingers on the plate for the last crumbs. He straightened and stretched his arms high and wide. He seemed to stretch and stretch until he was a tremendous tower of strength reaching up into the late afternoon sun. He swooped suddenly to grab the plate and toss it to me. Still in the same movement he seized the axe and swung it in a great arc into the root he was working on. Quick as he was, Shane was right with him, and together they were talking again to that old stump.

I took the plate in to mother. She was peeling apples in the kitchen, humming gaily to herself. "The woodbox, Bob," she said, and went on humming. I carried in stove-lengths till the box would not hold any more. Then I slipped out before she might think of more chores.

I tried to keep myself busy down by the river skipping flat stones across the current all muddy still from the rain. I was able to for a while. But that steady chopping had a peculiar fascination. It was always pulling me toward the barn. I simply could not grasp how they could stick at it hour after hour. It made no sense to me, why they should work so when routing out that old stump was not really so important. I was wavering in front of the barn, when I noticed that the chopping was different. Only one axe was working.

I hurried around back. Shane was still swinging, cutting into the last root. Father was using the spade, was digging under one side of the stump, bringing the dirt out between the cut roots. As I watched, he laid the spade aside and put his shoulder to the stump. He heaved against it. Sweat started to pour down his face. There was a little sucking sound and the stump moved ever so slightly.

That did it. Of a sudden I was so excited that I could hear my own blood pounding past my eardrums. I wanted to dash to that stump and push it and feel it move. Only I knew father would think I was in the way.

Shane finished the root and came to help him. Together they heaved against the stump. It angled up nearly a whole inch. You could begin to see an open space in the dirt where it was ripping loose. But as soon as they released the pressure, it fell back.

Again and again they heaved at it. Each time it would angle up a bit farther. Each time it would fall back. They had it up once about a foot and a half, and that was the limit. They could not get past it.

They stopped, breathing hard, mighty streaked now from the sweat rivulets down their faces. Father peered underneath as best he could. "Must be a taproot," he said. That was the one time either of them had spoken to the other, as far as I knew, the whole afternoon through. Father did not say anything more. And Shane said nothing, He just picked up his axe and looked at father and waited.

Father began to shake his head. There was some unspoken thought between them that bothered him. He looked down at his own big hands and slowly the fingers curled until they were clenched into big fists. Then his head stopped shaking and he stood taller and he drew a deep breath. He turned and backed in between two cut root ends, pressing against the stump. He pushed his feet into the ground for firm footholds. He bent his knees and slid his shoulders down the stump and wrapped his big hands around the root ends. Slowly he began to straighten. Slowly that huge old stump began to rise. Up it came, inch by inch, until the side was all the way up to the limit they had reached before.

Shane stooped to peer under. He poked his axe into the opening and I heard it strike wood. But the only way he could get in position to swing the axe into the opening was to drop on his right knee and extend his left leg and thigh into the opening and lean his weight on them. Then he could bring the axe sweeping in at a low angle close to the ground.

He flashed one quick glance at father beside and behind him, eyes closed, muscles locked in that great sustained effort, and he dropped into position with the whole terrible weight of the stump poised above nearly half of his body and sent the axe sweeping under in swift powerful strokes.

Suddenly father seemed to slip. Only he had not slipped. He had straightened even further. The stump had leaped up a few more inches. Shane jumped out and up and tossed his axe aside. He grabbed one of the root ends and helped father ease the stump down. They both were blowing like they had run a long way. But they would not stay more than a minute before they were heaving again at the stump. It came up more easily now and the dirt was tearing loose all around it.

I ran to the house fast as I could. I dashed into the kitchen and took hold of mother's hand. "Hurry!" I yelled. "You've got to come!" She did not seem to want to come at first and I pulled her. "You've got to see it! They're getting it out!" Then she was excited as I was and was running right with me.

They had the stump way up at a high angle. They were down in the hole, one on each side of it, pushing up and forward with hands flat on the under part reared before them higher than their heads. You would have thought the stump was ready to topple over clear of its ancient foundation. But there it stuck. They could not quite push it the final inches.

Mother watched them battling with it. "Joe," she called, "why don't you use some sense? Hitch up the team. Horses will have it out in no time at all."

Father braced himself to hold the stump still. He turned his head to look at her. "Horses!" he shouted. All the pent silence of the two of them that long afternoon through was being shattered in the one wonderful shout. "Horses! Great jumping Jehoshaphat! No! We started this with manpower and, by Godfrey, we'll finish it with manpower!"

He turned his head to face the stump once more and dropped it lower between his humped shoulders. Shane, opposite him, stiffened, and together they pushed in a fresh assault. The stump quivered and swayed a little— and hung fixed at its crazy high angle.

Father grunted in exasperation. You could see the strength building up in his legs and broad shoulders and big corded arms. His side of the upturned stump rocked forward and Shane's side moved back and the whole stump trembled like it would twist down and into the hole on them at a grotesque new angle.

I wanted to shout a warning. But I could not speak, for Shane had thrown his head in a quick sideways gesture to fling his hair from falling over his face and I had caught a glimpse of his eyes. They were aflame with a concentrated cold fire. Not another separate discernible movement did he make. It was all of him, the whole man, pulsing in the one incredible surge of power. You could fairly feel the fierce energy suddenly burning in him, pouring through him in the single coordinated drive. His side of the stump rocked forward even with father's and the whole mass of the stump tore loose from the last hold and toppled away to sprawl in ungainly defeat beyond them.

Father climbed slowly out of the hole. He walked to the stump and placed a hand on the rounded bole and patted it like it was an old friend and he was perhaps a little sorry for it. Shane was with him, across from him, laying a hand gently on the old hard wood. They both looked up and their eyes met and held as they had so long ago in the morning hours.

The silence should have been complete. It was not because someone was shouting, a high-pitched, wordless shout. I realized that the voice was mine and I closed my mouth. The silence was clean and wholesome, and this was one of the things you could never forget whatever time might do to you in the furrowing of the years, an old stump on its side with root ends making a strange pattern against the glow of the sun sinking behind the far mountains and two men looking over it into each other's eyes.

I thought they should join the hands so close on the bole of the stump. I thought they should at least say something to each other. They stood quiet and motionless. At last father turned and came toward mother. He was so tired that the weariness showed in his walk. But there was no weariness in his voice. "Marian," he said, "I'm rested now. I don't believe any man since the world began was ever more rested."

Shane too was coming toward us. He too spoke only to mother. "Ma'am, I've learned something today. Being a farmer has more to it than I ever thought. Now I'm about ready for some of that pie."

Mother had been watching them in a wide-eyed wonder. At his last words she let out a positive wail. "Oh-h-h —you—you—men! You made me forget about it! It's probably all burned!" And she was running for the house so fast she was tripping over her skirt.

The pie was burned all right. We could smell it when we were in front of the house and the men were scrubbing themselves at the pump-trough. Mother had the door open to let the kitchen air out. The noises from inside sounded as if she might be throwing things around. Kettles were banging and dishes were clattering. When we went in, we saw why. She had the table set and was putting supper on it and she was grabbing the things from their places and putting them down on the table with solid thumps. She would not look at one of us.

We sat down and waited for her to join us. She put her back to us and stood by the low shelf near the stove staring at her big pie tin and the burned stuff in it. Finally father spoke kind of sharply. "Lookahere, Marian. Aren't you ever going to sit down?"

She whirled and glared at him. I thought maybe she had been crying. But there were no tears on her face. It was dry and pinched-looking and there was no color in it. Her voice was sharp like father's. "I was planning to have a deep-dish apple pie. Well, I will. None of your silly man foolishness is going to stop me."

She swept up the big tin and went out the door with it. We heard her on the steps, and a few seconds later the rattle of the cover of the garbage pail. We heard her on the steps again. She came in and went to the side bench where the dishpan was and began to scrub the pie tin. The way she acted, we might not have been in the room.

Father's face was getting red. He picked up his fork to begin eating and let it drop with a little clatter. He squirmed on his chair and kept taking quick side looks at her. She finished scrubbing the tin and went to the apple barrel and filled her wooden bowl with fat round ones. She sat by the stove and started peeling them. Father fished in a pocket and pulled out his old jack-knife. He moved over to her, stepping softly. He reached out for an apple to help her.

She did not look up. But her voice caught him like she had flicked him with a whip. "Joe Starrett, don't you dare touch a one of these apples."

He was sheepish as he returned to his chair. Then he was downright mad. He grabbed his knife and fork and dug into the food on his plate, taking big bites and chewing vigorously. There was nothing for our visitor and me to do but follow his example. Maybe it was a good supper. I could not tell. The food was only something to put in your mouth. And when we finished, there was nothing to do but wait because mother was sitting by the stove, arms folded, staring at the wall, waiting herself for her pie to bake.

We three watched her in a quiet so tight that it hurt. We could not help it. We would try to look away and always our eyes would turn back to her. She did not appear to notice us. You might have said she had forgotten we were there.

She had not forgotten because as soon as she sensed that the pie was done, she lifted it out, cut four wide pieces, and put them on plates. The first two she set in front of the two men. The third one she set down for me. The last one she laid at her own place and she sat down in her own chair at the table. Her voice was still sharp.

"I'm sorry to keep you men waiting so long. Your pie is ready now."

Father inspected his portion like he was afraid of it. He needed to make a real effort to take his fork and lift a piece. He chewed on it and swallowed and he flipped his eyes sidewise at mother and back again quickly to look across the table at Shane. "That's prime pie," he said.

Shane raised a piece on his fork. He considered it closely. He put it in his mouth and chewed on it gravely. "Yes," he said. The quizzical expression on his face was so plain you could not possibly miss it. "Yes. That's the best bit of stump I ever tasted."

What could a silly remark like that mean? I had no time to wonder, for father and mother were acting so queer. They both stared at Shane and their mouths were sagging open. Then father snapped his shut and he chuckled and chuckled till he was swaying in his chair.

"By Godfrey, Marian, he's right. You've done it, too."

Mother stared from one to the other of them. Her pinched look faded and her cheeks were flushed and her eyes were soft and warm as they should be, and she was laughing so that the tears came. And all of us were pitching into that pie, and the one thing wrong in the whole world was that there was not enough of it.

# Reviewing and Interpreting the Selection

Record your answers to these questions in your personal literature notebook. Follow the directions for each part.

**Reviewing**  Try to complete each of these sentences without looking back at the selection.

Understanding
Main Ideas

1. Joe and Shane don't talk at lunch because

    a. their minds are on the problem of the stump.

    b. they are angry with Marian.

    c. they are remembering their problems with the peddler.

    d. Marian is talking too much.

Identifying
Sequence

2. Just before the stump tears loose,

    a. the men attack its roots with their axes.

    b. Shane cuts its taproot.

    c. Father pushes on the stump alone.

    d. both men push at it with all their strength.

Identifying
Cause and Effect

3. The men work hard to remove the stump in one day because

    a. removing it has become a personal challenge.

    b. they know that it is dangerous.

    c. Shane may be leaving soon.

    d. the weather is good that day.

4. Because the two men keep fighting the stump, Mother says she thinks they are

    a. thoughtless.

    b. rude.

    c. splendid.

    d. impossible to understand.

5. The narrator in this story is

    a. Shane.

    b. Mother.

    c. Bob, the little boy.

    d. Father.

**Interpreting** To complete these sentences, you may look back at the story if you'd like.

6. The fact that the men don't speak to each other after the stump rolls out probably means that

    a. they don't like each other.

    b. their feelings are so deep that they cannot be expressed in words.

    c. they are too surprised to say anything.

    d. they are ashamed of what they have done.

7. A good word to use to describe Mother is

    a. silly.

    b. disappointed.

    c. determined.

    d. selfish.

8. Shane says that Marian's pie is "the best bit of stump I ever tasted" because he

   a. understands that her challenge was making the pie.
   b. thinks that the pie tastes like wood.
   c. wants to embarrass her.
   d. isn't used to talking with women.

9. Considering their actions, you would expect that the next time these characters have a problem they will probably

   a. find someone else to solve it for them.
   b. keep trying until they solve it themselves.
   c. give up without trying.
   d. try for a while to solve it but give up if it's too difficult.

10. The most important lesson Bob learns by watching the adults is that

    a. no job is too tough if you keep trying.
    b. you shouldn't talk while you are doing a job.
    c. it is best to remove all trees from your property.
    d. you should never take any help when you have a job to do.

Now check your answers with your teacher. Study the questions you answered incorrectly. What types of questions were they? Talk with your teacher about ways to work on those skills.

# Theme

Some important life events can change you and help you grow. Wonderful successes, disappointing failures, great friendships, and sad losses work together to create your unique way of looking at the world. From each memorable event, a person learns a lesson about the meaning of life and of human nature. That lesson can be expressed in a theme.

Often when writers write stories, their goal is to share some of life's themes. Sometimes readers can easily recognize those themes, especially when their own experiences are like the ones in the stories. At other times, however, readers encounter new ideas to think about. By sharing different themes, writers connect with readers in ways that enrich their readers' lives.

In this unit you will look at the themes in one chapter of the novel *Shane*. You will study some techniques that author Jack Schaefer uses to develop his themes:

1. Schaefer develops themes through the action of the story.

2. He uses the characters' words, feelings, and actions to suggest the themes.

3. He uses symbols to help illustrate the themes.

## 1 • Theme and Action

In every story there is a series of actions that make up the plot. When authors write, they carefully choose which actions to include. In the hands of a skilled writer, actions both advance the plot and develop the theme.

Read the following passage from *Shane*. See how Father's actions move the plot forward. Look for ways that his actions help to express a theme.

> Again and again they heaved at it [the stump]. Each time it would angle up a bit farther. Each time it would fall

back. They had it up once about a foot and a half, and that was the limit. They could not get past it. . . .

Father began to shake his head. There was some unspoken thought between them that bothered him. He looked down at his own big hands and slowly the fingers curled until they were clenched into big fists. Then his head stopped shaking and he stood taller and he drew a deep breath. He turned and backed in between two cut root ends, pressing against the stump. He pushed his feet into the ground for firm footholds. He bent his knees and slid his shoulders down the stump and wrapped his big hands around the root ends. Slowly he began to straighten. Slowly that huge old stump began to rise. Up it came, inch by inch, until the side was all the way up to the limit they had reached before.

The men have reached a point where most people would give up. They have tried to budge the stump again and again. Father reaches down inside himself and decides that he will not be conquered by the stump. He prepares himself—clenches his fists, takes a deep breath, plants his feet—and then pushes against the stump with all his might.

Father's actions set the stage for the final effort to dislodge the stump. His actions also develop one of the main themes of the story. If Father had given up at this point, the story would have expressed a different theme, perhaps "It is good to recognize your own limits." But instead he keeps trying, and he teaches us that "determination, perseverance, and hard work will eventually bring success."

## Exercise 1

Read the following passage, in which Mother has just given the two men a plate piled high with biscuits. Then use what you have learned in this lesson to answer the questions after the passage.

The two of them stared after her till she was out of sight. They turned to stare at the biscuits. Father gave a deep sigh, so deep it seemed to come all the way from his heavy work shoes. There was nothing sad or sorrowful about it.

There was just something in him too big to be held tight in comfort. He let his axe fall to the ground. He leaned forward and separated the biscuits into two piles beside the plate, counting them even. One was left on the plate. He set this by itself on the stump. He took up his axe and reached it out and let it drop gently on the lone biscuit exactly in the middle. He rested the axe against the stump and took the two halves of the biscuit and put one on each pile.

He did not say a word to Shane. He pitched into one pile and Shane did into the other, and the two of them faced each other over the last uncut roots, munching at those biscuits as if eating them was the most serious business they had ever done.

1. Why does Father take such pains to make the two piles of biscuits equal? What do his actions show about the way he thinks friends should be treated?

2. Father and Shane say nothing to each other as they eat. They seem to have come to an unspoken understanding. What do their actions suggest about the meaning of friendship and how real friends act toward each other?

Now check your answers with your teacher. Review this part of the lesson if you don't understand why an answer was incorrect.

## Writing on Your Own 1

In this exercise you will choose a theme and write a paragraph explaining how your story will illustrate your theme. Follow these steps:

- Review your answers to the questions in Developing Themes on page 149. Look over your list of themes. Choose the two that you feel most strongly about. What actions would get across these themes best? For each theme, think about a character who might be in a situation where those actions would be natural. Jot down ideas about both themes, actions, and characters. Then choose the set of ideas that you like better.

- Write a brief outline of a story that would express your chosen theme. Include the main events that will move the story along.

- Write a paragraph explaining how the events you have outlined will illustrate your chosen theme.

## 2 • Theme and Character

If you are unsure about the theme of a story, pay attention to the characters. How are they described? What do they do and say? How do you feel about them? Themes are often developed through the attitudes and actions of the characters in a story. For example, read this passage from *Shane* and see how Schaefer uses Mother's words to help convey the theme.

> Along the middle of the afternoon, I wandered into the barn. There was mother by the rear stall, up on a box peering through the little window above it. She hopped down as soon as she heard me and put a finger to her lips.
> "I declare," she whispered. "In some ways those two aren't even as old as you are, Bob. Just the same—." She frowned at me in such a funny, confiding manner that I felt all warm inside. "Don't you dare tell them I said so. But there's something splendid in the battle they're giving that old monster." She went past me and toward the house with such a brisk air that I followed to see what she was going to do.
> She whisked about the kitchen and in almost no time at all she had a pan of biscuits in the oven. While they were baking, she took her hat and carefully sewed the old ribbon into its old place. "Humph," she said, more to herself than to me. "You'd think I'd learn. This isn't Dodge City. This isn't even a whistle stop. It's Joe Starrett's farm. It's where I'm proud to be."

Everything that Mother says and does suggests that she approves of the men's efforts. She says they are "splendid" and then makes it clear that she is proud to be associated with them, proud to be on Joe Starrett's farm. Her words and actions support the theme of the importance of self-reliance, hard work, and pride.

## Exercise 2

Read the following passage, which takes place toward the end of the men's effort to remove the stump. Use what you have learned in this lesson to answer the questions that follow the passage.

They had the stump way up at a high angle. They were down in the hole, one on each side of it, pushing up and forward with hands flat on the under part reared before them higher than their heads. You would have thought the stump was ready to topple over clear of its ancient foundation. But there it stuck. They could not quite push it the final inches.

Mother watched them battling with it. "Joe," she called, "why don't you use some sense? Hitch up the team. Horses will have it out in no time at all."

Father braced himself to hold the stump still. He turned his head to look at her. "Horses!" he shouted. All the pent silence of the two of them that long afternoon through was being shattered in the one wonderful shout. "Horses! Great jumping Jehoshaphat! No! We started this with manpower and, by Godfrey, we'll finish it with manpower!"

1. Father and Shane have been battling the stump for most of the day now. Why doesn't Father want to use the horses? What theme does Father's attitude suggest?

2. Bob is remembering this scene as an adult. Do you think he remembers his father's actions as being foolish or heroic? What lesson or lessons do you think Bob learned about life from his father and Shane that day?

Now check your answers with your teacher. Review this part of the lesson if you don't understand why an answer was incorrect.

## Writing on Your Own 2

In this exercise you will write a character description and explain how your character reacts to conflict. Follow these steps:

- Review the plot outline you prepared for Writing on Your Own 1. Think about a character who could appear in your story. What would that character look like? How would he or she sound and move? What adjectives would you use to describe his or her personality? Write a short paragraph describing the main character in your story. Give particular attention to whatever quality will come into play to help illustrate the theme.

- How would this character react to the events you outlined earlier? Write a short paragraph explaining how the character will act in this conflict. Remember to give the conflict a focus that brings out your theme.

## 3 • Theme and Symbolism

One of the major themes of this chapter from *Shane* is that sometimes people must work long and hard to overcome a problem: they must meet the challenge with courage and refuse to give in to failure. The author has developed that theme, as well as several other themes, through the actions, attitudes, and words of Father, Shane, and Mother.

Another way to develop a theme is by using symbols. A *symbol* is a thing, a person, or an action that stands for something else. For example, in the United States, a voting booth stands for the right of every citizen to participate in government. The person who votes stands for all the people who care about how their country is run. The act of voting represents an act of faith in the decisions and actions of the government.

In this chapter of *Shane*, one of the important symbols is the tree stump. Bob is only a child, and at first he sees the stump as just a minor problem.

I tried to keep myself busy down by the river skipping flat stones across the current all muddy still from the rain. I was able to for a while. But that steady chopping had a peculiar fascination. It was always pulling me toward the barn. I simply could not grasp how they could stick at it hour after hour. It made no sense to me, why they should work so when routing out that old stump was not really so important.

Father and Shane come to see the stump as much more than just an annoyance. The stump becomes a challenge to them, and removing it becomes a symbol of their mastery over nature and any difficulty that comes their way. When you read this description of Shane's appearance and actions as he tackles the stump, you know that he feels he is doing more than just yard work.

I wanted to shout a warning. But I could not speak, for Shane had thrown his head in a quick sideways gesture to fling his hair from falling over his face and I had caught a glimpse of his eyes. They were aflame with a concentrated cold fire. Not another separate discernible movement did he make. It was all of him, the whole man, pulsing in the one incredible surge of power. You could fairly feel the fierce energy suddenly burning in him, pouring through him in the single coordinated drive.

By the end of the chapter, even young Bob realizes that there is more at stake in the battle against the stump than just whether the yard will be clear or not.

## Exercise 3

Read the following passage, which takes place after Mother learns that her pie has burned. Then use what you have learned in this lesson to answer the questions that follow the passage.

We sat down and waited for her to join us. She put her back to us and stood by the low shelf near the stove staring at her big pie tin and the burned stuff in it. Finally father spoke kind of sharply. "Lookahere, Marian. Aren't you ever going to sit down?"

She whirled and glared at him. I thought maybe she had been crying. But there were no tears on her face. It was dry and pinched-looking and there was no color in it. Her voice was sharp like father's. "I was planning to have a deep-dish apple pie. Well, I will. None of your silly man foolishness is going to stop me."

She swept up the big tin and went out the door with it. We heard her on the steps, and a few seconds later the rattle of the cover of the garbage pail. We heard her on the steps again. She came in and went to the side bench where the dishpan was and began to scrub the pie tin. The way she acted, we might not have been in the room.

Father's face was getting red. He picked up his fork to begin eating and let it drop with a little clatter. He squirmed on his chair and kept taking quick side looks at her. She finished scrubbing the tin and went to the apple barrel and filled her wooden bowl with fat round ones. She sat by the stove and started peeling them. Father fished in a pocket and pulled out his old jackknife. He moved over to her, stepping softly. He reached out for an apple to help her.

She did not look up. But her voice caught him like she had flicked him with a whip. "Joe Starrett, don't you dare touch a one of these apples."

1. How are Mother's actions similar to the actions of Father and Shane? What has the pie come to symbolize for Mother?

2. Think about some symbols in your own life. What things, people, or actions stand for something else? Why are these symbols important to you? What themes that you live by are connected with these symbols?

Now check your answers with your teacher. Review this part of the lesson if you don't understand why an answer was incorrect.

## Writing on Your Own 3

In this exercise you will decide what symbols best illustrate your theme and explain why. Follow these steps:

- Recall the theme that you chose. Think of things, people, or actions that would best symbolize your theme. For example, if your theme is working hard to achieve a goal, the symbol could be a trophy, a report card, or a paycheck. If your theme is how much we depend on our families, the symbol could be your grandmother. Make a list of possible symbols for your theme.

- Choose the symbol that you like best. Write a short paragraph explaining how that symbol stands for your theme.

## Discussion Guides

1. Do you think you would have liked living on the American frontier? With a partner, create a chart listing some of the positive and negative things about life on the frontier. When you have finished, discuss whether or not you would have liked living in the United States during frontier times.

2. Some people say that the character of Shane is a symbol of the spirit of the Old West—that Shane represents all the positive qualities of the American cowboy. With a small group of classmates, list the qualities of cowboys, as they are represented in popular books and movies. Compare those qualities with Shane's personality. Do you agree that Shane stands for the ideal American cowboy? Why or why not?

3. One of the challenges that the Starrett family faces is taming the land that they live on. What challenges does your community face right now? What challenges does the country face as a whole? Discuss these questions with your classmates. Have one student record the class's answers on the board. Then select one problem that you can begin working on today. Try to come up with some first steps toward solving that problem.

# Write a Dialogue

In this unit you have been looking at ways to express a theme. Now it is time to write an original dialogue that expresses a particular theme. Remember that a dialogue is a conversation between two or more people, so you will need to use quotation marks.

If you have questions about the writing process, refer to Using the Writing Process (page 295).

- Assemble the writing you did for this unit: *a*) a list of personal lessons that you learned in life, *b*) a list of plot events that would help develop your theme, *c*) a description of a main character and how he or she would react to those events, *d*) an explanation of how a particular symbol can stand for a theme.

- Review all of your writing assignments, and then choose a theme for your dialogue. It may be the theme you chose earlier, or you may want to write about a different one. Make sure that whatever you choose is a theme that you agree with.

- Next, think about the characters who might be talking to each other to express that theme. For example, if you choose the theme "Life was simpler in the old days," your dialogue could feature a girl and her grandmother talking about what it was like to grow up 50 years ago.

- Write a first draft of your dialogue, making sure that your readers can clearly identify each speaker. Make sure that the theme comes through clearly in what they say.

- Read your dialogue aloud to one or more classmates. Have them suggest changes that would improve it. See if your listeners can identify the theme you intended. If necessary, ask them for ways to make it more apparent. Make any revisions you agree with.

- Proofread your dialogue to find spelling, grammar, punctuation, and capitalization errors. Make a final copy and save it in a portfolio of your writing. If possible, share your dialogue with the class by reading it aloud with some volunteers.

# Unit 6 Use of Language

# I, Juan de Pareja
by Elizabeth Borton de Treviño

## About the Illustration

Who is in this scene, and what are they doing? Discuss what you think is happening. Use details from the illustration to support your answer. Then use the following questions to begin thinking about the selection:

- Where and when do you think this story takes place? What makes you think as you do?

- What might be the job of each person in the illustration?

- What do you think the relationship is between these two people?

# Unit 6

## Introduction

## About the Novel

The title character in *I, Juan de Pareja* is based on a real person, a black man who appears in a famous portrait by a master Spanish painter named Diego Velázquez. The real-life Juan de Pareja was also a painter; a small number of his works are displayed in art museums today.

Almost nothing is known about de Pareja's life, except that he was both a slave and friend of Velázquez. Elizabeth Borton de Treviño blends research and her own imagination to fill in the details of de Pareja's life. His story is narrated by Juan himself, as an old man looking back at his life. He was born to a black slave woman in Seville, Spain, in about 1610—a time when slavery was still accepted throughout Europe. His mother died when he was about five.

Doña Emilia, the wife of Juan's owner, treats him well and gives him light tasks to do. She teaches him to read and write so he can help her write letters. But when Juan is about twelve, first his master and then his mistress die. Juan, along with the rest of Doña Emilia's belongings, is left to her painter nephew, Diego Velázquez of Madrid.

A gypsy named Carmelo is hired to take Juan and the belongings to Madrid, a journey of several weeks. Along the way, he refuses to feed Juan. The boy runs away and tries to travel to his new master alone, but the gypsy finds him and beats him before delivering him to Velázquez. Once Juan arrives, the painter assures the frightened boy that he will never be beaten again.

## About the Author

Elizabeth Borton de Treviño was born in California in 1904 but has lived most of her life in Mexico. She graduated from Stanford University, studied violin at Boston Conservatory of Music, held various jobs in Boston publishing companies, and had her first book for young readers published in 1931. Since she married in 1935 and moved to Mexico, she has worked as a publicist for the Mexico City Tourist Department, has served as first violinist in the Vivaldi Orchestra, and has written more than twenty books for adults and young adults. Her best-known work—from which this selection is taken—is *I, Juan de Pareja,* which won the Newbery Medal in 1966. Many of her novels have been translated into several languages.

## About the Lessons

The lessons that follow this chapter from *I, Juan de Pareja* examine how the rich language of this novel helps make it a prize winner. Language is a very personal characteristic. From your own conversations with friends, you know that everyone has a unique style of speaking. Even when you can't see a group of your friends communicating, you can usually tell who is speaking, and when, by what they are saying and how they are saying it. You can often tell how your friends feel, too, by listening for slight changes in their usual styles.

Just as the use of language is important in oral communication, it is also important in novels and other forms of written communication. A writer takes the time to choose specific words and arrange them for different effects. Even when you may not be aware of individual words or phrases, the writer's decisions about how to use language affect how you think and feel about a story. You may appreciate a story even more when you look more carefully at the writer's techniques.

## Writing: Developing a Travel Brochure

Writers use language in specific ways to produce the effects they want. In the course of this unit, you will discover ways to present more realistic settings and more believable characters through the use of sensory details and clear, unique comparisons. You will put your new skills to use in a travel brochure written from the point of view of an imaginary tour guide. These suggestions will give you a good start on your project:

- Think of several places that you know well, either from having been there or from having read about them. Imagine that you are the publicity director for each place. What features make it attractive to visitors? For example, would people go there for a restful vacation or to see beautiful sights? Would they go to learn about something that happened there, such as a battle, a famous speech, or an unsolved crime? For each place, list some characteristics that make it attractive and interesting.

- Think of guided tours you have taken of different places, such as a museum, a business, a zoo, or a national park. What do you remember about the people who led the tours? Were some of them more knowledgeable than others? Were some funnier? Did some move too fast or give you more facts than you could take in? How did the tour guides influence your opinion of the places? Jot down your memories and opinions of each tour guide. Save your writing. You will use it later in this unit.

# Before Reading

The questions below will help you see how de Treviño develops rich language in *I, Juan de Pareja*. As you read the selection, keep these questions in mind:

- In which passages does the author use very descriptive details? To what sense or senses do the details appeal?

- Why do you suppose the author includes so many descriptive details? Do they help develop any story element besides the setting?

- Be alert for comparisons between unlike things. What similarities do the comparisons point out? Are there any comparisons that you must stop and reread to get their full impact?

# Vocabulary Tips

This selection uses some words that may be unfamiliar to you but that are important for understanding the story. Below, you will find some of the more difficult words and their definitions, as well as sentences that show how the words are used. Look them over before you begin reading the selection.

**austere**
very plain. Considering how rich she is, the movie star's home is surprisingly <u>austere</u>.

**furbelows**
showy, decorative trimmings. All the <u>furbelows</u> on Susan's prom dress made it stand out from the other girls' dresses.

**quiver**
to tremble or shake. The scary movie made me <u>quiver</u> with fright.

**detached**
not involved emotionally; separate. To settle this quarrel, we must find someone who is <u>detached</u> and can be fair.

**qualms**
feelings of uneasiness. Before the performance, the actor had <u>qualms</u> about stepping onto the stage.

**cryptic**
mysterious; having a hidden meaning. Slowly the detective made sense out of the case's <u>cryptic</u> clues.

**unerringly**
without making mistakes; sure and exact. No matter where I hide my slippers, my dog <u>unerringly</u> finds them.

**mortar and pestle**
hard bowl (mortar) in which a softer substance, such as corn or nuts, can be pounded or ground into a powder with a club-shaped tool (pestle). The woman used a <u>mortar and pestle</u> to ground the corn into meal.

**palette**
thin, oval-shaped board with a thumb hole at one end, on which an artist holds and mixes paints. The artist rarely looked at his <u>palette</u> as he dabbed his brush into the paint.

# I, Juan de Pareja

Elizabeth Borton de Treviño

### *In which I learn my duties*

What do I remember of my youth? I remember Master
and his studio.

Within a week I was quite well and had been given
new clothes. They pleased me, for Master did not dress
me up like a pet monkey in bright silks and turbans as
Doña Emilia had done in her innocent fancy. He was
an austere man himself, uninterested in furbelows
except when he had to paint them. He bought me a
good, serviceable jacket and knee trousers of country-
woven wool, dyed dark brown. I felt a momentary
quiver of distaste as I saw my brown hands and wrists
emerging from the brown stuff; I thought I must look in
this suit as if I were covered with a second skin. Master
himself stood back and stared at me with his detached,
impersonal regard.

"One gold earring came among my aunt's things," he
said suddenly. "It would look well on you."

"Perhaps it is the other of a pair that were my
mother's," I told him. "Mistress gave me one, but I lost it
on the road. She told me she would keep the other for me."

No doubt the gypsy had stolen my earring as I lay
unconscious. My *real* was gone, also.

Master brought the earring, and I took it with rever-
ence and worked it through the hole in my ear. It was
my mother's; I was glad to feel it bobbing against my

cheek. Master looked pleased to see the sparkle of gold against all the brown.

I wore that hoop for many years, until I sold it one day in Italy. But that was much later. I will tell you about that in good time.

Our household was a simple one, but ample and comfortable. The Mistress, Doña Juana de Miranda, was a round, bustling little woman, very active and competent in managing everything. She had a cook and a house-maid, between whom she divided all the household chores. I wondered just how much she would require of me, but I had no qualms, and I was determined to be trustworthy and careful and to do whatever she wished. I gave thanks daily that I had found a good Master and that I would never again be in the power of creatures like Carmelo.

I ate in the kitchen with the cook, who soon pampered me with tidbits, and I had a small room to myself, off the kitchen. It had been made for the pot boy and stable help, but Master kept neither horse nor carriage. He walked when he had to go somewhere, and Mistress hired a carriage once a week to make her calls and go shopping.

However, I soon found that I was not to do anything but serve Master, and he did not even want me to help him dress or to lay out his clothes. I brushed them and rubbed oil into his belts and boots, but Mistress herself, like a good wife (and I suspect because she adored him, and loved to work over and touch his things), sewed and mended his linen and saw that it was fresh. Master had other plans for me.

He had allowed me to rest and heal in those first days in his home. As soon as I was well, he said, "Come," and he took me into his studio.

This was a large room on the second floor of the house. It was almost bare, with a great window to the north that let in a pure cold light. Several easels, strong and sturdy, stood about, a chair or two, and there was a long table with a palette on it, a vase full of brushes, rags, and bits of canvas and wood for frames. In winter the studio was bitter cold, and in summer it was hot as an oven. During the heat it was full of smells, as well, for with the windows flung wide open, there ascended to us from the street the odor of refuse, of horse dung, and of tanning leather, for there was a leather craftsman nearby. The smells were awful, but Master never noticed anything . . . heat nor cold nor bad smells nor dust. All he thought about was light, and the only days when he was nervous were days of low fog or rain that changed the light he lived by.

One by one, he taught me my duties. First, I had to learn to grind the colors. There were many mortars for this work, and pestles in varying sizes. I soon learned that the lumps of earth and metallic compounds had to be softly and continuously worked until there remained a powder as fine as the ground rice ladies used on their cheeks and foreheads. It took hours, and sometimes when I was sure the stuff was as fine as satin, Master would pinch and move it between his sensitive fingers, and shake his head, and then I had to grind some more. Later the ground powder had to be incorporated into the oils, and well-mixed, and much later still, I arranged Master's palette for him, the little mounds of color each in its fixed place, and he had his preferences about how much of any one should be set out. And, of course, brushes were to be washed daily, in plenty of good Castile soap and water. Master's brushes all had to be clean and fresh every morning when he began to work.

Much later, I had to learn to stretch cotton canvas to the frames, and when I had learned the trick of it, I was set to doing the same with linen. This was, for me, the hardest task of all.

Master had all the tools for framing the canvas sharpened and put into good order and bought me plenty of wood to practice with. Each time I built a frame and stretched a canvas, holding the frame taut with wooden pins, and nailing the canvas on around the frame, he showed me the flaws in my work by his expression. For some time the trouble was with my carpentry. My corners didn't fit, or the side pieces were not precisely to measurement, or the pegs were too clumsy. Oh, it took care and thought, and I shed many tears. Doña Emilia had never asked more of me than to fan her or hand her a sweet or hold her parasol, until she taught me to write. But this work was a man's, and I grieved that I could not learn it.

One day when I had failed for the third time at trying to fit a frame on which he wanted to stretch a good linen canvas, Master put down his palette, left his model fretting on the model stand, and showed me just how. His fingers were slim and sensitive, with dark hairs on the second knuckle; his nails were almond-shaped. Many a woman would have been proud to have such delicate hands as his. He cut and fitted the pieces precisely, so easily, so quickly, that I lost heart. I had spoiled so many. I put my head in my hands and sobbed.

He lifted my head at once, smiled briefly, a mere flash of white teeth under the small dark mustache, and hurried back to his easel. I took the wood and the tool, held them just as he had and tried again, and this time it came right. I never failed again, and from then on I stretched all his canvases.

But this was but the beginning. Once properly stretched on the frame, the cloth had to be prepared to take the paint. We had many coatings we put on; Master taught me all the formulae from memory. In an excess of enthusiasm, I told Master I could write and that I would note down all the preparations.

"No," he said. "These are professional secrets. Keep them in your head."

And so I had to train my memory for each sort of finish to spread on the canvas, according to what use Master would have for it.

He usually rose and had his breakfast by six, earlier in summer. His breakfast was always the same: a piece of grilled meat and a small trencher of bread. Occasionally he would take an orange into the studio, and there eat it thoughtfully as he planned his work for the day. He liked the early light when it was still fresh from the dew and without any dancing dust motes in it. He was always in the studio until the light went in the afternoon, but he was not always painting. He made drawings, many drawings, though he did not save them, but tossed them aside. (I was able to keep a few.) He drew so much, so easily, so perfectly, that when at last he stood before a frame of prepared canvas, he could sketch in the outlines of his subject in one moment of flashing charcoal, never having to correct more than a knife-edge of line.

And often he simply sat staring . . . now at a piece of draped velvet, now at a copper bowl, now at me.

When I felt a little more confidence in his presence, and did not fear disturbing him in one of his reveries, I asked him why he did this.

"I am working, Juanico," was his answer. "Working, by looking."

I did not understand and so I held my tongue, thinking that this was what he meant me to do with this cryptic answer. But a week or more later, he spoke to me as if I had put my question but a moment before, answering, "When I sit and look at something I am feeling its shape, so that I shall have it in my fingers when I start to draw the outline. I am analyzing the colors, too. For example, do you see that piece of brocade on the chair? What color is it?"

"Blue," I answered promptly.

"No, Juanico. There is a faint underlay of blue, but there is violet in that blue, the faintest touch of rose, and the highlights are red and bright green. Look again."

It was magical, for suddenly I could see them, the other colors, just as he said.

"The eye is complicated. It mixes the colors for you," explained Master. "The painter must unmix them and lay them on again shade by shade, and then the eye of the beholder takes over and mixes them again."

"I should like to paint!" I cried out in my joy at this revelation.

"Alas, I cannot teach you," said Master, and then he became silent again and returned to his easel.

I pondered this remark and lay awake at night thinking of it after dark, for I could not understand why he could not teach me. I decided that he had meant to say, "I will not teach you," or "I do not wish to teach you." I put this thought away deep in my memory because it made me so sad. I had begun to love him, you see, and to wish to offer him all my heart's loyalty. But these words were a little worm, gnawing away at my affection.

The thought kept coming into my mind as I ground colors, or moved a vase or a flower jug when he was painting, or stretched linen on a frame. Perhaps he was simply too busy? That could be. Or perhaps he hated teaching. That could be, also. Then one day I learned the reason, but not from him.

Our life was very tranquil. Mistress was a careful and thrifty woman who watched over all the expenses of the household and was always busy mending or sewing or working at her tapestries. She was merry and gay, too, and often sang as she went about the rooms. The children, two little girls, Francisca and Ignacia (*la niña*) were toddlers, and very endearing, with their big soft eyes and their baby prattle. Master often held them on his knee, silently studying them, feeling the curve of the tender baby cheeks with his fingers. I would have been happy to help care for the little ones, but I was seldom asked to do it. It was accepted in our house that I belonged to Master. This suited me well, and in all except that little nagging wish to paint, I was content, having every reason to look forward to a pleasant and comfortable life.

The rooms of the house were large, well-carpeted, and with shutters to hold out the strong sun of summer and the bleak wind of winter. The curtains and the chairs were of red velvet mostly, with here and there an occasional note of sober deep blue. There was a crucifix over each bed, even mine, and when it was very cold there were many brasiers in the rooms, giving off a delicate but pervasive heat from glowing coals. There were no paintings by Master about. The walls were covered with rugs or hangings; all Master's work was kept in the studio.

One day Mistress called me and asked me to help her tidy a great carved chest she had at the end of her bed, in which I supposed she might have stored blankets and other woolen things, against the winter. But when she lifted the lid I saw a rainbow of silks in many colors that had been rumpled and stuffed back just any way.

"Help me fold these, Juanico," she directed me. "Then we will arrange them, all the darker shades at the bottom, and brighter ones toward the top. Your Master will keep this chest in his studio and you are to see that the stuffs are always in order, and bring them to him whenever he wants a spot of color, or a background of some cloth to catch the light. You will be very busy helping him now, for he is going to take in some apprentices."

"I thought he did not like to have apprentices about," I faltered.

"The court has asked him to do so," she told me. "Your Master is very deeply obligated to certain men of the court and could not refuse. Besides, he has many church commissions now and cannot do them all. He will have to have help, for backgrounds and so on, and perhaps even to make copies of his works."

"I wish I could learn to paint also!" I blurted out, forgetting that I had promised myself not to mention the matter again.

"I wish you could," Mistress answered, "but there is a law in Spain which forbids slaves to practice any of the arts. The crafts, some manual skills, yes. But not art. However, do not grieve. Move back now, and do not let your tears fall on this taffeta; they will spot it. I know you love color, Juanico. You may help me choose the colors for my embroidery, and I will ask Master to give you sole charge of this chest."

I remembered that Mistress had been daughter of a great painter before she became wife of one, and so I took her word.

So that was why I would not be taught to paint, could never transfer my vision to canvas. I felt sad, but I did not feel, at that time, any resentment at being a slave. God knows I was happy with Master and Mistress. I felt useful and appreciated. Freedom? I had had a taste of it on the road, and it was cruel to a black boy. I swallowed my disappointment, and as I dragged the laden chest through the halls to the studio I felt a kind of comfort. Master had not denied me of his own free will, but because he was forced to do so, by the law.

That very day we began to make ready a room for the apprentices to live in. A carpenter was called to come and fill in walls where some old stables stood open on one side, in the back patio. He was a merry fellow, singing as he cut and fitted his lumber, and in a few days there were two snug little rooms, each with a wide wooden bench to sleep on and a good chest with a lock, in which the apprentices could keep their possessions. I would have liked a chest with a lock, too, but none was given me, and so I supposed that this, too, was something slaves could not have. I therefore put the matter out of my mind and devoted myself to the tasks at hand.

The apprentices were, of course, free white boys, but they were under special obligations to Master and bound to obey him, just as I was, and in truth I had more freedom than they, for I was part of the household. I had Master's confidence, and he revealed himself to me in many small intimate ways. The apprentices were kept on a footing of severe formality. We all called him Master, slave and white boys alike, for Master means Teacher, Authority, Chief.

One of our apprentices was only a few years older than I, about sixteen. He was round-faced, pink-cheeked and blue-eyed, with blond hair and he had the most innocent smile in the world. His name was Cristobal; his father was a carver of religious images. We all thought Cristobal a simple soul, at first. But he was a schemer and a trouble maker, and it was soon clear why his father had not taken him on as one of his own apprentices, to learn the family skill.

Cristobal was a liar and a thief. He used to take things and then try to pretend that I had stolen them. Master set a trap and caught him at this, and promised to send him home to his father for a good whipping the next time anything of the sort happened. Then Cristobal let me be, though sometimes he could not resist pinching me or tripping me.

Once when Cristobal stole a piece of Master's azure silk, I was in hopes he would get rid of the boy for good, but he merely sent him to bed without supper. Master never beat anyone. I think he kept Cristobal because the boy was remarkable at drawing. He could sketch swiftly, catching the movement of a bird on the wing or a cat leaping after a drifting feather with but a few telling lines, and he could suggest a likeness which seemed to me miraculous in one so young.

I heard Master and Mistress talking about the apprentices one evening after supper, as Master sat with his glass of ruby wine and a few raisins.

"Send him home," suggested Mistress. "He makes me nervous and I am afraid he will hurt one of the babies."

"No, for they would cry and point him out. He is a real sneak," said Master sadly.

"I don't like him."

"Nor do I. But he has a remarkable talent."

"What about the other one, Alvaro?"

"A good boy. Dutiful, well-mannered, correct. He will never be a painter, though. A good copyist, perhaps."

Alvaro was the son of a scrivener at court. He was little and thin and he stuttered. Also, he had a delicate stomach. I liked Alvaro, but I paid more attention to Cristobal. I had to, in order to protect myself, my clothes, and the things which Master had put into my charge.

When Master had a portrait commission (and at certain times of the year he had many) I had to be near to arrange tables and chairs on the model's dais; I had to have good sketching paper ready, fixed firmly against a backing of light wood. I had to provide well-burned charcoal sketching sticks. To make them, I built a little fire and closed it in with bricks, all but a small vent, in the back patio, and then I toasted thin twigs and branches of olive until they were charred through.

Always I had to adjust the windows, so as to keep the light striking the same spot on a lady's gown or a gentleman's coat. It was very delicate work, and I had to be most attentive.

Master was curiously exacting about all of these matters, but when the sitting began, I alone knew how strange he was about his work. He always kept a drape that could be let down over his canvas, so that no one could see what he was doing; he never allowed sitters to see his paintings until they were finished. Many times, days would pass, and Master had done little more than stand and think, in front of a model, sometimes drawing a line or two.

And yet when he had decided upon every detail in his mind, when he had thought out the whole composition and had analyzed all the colors and lines, then he seized his brush and worked swiftly. He held the brush about four inches above where the hair began, and his palette —a large, smooth, kidney-shaped piece of wood —was always prepared with small mounds of colors in an unchanging order. Nearest his thumb were the cool, earth colors, gradually becoming warmer and more glowing until they ended in a larger mound of white. When Master was working intensely, he did not even glance at his palette, but put his brush unerringly into the colors he wanted, taking the amounts he needed and blending them in the middle to the shades he required. I have seen him thus mix up the same shade time and time again, without glancing, and taking them straight to the canvas; they were always perfect.

His strokes on the canvas, too, sometimes seemed slapdash, rough and unintelligible, if one stood as close to the canvas as he. But a little distance away, and those spots and dashes of light cream or ivory would resolve themselves into a delicate frill of lace, or the daintiest of highlights on satin. Time after time I verified this, and it always seemed magical to me. Master never commented on my astonishment, but often I saw a slight smile curl the quiet mouth beneath the dark silky mustache.

And he never chatted while he worked. It was the sitter who spoke, and Master merely put in a word now and again, should there come an expectant silence. Then he would murmur, "Ah?" or "Possibly," or "Just so."

But he studied people. Once he said to me, when the sitter had gone home, and Master was working on a background, "I like to watch people when they talk about themselves, Juanico. Then they reveal to you what they really are. Women, for instance, love themselves; they speak of themselves as if they were talking about a beloved relative who is to be pardoned any foolishness. Men, on the other hand, seem to admire themselves. They speak of themselves like judges who have already brought in a verdict of 'Not guilty.'"

I ventured, "Isn't it difficult to show people their true selves when you paint them, Master?"

"No. Nobody ever knows what he really looks like. Bring me some more of the ochre."

And he was silent again.

Once in a while he would paint me, to keep his hand in, or would ask me to model some difficult fabric.

After he had taught the apprentices to draw vases and fruits and cheeses and hams and all manner of objects, he began to let them sketch people. Then I was often told to pose for them. Then I had my revenge on Cristobal and I helped Alvaro, turning myself subtly so as to ruin Cristobal's drawing and holding myself very still when I noticed Alvaro's eyes on me. Master scolded me for this and watched me, but all the same I was sometimes mischievous. I was always sorry when Master criticized Alvaro's work and praised Cristobal's, and one day he answered the distress he saw that this caused me, by telling me his reason.

"Art must be true," he said. "It is the one thing in life that must rest on solid truth. Otherwise, it is worthless."

Then one day there was a knock at the door, and soon after, Mistress came running into the studio, pale with excitement. Behind her, pacing slowly, followed a messenger from the King. He handed a rolled parchment to Master, bowed, and turned. Mistress ran ahead of him to open the door for his departure. The apprentices and I stood silent and respectful as Master unrolled the parchment and read it. He rolled it up again, and took up his palette and brush once more. I remember that he was painting a bronze vase, and I had been at great pains to keep moving it so that the sunlight should continue to strike it at the same point every moment.

"Diego!" burst forth Mistress. "Tell me, please! Don't make me wait to know! What was in the King's message?"

"I am to paint his portrait," he answered at length, frowning.

"Oh, God be praised! How wonderful!"

"And I am to be given a studio in the palace."

Mistress collapsed onto a chair, which creaked ominously, and she had to fan herself. Little black curls escaped from her pompadour and fell down over her forehead. This meant she was to move in court circles. It meant a fortune, dignity, honors, position beyond anything she had dreamed of.

But Master was silent and pale as he continued to paint the vase. At last he murmured, under his breath, and only I heard, "I hope they haven't sent some courtier to select and prepare a studio for me. It must have light. Light. Nothing else matters. . . ."

# Reviewing and Interpreting the Selection

Record your answers to these questions in your personal literature notebook. Follow the directions for each part.

**Reviewing**  Try to complete the following sentences without looking back at the selection.

Recognizing
Literary
Elements
(Setting)

1. The following detail shows that this novel is set about 300 years ago:

   a. Juan thinks that his brown clothing looks like a second skin.

   b. Juan's Mistress employs both a cook and a housemaid.

   c. Master teaches Juan how the eye combines different colors into a single color.

   d. when the weather is very cold, the family heats the rooms with brasiers filled with glowing coals.

Understanding
Main Ideas

2. From Juan's detailed description of the stages of framing a canvas and preparing it for use, you can tell that

   a. Juan enjoys the job and thinks it is great fun.

   b. artists of the Renaissance spent too much time on this stage of their job.

   c. a properly prepared canvas is essential to a good work of art.

   d. the materials that Master worked with were not very good to begin with.

3. According to Juan, the only thing that Master is concerned with in his studio is the

    a. smells coming in from the street.

    b. light.

    c. arrangement of the furniture.

    d. temperature.

4. Of the four events listed below, this one occurs after the apprentices arrive in the household:

    a. Master is invited to paint a portrait of the King.

    b. Master takes on many church commissions.

    c. Juan discovers why Master cannot teach him how to paint.

    d. a carpenter turns some old stables into two snug little rooms.

5. Master cannot teach Juan how to paint because

    a. he knows he'll be too busy with his apprentices.

    b. the law forbids slaves to practice the arts.

    c. Juan must take care of the chest of silks for background color.

    d. he does not like to teach.

**Interpreting**  To complete these sentences, you may look back at the selection if you'd like.

Making
Inferences

6. Master does not explain why he cannot teach Juan to paint because he

   a. isn't very interested in the subject.
   b. knows the rule is unkind, and he doesn't want to hurt Juan.
   c. doesn't think Juan deserves an explanation.
   d. thinks Juan has expressed interest in painting simply to make conversation.

Analyzing

7. Master's habit of talking is like his method of painting in that he

   a. thinks about the topic for a long time before taking action.
   b. does everything quickly and easily.
   c. spends too little time at each activity.
   d. tends to make colorful, even outrageous, statements.

Predicting
Outcomes

8. From what you know of the two apprentices, it is probable that

   a. Alvaro will shortly give up painting altogether.
   b. Alvaro will go to work for Cristobal.
   c. Cristobal is sure to be a successful painter.
   d. Cristobal will be a successful painter if he can stay out of trouble.

9. Of all Master's statements, this one is the best guide to appreciating art from any era:

   a. "The painter must unmix them [colors] and lay them on again shade by shade, and then the eye of the beholder takes over and mixes them again."

   b. "Nobody ever knows what he really looks like."

   c. "Art must be true. It is the one thing in life that must rest on solid truth. Otherwise, it is worthless."

   d. "I am working. . . . Working, by looking."

10. Juan's attitude toward slavery is that

   a. slaves have nothing to complain about as long as their owners treat them decently.

   b. the institution of slavery is totally evil and should be outlawed.

   c. there is nothing wrong in slavery itself, but he personally is bitter about being a slave.

   d. if he were offered freedom, he would refuse it.

Now check your answers with your teacher. Study the questions you answered incorrectly. What types of questions were they? Talk with your teacher about ways to work on those skills.

# Use of Language

Cartoons and comic books use pictures to tell stories. Mimes and dancers use movement. But writers and speakers use words. Some people have a way of telling stories that makes their spoken words come alive. The same thing is true of good writers. While you are reading their written words, you can almost see, smell, taste, and touch the things that they describe. You feel you have shaken hands with the characters they create.

How do good storytellers and writers use language so powerfully? If we look closely at their work, we can see the techniques they use. We can understand a bit better how they get the effects they want. In these lessons, we will look at some of the ways in which Elizabeth Borton de Treviño uses language to make her novel more effective:

1. She uses many sensory details to help readers imagine the setting.

2. She uses fresh comparisons that help readers see familiar things in new ways.

3. She pays great attention to visual detail to help readers understand what the two artists see, think, and feel.

## 1 • Setting, Details, and the Senses

The story of *I, Juan de Pareja* takes place hundreds of years ago in the country of Spain. Therefore, we can expect many differences between that setting and our own. Since the setting is so different, the writer must use exact, descriptive details to help us imagine how things look, sound, smell, taste, and feel. Notice how this description of Juan's outfit suggests not only its color but its texture and style as well.

Within a week I was quite well and had been given new clothes. They pleased me, for Master did not dress me up like a pet monkey in bright silks and turbans as Doña Emilia had done in her innocent fancy. He was an austere man himself, uninterested in furbelows except when he had to paint them. He bought me a good, serviceable jacket and knee trousers of country-woven wool, dyed dark brown. I felt a momentary quiver of distaste as I saw my brown hands and wrists emerging from the brown stuff; I thought I must look in this suit as if I were covered with a second skin.

Not only does the author tell us that Juan's clothes are made of wool, she describes it as "country-woven wool," a detail that suggests a heavy, somewhat rough material. The practical nature of the material is further explained by its contrast with the "bright silks and turbans" given Juan by his previous owner.

The author also tells us that Juan's trousers are knee-length, and his jacket ends just short of his wrists. In addition, her comparison between the suit and "a second skin" suggests a snug fit and a color that closely matches Juan's skin.

In the following description of Master's house, the details tell about the rooms and the weather. They appeal to the senses of sight and touch as they tell us how people lived during the 1600s.

The rooms of the house were large, well-carpeted, and with shutters to hold out the strong sun of summer and the bleak wind of winter. The curtains and the chairs were of red velvet mostly, with here and there an occasional note of sober deep blue. There was a crucifix over each bed, even mine, and when it was very cold there were many brasiers in the rooms, giving off a delicate but pervasive heat from glowing coals.

Although we are not familiar with brasiers, the paragraph suggests that they held hot coals and were used to warm rooms in winter. We can picture basins or bowls, probably of metal, scattered around large, shuttered rooms, and the coals inside them giving off heat, smoke, and a dim orange-red glow. Again, the author's use of sensory details helps us imagine ourselves in another place and time.

## Exercise 1

Read the following passage, which describes Master's studio. Then use what you have learned in this lesson to answer the questions that follow the passage.

> This was a large room on the second floor of the house. It was almost bare, with a great window to the north that let in a pure cold light. Several easels, strong and sturdy, stood about, a chair or two, and there was a long table with a palette on it, a vase full of brushes, rags, and bits of canvas and wood for frames. In winter the studio was bitter cold, and in summer it was hot as an oven. During the heat it was full of smells, as well, for with the windows flung wide open, there ascended to us from the street the odor of refuse, of horse dung, and of tanning leather, for there was a leather craftsman nearby. The smells were awful, but Master never noticed anything . . . heat nor cold nor bad smells nor dust. All he thought about was light, and the only days when he was nervous were days of low fog or rain that changed the light he lived by.

1. Which detail or details appeal to the sense of sight? of smell? of touch, or heat and cold?

2. In Juan's day, was it common for craftspeople to work at home? Identify details that support your answer.

3. What transportation did people use at that time? How can you tell?

4. What did people depend on most to light their homes? What details suggest your answer?

Now check your answers with your teacher. Review this part of the lesson if you don't understand why an answer was incorrect.

**Writing on Your Own 1**

In this exercise you will use what you have learned to write a description whose details appeal to any sense except sight. Follow these steps:

- Choose one of the places you listed for item 1 under Developing a Travel Brochure on page 183. Imagine yourself at your chosen place, with your eyes closed. What do you hear nearby? What sounds and smells come from far off? Be specific. For example, if you hear birdcalls, are they sweet and pleasing or harsh and grating? Write descriptions—each at least a sentence long—of three or more of the things you hear and smell.

- Once again, imagine yourself at the place with your eyes closed. It is a summer day, and no other people are there. You are shoeless and wearing a swimsuit. What do you feel? Are you standing on mud, pavement, or plush carpeting? Do you feel hot sun, a cool breeze, or something else? Is the air dry or humid? Are insects attacking you? Is sand blowing at you? When you reach out, what do you touch? How does it feel? Write as many details as you can about what you will be aware of through your sense of touch, both at your fingertips and across your body.

- Now combine your details in a description of the place. Remember to begin by telling what place you are in and where it is.

## 2 • Comparisons and Connections

Frequently, when we come across a new object or situation, we see similarities between it and a familiar object or situation. To describe the new thing more exactly, we can compare it to the familiar thing. This helps our audience react to the thing just as we did.

For example, the color of clouds at sunset might be orange one evening. How could you let someone else know the exact shade of orange that you see? You could say the sunset looks like orange juice. Your comparison would tie together two unlike things—the sunset and orange juice—and would make your listener stop and think about the image.

Writers take advantage of comparisons to present things more exactly and powerfully. In one passage of *I, Juan de Pareja*, for example, the author describes the fine powder used in making paints. She could have said that the raw materials are ground as fine as chalk. The comparison with chalk is exact, but it is too common and familiar. Everyone has heard it before, and no one has any particular reaction to it. In the following passage, find the comparison that de Treviño uses instead.

> I soon learned that the lumps of earth and metallic compounds had to be softly and continuously worked until there remained a powder as fine as the ground rice ladies used on their cheeks and foreheads.

The narrator says that the raw materials are worked into a powder as fine as the face powder that women wear. This unexpected comparison does more than describe how fine the materials must be ground to be used in paint. It also suggests that the "lumps of earth and metallic compounds" are changed into something of a higher quality. They are now linked to beauty.

## Exercise 2

Read the following passage, in which Master is speaking to Juan. Then use what you have learned in this lesson to answer the questions that follow the passage.

> I like to watch people when they talk about themselves, Juanico. Then they reveal to you what they really are. Women, for instance, love themselves; they speak of themselves as if they were talking about a beloved relative who is to be pardoned any foolishness. Men, on the other hand, seem to admire themselves. They speak of themselves like judges who have already brought in a verdict of "Not guilty."

1. According to Master, when women speak of themselves, with what do they compare themselves? How does this show their love of themselves?

2. According to Master, how do men act when they speak of themselves? How does this show their pride in themselves?

3. From what Master says, do you think he is more interested in capturing people's appearances or attitudes in his paintings? Support your answer.

Now check your answers with your teacher. Review this part of the lesson if you don't understand why an answer was incorrect.

## Writing on Your Own 2

In this exercise you will use what you have learned to write comparisons that show a thing in different lights. Follow these steps:

- Review your answers to the questions in Writing on Your Own 1 on page 207. Choose one item that might be found at the place you described, or one characteristic about it. For example, you might choose the huge trees at a park, or the atmosphere there.

- Think of two different comparisons to describe the item or characteristic you chose. In one comparison, show what the thing has in common with an unlike thing that is beautiful, useful, or otherwise desirable. In the second comparison, show what the thing has in common with an unlike thing that is ugly, or dangerous, or otherwise undesirable. The first comparison should make readers feel good about the item or characteristic, while the second comparison should leave them uneasy about it. Here are examples:

  The trees were strong pillars that tickled the clouds.

  The trees towered over us like threatening ogres.

## 3 • Language and Character

If you could recite the batting order of your favorite team and quote hitting and pitching statistics, anyone would be able tell you are a baseball fan. If you could discuss the strengths and weaknesses of all the popular video games, people would know that you love video games. If you like to debate which restaurants serve the most delicious meals, people would be able to guess that you enjoy food.

It is no surprise that what we like to talk about reveals something about our personality. Describing what a character enjoys gives a writer a useful way to reveal what a character is like without being obvious about it. The writer just lets the character talk. The character's choice of topics and words suggests his or her nature.

In *I, Juan de Pareja*, the narrator is Juan himself. His language throughout the entire novel provides clues to his character. Here is his description of how Master helps him learn to make a frame for a painting canvas. Watch for details about what he sees and how he describes it.

> One day when I had failed for the third time at trying to fit a frame on which he wanted to stretch a good linen canvas, Master put down his palette, left his model fretting on the model stand, and showed me just how. His fingers were slim and sensitive, with dark hairs on the second knuckle; his nails were almond-shaped. Many a woman would have been proud to have such delicate hands as his. He cut and fitted the pieces precisely, so easily, so quickly, that I lost heart. I had spoiled so many. I put my head in my hands and sobbed.

Juan sees the swift, sure movements of Master's hands. He also sees the dark hairs on the second knuckle and the almond shape of the fingernails. In the background he is aware of the impatient model and of Master's abandoned palette. Even at his young age, Juan notices and memorizes tiny details about the appearance of people and things. Clearly he has the eye of an artist, even before he is aware that he would like to be one.

By giving Juan language that is packed with visual details, de Treviño develops an essential part of his character. Juan cannot stop himself from seeing with exactness. In time he cannot stop himself from recreating what he sees. His language shows that he is destined to become a painter.

## Exercise 3

Read the following passage, in which Juan first states his desire to paint. Then use what you have learned in this lesson to answer the questions that follow the passage.

"I should like to paint!" I cried out in my joy at this revelation.

"Alas, I cannot teach you," said Master, and then he became silent again and returned to his easel.

I pondered this remark and lay awake at night thinking of it after dark, for I could not understand why he could not teach me. I decided that he had meant to say, "I will not teach you," or "I do not wish to teach you." I put this thought away deep in my memory because it made me so sad. I had begun to love him, you see, and to wish to offer him all my heart's loyalty. But these words were a little worm, gnawing away at my affection.

. . . It was accepted in our house that I belonged to Master. This suited me well, and in all except that little nagging wish to paint, I was content, having every reason to look forward to a pleasant and comfortable life.

1. Explain Juan's statement that "these words were a little worm, gnawing away at my affection."

2. In the last paragraph, what word does Juan use to describe his wish to paint? Is he happy to have this wish to paint, proud of it, or embarrassed by it? What internal conflict does Juan's choice of words hint at?

Now check your answers with your teacher. Review this part of the lesson if you don't understand why an answer was incorrect.

## Writing on Your Own 3

In this exercise you will use what you have learned to write two short monologues from very different characters. Follow these steps:

- Review the notes you made in response to the second item under Developing a Travel Brochure on page 183. From among the tour guides you described, choose one with a definite attitude and/or strong opinions.

- Imagine that the tour guide you have chosen is leading a group of children through a zoo. He or she stops to talk about one of these types of animals: monkeys, elephants, penguins, or frogs. Choose an animal group that your tour guide will have strong feelings about. Then write a monologue, about one paragraph long, that your guide would use to describe that animal. Include at least two details about the sight, sound, smell, or feel of the animal. Also include at least one comparison that would make the tour group feel strongly about the animal, either in a good way or in a bad way. For example, a tour guide who is easily frightened might concentrate on the size and strength of the elephant, and compare its weight to that of a tank.

  Tour guides who are poorly prepared, not comfortable with children, or very witty would focus on different characteristics or describe them differently. In any case, their comparisons and speaking styles should match their personality.

- Now imagine a tour guide who is the opposite of your first one. For example, if the first one was fearful, the second one should be fearless. If the first one was poorly prepared, the second one should be a "walking encyclopedia."

- Write a second monologue. Have the second tour guide describe the same animal in the way he or she sees it, with new sensory details and a new comparison. Make sure the differences between the monologues bring out the differences between the guides' personalities.

- Invite a classmate to read both monologues. Ask your classmate to tell which tour guide he or she would prefer to have, and why.

# Discussion Guides

1. Juan posed differently for Cristobal and Alvaro. Imagine that Cristobal complains to Master about Juan, and that Master asks both apprentices for their opinions of Juan. With two partners, develop a conversation among Master and the two apprentices concerning Juan. Present your skit for the class.

2. Some critics feel that mixing historical fact and imaginative fiction is unfair to history. They would object to *I, Juan de Pareja* because it goes beyond what can be proved in historical records. Others feel that, as long as an author clearly states that a story is based on limited records, but is true to known facts, a novel like this one is an exciting way to teach historical events. Where do you and your classmates stand on this issue? Hold a debate on whether or not writers should be allowed to write novels based on historical figures like Juan or Julius Caesar or George Washington.

3. Another writer who often uses a first-person narrator and a great number of sensory details is Edgar Allan Poe. Work with a small group to select a Poe short story, such as "The Masque of the Red Death," "The Cask of Amontillado," or "The Fall of the House of Usher." Take turns reading aloud several paragraphs from your selection. Then discuss this chapter from *I, Juan de Pareja* and the Poe tale, focusing on the language in each piece. Compare, for example, both authors' uses of detail and comparisons. Does Poe use fewer details than de Treviño, more, or about as many? Do the sensory details in the Poe selection appeal to as many different senses as those in the novel selection? What mood do Poe's comparisons convey? Which selection uses language that is closer to the language your group uses? Which do individual members of the group prefer? Group members should give reasons for all their answers. After all the groups have finished their discussions, each group should share its observations with the class.

# Write a Travel Brochure

In your previous writing assignments, you have used language for specific effects. You have chosen sensory details for describing a place exactly. You have developed comparisons that influence readers' feelings. You have used language to reveal a speaker's character. Now you will use your new skills to create a travel brochure, as written by an imaginary guide.

If you have questions about the writing process, refer to Using the Writing Process on page 295.

- Assemble the writing you did for all of the exercises in this unit. You should have *a*) your notes about places to visit and tour guides you have known; *b*) your description of a particular place, full of sensory details; *c*) two comparisons involving the same thing, with different effects; *d*) two monologues describing the same animal, from two different characters.

- First decide whether you will write your brochure about the same place you described earlier or whether you will choose a new place. Then decide whether your speaker will be one of the tour guides you used in the monologues or a new person. If it is a new person, write some brief notes to help you keep his or her habits and attitudes in mind.

- Imagine that your tour guide is looking for people to take on his or her tour. The guide decides to write a one-page brochure describing the highlights of the tour—as he or she sees them. This brochure will be posted on supermarket bulletin boards to attract business.

   Repeat any exercises in the first item above that will help you discover the features of the place that are important to this guide. List all the sensory details and comparisons that your guide might use to describe those features. Remember that these items should reveal the guide's attitudes, not your own. Then write your guide's one-page travel brochure.

- Read your brochure to one or more classmates who can point out passages that should be improved. Make any revisions you agree with.

- Proofread your brochure to find spelling, grammar, punctuation, and capitalization errors. Then make a final copy and share it with the class. If you have written about the same place as any of your classmates, compare your brochure with theirs. Are your descriptions very similar, or are they different—and why? After you have shared your writing, save it in your writing portfolio.

# Unit 7 Historical Fiction

# Message to Hadrian
by Geoffrey Trease

## About the Illustration

This picture illustrates a scene from the chapter you are about to read. Following are some questions that will help you begin to think about the chapter. Use details from the drawing as clues to answer the questions. Give reasons for your answers.

- In what period of history do you suppose this action is taking place? In what part of the world might it be happening?

- What kind of event is the crowd watching?

- Who do you suppose may be important characters in the story? How might the outcome of this event be important to them?

# Unit 7

## Introduction

## About the Novel

In Britain, around A.D. 117, 14-year-old Paul is visiting his father, a Roman army officer at a dangerous outpost. When Britons destroy the fort in a lightning attack, Paul must run for his life to the nearest town. He arrives just as the last ship of fleeing Romans pulls away from the wharf. One passenger, Lucius Fabius Severus, orders the captain to wait until he can help Paul board. Severus invites Paul, now an orphan, to travel with him.

Paul soon learns that his new friend is a poet. A few years before, Severus had tried to publish a poem attacking a rich Roman named Calvus, a crime boss with friends in the government. Calvus, however, bribed Severus's secretary to change the poem to attack the emperor. As a result, Severus was exiled to far-off Britain. Calvus's friends and spies have prevented Severus from getting the truth to the emperor. So Severus remains in exile and can never go home again.

News arrives that the old emperor has died and that the new emperor is Hadrian, an old friend of Severus. Paul volunteers to take Severus's message to Hadrian. Calvus's henchmen, Mucius and the Killer, try repeatedly to stop the boy, and Paul barely survives the trip. At one point, he receives help from Manlius, a chariot driver on his way to Rome to race in the Coliseum. When Paul reaches Rome, he is lucky enough to talk to Hadrian, but the emperor demands proof of Severus's charges.

Paul goes to Severus's home, a simple villa outside Rome, for help. He is welcomed by the poet's teenage daughter, Antonia, who has been left in charge of the house and servants while her mother visits relatives. "Tonia" tells Paul that, after a long disappearance, the bribed secretary, Theodore, has been seen recently in Rome. The two young people wait for Tonia's mother to return, but one evening three men invade the home.

Despite their disguises, Paul recognizes Mucius and the Killer, and once more he escapes, this time with Tonia. She suggests they flee to Rome, where she can stay with an uncle. When their horses tire, Paul and Tonia hitchhike to the city, arriving very late that night. Tonia insists on waiting until morning before going to her uncle's home, so the two rent a room at an inn, where they fall into an exhausted sleep. As this excerpt from *Message to Hadrian* begins, Paul is describing what happens the next day.

## About the Author

Born in 1909 in Nottingham, England, Geoffrey Trease gave up scholarships to college because he wanted to become a full-time writer. Today he is the author of over 100 novels, plays, and nonfiction books for adults and young adults. He is also widely recognized as the writer who gave a strong sense of history to the young adult historical novel. Before Trease's first book was published in 1934, historical novels were strong on adventure but weak on accuracy. Trease's *Bows Against the Barons* changed that, however, with its realistic portrayal of Robin Hood.

Trease's second contribution to young adult novels was the

appearance of strong female characters in historical adventures—females whose courage and intelligence matched those of the males with whom they were paired.

Trease's novels usually present imaginary young people from England, involved in actual events in English or European history. A few of them include *Cue for Treason* (1940), set in the times of Elizabeth I; *Shadow of the Hawk* (1949), about the Renaissance; *Web of Traitors: An Adventure Story of Ancient Athens* (1952); and *The Red Towers of Granada* (1966), set in the Middle Ages. In his eighties, Trease noted, "I do as I have always done—I write about what interests me and hope it will find enough readers to keep my publishers happy."

## About the Lessons

The lessons that follow the selection from *Message to Hadrian* focus on characteristics of the historical novel. Like any other fictional novel, a historical novel is meant to entertain and to make readers think. In addition, however, a historical novel is meant to give readers an understanding of a specific time and place in history—to help readers share the thoughts and feelings of people from that past era. In a good historical novel, details about the era are not merely colorful additions; rather, they are an essential part of the story and its action.

## Writing: Developing an Account of an Event of the Past

To create effective novels about the past, authors must have a broad knowledge of the time period. They must know what people of that time ate and wore; how they worked and played; and what their families, government, and religion were like. What stories, songs, and poems were their favorites? Who were their heroes and villains? Often, authors of historical novels do months of research before beginning to write.

In the course of this unit, you will limit your research to a single aspect of life in the past. You will focus on a competitive sport in a time period of your choice. Then you will write an account of a sporting event from that period. The suggestions below will help you get started.

- Consider various periods in world history that you have learned about through classes, movies, and your own reading. If you could go time-traveling, which times and places would you most like to visit? Why? Jot down some notes about your choices.

- List ways in which you could learn more about the periods of history you are interested in. Be as specific as possible. Don't forget electronic media. When you begin to use the sources you've listed, remember to look for evidence that each source is factual and as accurate as possible.

- Beginning with the eras you listed for the first item and the reference sources you listed for the second item, determine what sports were important to the people of each era. For example, during the Middle Ages, popular sports were jousting and wrestling. Look for descriptions of competitions, the athletes, and the audiences. Keep notes of your findings. You'll use them later in the unit.

# Before Reading

The questions below will help you see how Geoffrey Trease blends historical detail and imagination into an exciting story. As you read the excerpt from *Message to Hadrian,* keep these questions in mind:

- What do you learn about the food, clothing, customs, and daily activities of Romans during the days of the emperors?

- How do the conditions of the time affect the problems that the characters face and the actions that they take to solve them?

- In what ways are the attitudes and beliefs of the characters typical of their time and place—and different from ours?

# Vocabulary Tips

This selection uses some words that may be unfamiliar to you but that are important for understanding the story. Below, you will find some of the more difficult words and their definitions, as well as sentences that show how the words are used. Look them over before you begin reading the selection.

**aghast**     feeling great horror or dismay. We were <u>aghast</u> at the damage that the hurricane caused in our town.

**convention**     usual custom or practice. Shaking hands upon greeting is a <u>convention</u> based on showing a stranger you are unarmed.

**ravenous**     extremely hungry. When I'm dieting, I'm always <u>ravenous</u>.

**blanch**     turn pale. These almonds will <u>blanch</u> when they're steamed.

**luminous**     glowing. In the dark room, the radio dial was <u>luminous</u>.

**innate**     already existing in a person or thing naturally; not added. A great athlete must have <u>innate</u> ability, but she must also train regularly.

**magistrate**     government official. Is a justice of the peace an elected <u>magistrate</u> or an appointed one?

**pawn**     person used by another person as a tool, like the least valuable playing piece in a chess game. The critic called the mayor a <u>pawn</u> of the rich businessmen in town.

**rile**     anger. Don't <u>rile</u> the animal by poking that stick into its cage!

**manifold**     many; of many sorts. The museum was known for its <u>manifold</u> collections.

**disconsolately**     in an unhappy manner; beyond comfort. The child stared at the dropped ice cream cone <u>disconsolately</u>.

**bar**     except; leaving out. Our team is the best in the league, <u>bar</u> none.

**tunic**     a shirt-like garment, knee-length or longer. Elena wore a long-sleeved velvet <u>tunic</u> to the party.

**toga**     a loose, robe-like outer garment. The <u>toga</u> was worn by men in ancient Rome.

# Message to Hadrian

Geoffrey Trease

When I woke up it was broad daylight. The air had almost a noonday warmth. Tonia sat up yawning.

"Oh, I'm hungry!" she announced.

"Your uncle will no doubt give you lunch." Privately, I hoped he would extend that hospitality to me as well.

Tonia swung her feet to the floor and started to comb her hair. "Paul," she began doubtfully.

"Yes?"

"I hope you're not going to be angry with me—"

"Why on earth should I be angry with you?"

"I haven't an uncle."

*"You haven't an uncle?"*

"Not in Rome, anyway—or within a hundred miles of Rome."

I stared at her aghast. "Then why did you say you had?"

She dropped her eyes. "I was afraid you wouldn't bring me if you thought there wasn't anybody—"

"Do you mean you have no friends or relations in Rome at all? Nowhere to go?"

The bowed head nodded. I was appalled. It looked as though we should have to go on to her mother at Terni. Heaven knows how far that was—and I had spent nearly all my money.

"I don't understand," I said sharply. "Why did you tell me a lie?"

She flung up her head. She was pink and defiant.

"There wasn't time to argue and explain. If I hadn't, we shouldn't *be* in Rome now."

"True enough," I retorted. Nobody likes being tricked. I felt sure now that, if she had been honest with me, I could have taken her to someplace of safety nearer to her own home. Instead, I was back in the city with a girl on my hands. The responsibility was alarming. "Well, as your uncle is nonexistent, perhaps you'll tell me where you want to go from here?"

"Certainly—and don't look so cross, Paul, please! I want to find that wine shop where Theodore is living."

## An Hour at the Races

"You never thought much of that idea," I reminded her.

"No, but we agreed to try. I did get you the address from Naso."

"It's a slim chance—"

"Yes, it's slim, Paul—and that's all the more reason why we should do something before it snaps!"

"What do you mean?"

"Can't you see? It came to me in a flash, last night. Theodore may not help us, but who knows? While he lives there is one man who knows the true story. I want to see Theodore while he *is* still alive. Calvus knows the whole case of Father's exile may be re-opened. He knows that you have reached Rome after all and seen the Emperor—he knows that you and I have made contact—he will soon know, if he doesn't yet, that we've escaped together, though he may not guess we've come to Rome. Anyhow, he will realize that things are moving. At any moment he may decide to get rid of any awkward evidence, just to be on the safe side."

She was right. Once Calvus learned that I had given his men the slip he would have to do some fresh thinking. It might occur to him, then, that Theodore would be better if tidied away into the grave. We had better see Theodore before anyone else did.

"I'll go at once," I said.

"*We'll* go."

"The Subura's a low part of town. No place for you."

"Remember, I know him. He may talk to me."

"All right, but it isn't a district for a respectable young girl—"

"Do I *look* respectable?"

I had to laugh. She did not, after the night's adventures. I must have looked a pretty sight myself. But we could not do much about it. We had nothing but the clothes we stood up in.

In the crowded, noisy, raffish Subura nobody is surprised at anything. Crooks, runaways, tricksters of every color and nationality swarm there amid thousands of others whose only fault is that they are poor. There are hundreds of poky little shops—some giving honest value and some not. In the Subura you can buy almost anything. And almost anybody. Above and behind the shops is a honeycomb of sordid tenements, a honeycomb of no sweetness whatever. Mystery hangs, like an invisible curtain, at the entrance to every narrow alley, every darkly shadowed arcade. No wonder the treacherous Greek had gone to ground in the Subura. No awkward questions are asked there, it is the town-within-the-town, the place of forgotten men.

And also of forgotten women. Elsewhere in Rome, Tonia would have been noticeable, a girl walking in the public street with a boy. In the Subura there are no conventions.

Our directions were precise. We never needed to ask the way—which was as well. We paused only to buy some bread from a stall. We ate as we walked. We were ravenous.

Theodore lived three flights up, above the wine shop. He was at home. I shall never forget his expression as he looked up from his copying and recognized Tonia. His weak face blanched. His pen fell from his fingers, spattering his manuscript.

"Miss Tonia!" he almost whispered.

He was about thirty, I judged. He had big, luminous eyes—the melting eyes of an Asiatic Greek. There had once been a gentle sort of charm in that face, but it had faded, gone rotten somehow, like a flower.

"Yes," she said curtly, " 'Miss Tonia!' "

He stood up. The old habit of respect clung to him. "What do you want?" he asked hoarsely. His gaze shifted anxiously to me, standing with my back against the door.

"My father," said Tonia.

"I am sorry—I know nothing—"

"You know everything there is to be known." Her voice reminded me suddenly of her father's. It had the same ring of innate authority. I saw him wilt before it— and before the fire which I could imagine in her eyes. "The game's up, Theodore. If you value your skin—" She paused significantly.

"You can't frighten me," said the slave, licking his lips—it was only too obvious that she could. "I was promised protection—"

"Do you call this protection?" She laughed, and glanced over her shoulder toward me. I played up to the part. I looked as grim as I could, as though only waiting for the word to tear him apart. "Calvus has finished with you. You've served your purpose. You're safer dead than alive, so far as *he's* concerned. You don't deserve any consideration from us," she went on scornfully, "but you *were* once our slave—still are, indeed. So I've come to warn you."

"Warn me?"

"To expect a visit from the Killer, very soon."

"No! No, Miss Tonia—"

"Yes, Theodore. My father's case is to be re-opened. Calvus wants to destroy the last of the evidence while he can."

His resistance crumbled. He believed her. The names—the Killer, far more than Calvus—proved that she knew more than he had thought possible. She spoke with such assurance, and what she said was so terribly likely, that he made no more attempt to bear it out. He dropped to his knees, babbling, excusing himself, begging forgiveness for the past, promising deathless fidelity for the future. He was a sickening sight.

"Pull yourself together!" Tonia checked his hysteria with a slap. (She told me afterward how wonderfully it had relieved her feelings.) "Tell me exactly what happened."

The sorry tale poured out. Tempted by hope of gain, Theodore had gone to Calvus with warning of the poem Severus was about to publish. With his usual cunning the racketeer had turned the tables on his enemy. Theodore had been dazzled by a far higher reward than he had ever expected, if he would desert his master completely and insert the forged passage in the poem.

"And then you vanished. Where to?" she demanded.

"To Baiae, Miss Tonia. They wanted me out of Rome for the time being. Vettius had a villa on the coast—I had to stay hidden there until—until—"

"My father had been shipped off to Britain! Very wise!" Her disdain was withering.

I remembered what Severus had told me about this man Vettius. He was a senator, an ex-magistrate, a former governor, a personage of importance—but as much a hireling of Calvus as Mucius was, or the Killer. Calvus had many well-known public men in his clutches. He lent them money, blackmailed them, got them somehow at his mercy, and then used them as pawns to advance his own schemes. Without their seals and signatures his various contracts would never have gone through.

"What did you do with my father's notes?"

"Vettius took them."

"Vettius? Not Calvus?"

"No. Calvus thought they had been destroyed—"

"And they weren't destroyed?" I broke in, unable to keep silent any longer.

No, Theodore explained. Vettius had quietly retained the tablets. Why? That was easy. It was a chance for Vettius to get something on Calvus. There was no love lost between them. In that company no one trusted anyone else. The day might come when Calvus tried to tighten his screw too far—or when Vettius saw the chance to break his chain. Vettius, the proud aristocrat, did not enjoy being at the beck and call of a hopped-up adventurer like Calvus.

So Theodore had picked up a useful extra bribe by handing over the tablets to Vettius and telling Calvus he had burned them. Vettius had hidden them in his library overlooking the sea. He had put them behind a painted panel, the one which showed the wooden horse at Troy—

"Did he let you see him?" Tonia interrupted, amazed.

"Oh, no, Miss Tonia!" Though his nerve had collapsed,

the Greek could not help a smirk of satisfaction at his own forethought and cunning. "Vettius thought he was alone. But I watched. So that now I can tell you, Miss Tonia—"

"So that you would have another little dirty secret to sell, you mean! Don't pretend you did it for our sakes. What a gang of scoundrels! No trust even for each other! Vettius insures himself against Calvus, you insure yourself against Vettius—I shall be sick if I hear much more."

There was not much more to hear. Theodore told us a little of the vast luxury villa at Baiae—how its foundations were driven into the sea, so that, walking its terraces, Vettius could almost fancy himself afloat in a giant galley of marble and glass and cedarwood and bronze. The library looked seaward to the lovely island of Ischia. Between the bookcases stood painted panels with scenes from history. Behind one of these—to the best of Theodore's knowledge—still lay the writing tablets which could prove the innocence of Severus.

Tonia eyed him thoughtfully for a moment. "If you were a man," she said, "I would tell you to get them back for us. As it is," she turned to me, "give me some money, Paul. He can't do anything more for us at the moment."

"If he had what he deserved—," I growled.

"I know. But for what he has told us now I must be thankful." Her lip curled. "Gold is all Theodore understands."

"There's hardly any left," I objected, fumbling with the bag hung around my neck.

"Never mind," she said impatiently. "It was Father's money in the first place."

That riled me. "It's still your father's—I've only used it as he told me. Do as you like, then, but don't blame me." I tossed down the last three coins on the table and returned to my place at the door. Tonia was his daughter. She was handling this affair.

"There, Theodore," I heard her say. "Now, if you're smart, you'll change your address—quickly. But send us word, secretly, in a week or two, so that we may know where to get hold of you again."

"Very well, Miss Tonia."

She turned in the doorway as we left. "And don't change sides any more," she warned him. "No, don't start vowing and promising. Just bear this in mind: from now on the winning side is going to be ours."

She swept out like a young empress. Down in the street she said: "Oh, Paul, it's good to breathe fresh air again!" And though that mean byway of the Subura was thick with the manifold stenches of the slums, I knew what she meant.

I had known what it would be—it had been easy to read Tonia's mind while she listened to Theodore's description of the villa.

Before she could say anything more I asked: "How far is this place, Baiae?"

"I'm not sure. Over a hundred miles, anyway. It's just this side of Naples."

"Listen," I said, "I'll do what I can. On one condition. I must see you safe somewhere first."

"We can't talk in the street, Paul—" That was true. It was hard even to walk two abreast, what with the narrowness and the crowds and the goods pushed out in front of the shops. "Anyway, I'm hungry, and you must be, too." That was also true.

We turned into an eating house which looked slightly less scruffy than most. I did not like taking a girl into such a place, but we both needed a cooked meal after all we had gone through. We sat down at a big three-legged table, and a slave girl, eyeing us with curious glances, brought us some kind of porridge and then a dish of pork, strongly flavored with garlic. At this early hour we were the only customers.

"I'll pay," said Tonia, "since I've still got money."

"Right. Now, first, what's to be done about you?"

"Nothing. I'm going to Baiae."

"You're not!"

"I am. You can't stop me. "

"Look," I said earnestly. "I feel sort of responsible for you. I owe a lot to your father. He'd never forgive me—"

She checked me with a hand laid on my arm. "He's *my* father, Paul. I haven't seen him for years. If this fails I shall never see him again. I used to say to myself, over and over again: 'If only there was something I could do—' This is it."

"I know. But this is a—a man's job," I said a little self-consciously.

She smiled at the word "man," but nicely. "Could you have gotten this information out of Theodore?"

"No—"

"And would you have brought me to Rome if I hadn't said that about an uncle? I don't *like* pretending things to you, Paul. And I'm telling you the absolute truth now—there is no one I can go to here, so, if it isn't safe to go home yet, I shall have to go and join Mother at Terni. How much time shall we have wasted by then?"

I considered for a moment. Terni was in the wrong direction—and I could not let her go alone. "You win," I said reluctantly. "But how are we going to get to Baiae?"

"Easy. It's a very good road—you see, all the best people go to Baiae—the Emperor, everyone. It's like Tibur, only more so, being seaside. Lots of carriages for hire on that road."

"But it's over a hundred miles! What about money?"

"H'm . . . we may need a lot. We may have to bribe servants at the villa, too."

"And you have no friends or relatives in Rome!"

"I know—couldn't you borrow from that friend of yours, Manlius? Charioteers make loads and loads of money."

It was an idea. Manlius was the sort of person from whom one *could* ask a great favor without feeling bad about it. He would be quite sure of getting his money back. Tonia's mother would see to that.

Now that we had agreed on a plan, I was as eager as she was to try it out. The sooner we started for Baiae, the greater our chances of recovering her father's notes. Things were moving fast. Calvus was worried, or he would not have sent the Killer in search of me. If this nervousness spread to his associates, Vettius might remember the evidence he had stored away in his library. He might take it out and make some deal with Calvus that would not help us in the least. We must lay our hands on those waxen tablets before anyone else remembered their existence—and their value.

Quickly we finished our meal and hurried to the Circus Maximus. It was the only place I knew where Manlius might be found. When we got there the crowds were streaming through the entrances. The afternoon racing was due to begin in an hour.

"Your friend's famous!" said Tonia. She pointed. There, in the shady arcades outside where men hawked wine and cakes or offered to tell your fortune, and flashy girls hung about waiting for their young men, the portraits of the most popular drivers were pinned up for sale. "He's *nice*," said Tonia warmly. "I love his funny black eyebrows."

We went in with the crowd. We had moderately good places, halfway up and fairly near the starting post. The marble seats in front were filled with well-to-do men and women, all dressed up for the occasion.

"That's where *I'd* like to be," Tonia admitted, "if I didn't look such a sight." She looked around her with bright eyes. "This is exciting. Mother doesn't approve of the races—"

"I don't think your father does," I recalled, "but it's the betting he really objects to."

"Yes—people go mad on the idea of money for nothing. Mother says it's the ruin of Rome."

"You stay here and keep my seat. I'm going to see if I can get through to Manlius."

I slipped along the gangway and, after sundry inquiries, found my way down to a doorway which led behind the scenes to the drivers' quarters. Here, however, I came up against a difficulty.

"Not a chance, my lad," said the stalwart attendant who barred my path.

"But I know him! I'm a personal friend—"

"They all say that." The man leered knowingly.

I jingled the small change which was all I possessed since I had given Tonia her father's gold. "It would be quite all right," I tried to wheedle him. "You see—"

"Can't be done! Why, he's driving in the first race."

It was no good. I could see he was not going to let me through. "All right," I said disconsolately, "I'll have to come around and see him after the meeting."

The attendant flung back his head and laughed. "Think it's as easy as that, do you? And you pretending you know Manlius personally! Why, he'll be mobbed!

Win or lose, he's got his fans, same as the others. They'll be round in their hundreds—their thousands, more like—fighting to get a glimpse of him close to, never mind speaking to him!"

I had not known, till then, what it meant to be a popular driver, one of the sporting heroes of Rome. "I see," I said. "Perhaps it would be better if I went to his lodgings afterward. If you could tell me his address—"

"Sorry," the doorkeeper interrupted. "Not allowed to. Why, if everyone knew where the drivers lived, they'd be pestered out of their minds. Now, run along, lad," he went on more kindly. "I know how you feel. But Manlius is only a man same as me—this crazy hero worship is all very well, but—"

"I'm not a hero worshiper," I snapped. "I want to borrow some money from him, that's all!"

" 'All'?" His laughter rang in my ears as I turned way. "Borrow money, eh? That's a good 'un, that is."

By the time I had squeezed back to my seat the first race was nearly due to begin. The presiding magistrate and his suite were filing into the royal box at the western end. Below were the twelve stable doors, with the starting ropes stretched in front between twin statues of Hermes. The Emperor was not here today. He was away from Rome, it was rumored, hunting.

"Well?" Tonia looked around eagerly.

"Couldn't get to him," I grunted. "It's going to be harder than I'd realized. It seems easier to speak to the Emperor than a star charioteer! Tonia, how much did you give that slimy Greek?"

"Just the one gold piece."

"I'm wondering—supposing we can't get through to Manlius today—how far the other two would carry us?"

"But we haven't *got* two," she said in a small voice.

"Well, near enough. I'd forgotten the dinner you paid for."

"Paul, we haven't any money at all."

I stared aghast. "What have you done with it?"

"I've given it to that man over there—the bookmaker. I felt sure you'd get plenty more from Manlius."

"You mean—" Words almost failed me. "You've been *betting* with it?"

"Yes. The first race."

Really! Girls . . . the last of our certain money, bar the few coppers I still had myself. I took a deep breath. "May I ask," I inquired with heavy sarcasm, "with all your expert knowledge of the sport, which team you decided to back?"

"Oh, Manlius', naturally. He's your friend—and blue is one of my favorite colors—and I *love* his funny eyebrows—"

"All of which," I groaned, "makes him a certain winner!"

"I'm so glad you think so. I always go by what you say."

Further conversation was impossible—which was perhaps as well. The presiding magistrate was on his feet, splendid in a scarlet tunic with a purple toga draped over it. On his head was a wreath of gold, in one hand he held an ivory scepter, in the other a white cloth with which to give the starting signal.

The stable doors were open. The teams were lining up, the horses bedecked with lucky charms and their stable colors. There was Manlius, a proud, erect figure in his chariot, helmeted and whip in hand. The reins were tied around his blue tunic at the waist, and I caught there the glint of a dagger, ready to cut himself free if he were thrown out.

The restless horses edged at last into a reasonable line. The white cloth fluttered down to the sand below, the trumpet blared—and they were off!

About two hundred thousand people promptly took leave of their senses. Or so it seemed.

"Come on, the Greens!"

"White—come on, White!"

"Red! Good old Reds!"

"Show 'em, the Blues!"

The course was a long narrow oval of sparkling, gritty sand. Down the center ran a marble barrier decorated with statues and ending in two turning posts of gilded bronze. These turning posts produced the biggest thrills in the race—the chariots had to wheel so sharply that a fraction of an inch too near might mean an upset, a driver thrown headlong, or a wheel torn from its axle. Then, too, there was the risk of collision with another chariot.

"Oh, come *on*, Manlius!" wailed Tonia. Her knuckles were white with anguish. She was bobbing up and down as though she herself were in the race.

But Manlius' new team was lying well back. There was a Red driver in the lead, then a Green and one of other Blues fighting for second place, and two others strung out in front of my friend.

The signal dolphins lining the embankment were turned to show that it was now the sixth lap, the last but one. . . .

"Manlius!" Tonia was screaming. She could have saved her breath. He had gained a little, but he was still only fifth. He didn't have a chance. From the odds that the bookmakers had been calling they must have known it all along. She might have saved her money as well as her breath, I reflected sulkily. I agreed with her father more heartily than ever. Betting was the ruin of the Roman character. The passion to get something for nothing—or almost nothing—would drive people to the silliest behavior.

The Green driver was overtaking the Red. The crowd was nearly delirious. The Green was using his whip like a maniac. He cut in riskily, too riskily. . . . A tremendous howl went up from the stands.

"Shipwreck! SHIPWRECK!"

For an instant the two chariots seemed locked together. A man shot out, a green tunic rolled over in the sand, a loose wheel ran wobbling away like a child's hoop—

The man behind me swore violently. Both chariots were out of the race. Green was unhurt, but by the time he had cut himself free from his reins it was far too late for him to regain control of his team. And it was poor Red who had lost a wheel.

The other chariots came thundering on behind. The attendants prepared to turn the bronze dolphin. Last lap!

"Blue! Come on, Blue!"

*"Manlius!"*

I could scarcely believe my eyes. Surely it had been one of the other Blue drivers in third place. But now Manlius was coming up, hand over fist. Out of the flying dust shot the four outstretched heads, and erect above them, serene as a god in the clouds, Manlius!

Tonia clutched my wrist as he neared the turning post. She was so frantic her nails dug into me. I was not exactly calm myself. He could never do it—he could never make the sharp left-handed turn at that appalling speed. It was too much to ask of the trace horses, the stallions on the outside. One must almost stop and act as the pivot, and the other had such a wide arc through which to swing.

They thundered on, those four silky bays, each with the Libyan star clear on its forehead. Manlius cracked his whip, but I could swear that he did not touch them with it. I closed my eyes as they came to the turn—

"*Shipwreck!*" The howl went up from a hundred thousand supporters of his rivals.

"No! He's gotten by!"

The chariot must almost have scraped the post. But his blue tunic was flashing down the straight for the last time. The next team was thirty yards behind. The roar of the crowd must have been heard on the other side of the Tiber.

"Blue wins! Manlius! Manlius!"

Tonia let go of my wrist. "Say," I began, "where are you going?" But she had vanished, leaving me to study her nail prints on my flesh. In a few minutes she came pushing her way back to me.

"The odds were very good," she whispered triumphantly. "No one else seemed to think he could possibly win." She slipped me a great handful of money. "Look after all this, will you? I'm scared of thieves now."

"Come on," I said sternly, jumping to my feet. "We're going. Before you bet it all on some driver whose nose you fancy."

"Yes, Paul." She followed me with surprising meekness. "But don't worry, I shall never, never want to bet again."

"Good."

"It's much too upsetting."

We walked out into the street and looked for a cab-stand. A few minutes later we were in a hired carriage, rolling along the Appian Way.

# Reviewing and Interpreting the Selection

Record your answers to these questions in your personal literature notebook. Follow the directions for each part.

**Reviewing**   Try to answer each of these questions without looking back at the selection.

Identifying
Cause and Effect

1. Which statement was *not* one of Tonia's reasons for lying to Paul about having an uncle in Rome?

   a. She was confused and scared when she had to flee her home.
   b. She knew that the secretary who had betrayed her father was in Rome.
   c. Paul would not take her to Rome unless she had relatives there.
   d. In Rome, she and Paul could do something to help her father.

Recalling Facts

2. Whom did Paul and Tonia go into the Subura to find?

   a. Manlius
   b. Calvus
   c. Severus
   d. Theodore

Identifying
Sequence

3. After talking to Theodore, what important decision does Tonia make next?

   a. She bets all her money on Manlius.
   b. She buys some bread from a stall.
   c. She decides to go to Baiae.
   d. She decides to borrow money from Manlius.

4. Why is Theodore important to his enemies and Severus alike?

   a. He knows people who work for both of them.

   b. He could give testimony about what really happened.

   c. He has accepted money from both sides.

   d. He is Greek.

5. Which of these passages is a metaphor—a comparison of two things that does not use the word *like* or *as*?

   a. She flung up her head. She was pink and defiant.

   b. Above and beyond the shops is a honeycomb of sordid tenements, a honeycomb of no sweetness whatever.

   c. "If you were a man," she said, "I would tell you to get them back for us."

   d. The Green was using his whip like a maniac.

**Interpreting**   To complete these sentences, you may look back at the selection if you'd like.

6. In modern society, the people who are treated most like the star charioteers of the Roman Empire are . . .

   a. television talk-show hosts.

   b. famous professional athletes.

   c. horse-racing jockeys.

   d. painters, sculptors, and other artists.

7. Paul doesn't want to keep Tonia with him because

   a. he knows that she will get frightened and do something foolish.

   b. she's somewhat bossy and usually argues for her own ideas.

   c. he wants to protect her reputation as a young lady.

   d. he doesn't want her to see that he is frightened.

8. Paul's surprise at the difficulty of seeing Manlius before the race indicates that

   a. in Britain, where Paul grew up, chariot races and drivers were not popular.

   b. before Manlius started racing, nobody paid any attention to chariot racers.

   c. Paul is easily surprised by things that are new to him.

   d. Severus had lied to him about sports events in Rome.

9. Now that Paul and Tonia have a good amount of money, they probably will

   a. have an easy time achieving their goals.

   b. fight over the money.

   c. bet only a small portion of it next time, instead of the whole amount.

   d. use it wisely, but still encounter problems and danger.

10. The best description of Theodore is that he
    is a

    a. minor character because he appears in
       the story so briefly.

    b. minor character because his actions do
       not affect the plot.

    c. main character because he is the ser-
       vant of one of the main characters.

    d. main character because his personality
       is so dramatic.

Now check your answers with your teacher. Study the questions
you answered incorrectly. What types of questions were they? Talk
with your teacher about ways to work on those skills.

# Historical Fiction

Many of us know stories that begin with the phrase "Once upon a time." As children, we quickly learned that "Once upon a time" is a clue that there never was such a time. The magical times, places, and characters in the story never really existed. Nobody ever really faced the problem of fire-breathing dragons. There never were people with the ability to climb beanstalks to the clouds.

In one way, historical fiction is somewhat like those fantasies. In a historical novel such as *Message to Hadrian*, many of the characters are imaginary. Even when a character is based upon a real person, the author makes up most of that character's actions and words.

But there the similarity to fantasy ends. A good historical novel uses its imaginary characters to bring life to historical fact. Every building, dish, or hat mentioned in the novel matches—in some way—real buildings, dishes, or hats of that historical period. Every action that the characters take was possible with the knowledge and tools of that time. Every opinion stated by a character was an opinion held by individuals at that time.

It would take the fun out of a historical novel to figure out which events really happened and which ones were created by the author. It is up to the author, then, to convince readers that he or she knows the time period well and can be trusted to present it accurately. The author uses a wealth of historical detail to develop that trust. In a good novel, this detail is not presented separately from the usual elements of a story. Instead, historical fact is a natural part of the setting. It is reflected in the characters' problems. It shapes the characters' attitudes, words, and actions.

In these lessons, you will look at how Geoffrey Trease develops particular qualities of setting, conflict, and characters to make *Message to Hadrian* a historical novel:

1. Trease uses accurate details of time and place to show that the story happens at a specific time in the past.

2. The problems that his characters face give readers an understanding of the time period and its attitudes.

3. His characters think, look, and act like actual people of that period in history.

## 1 • Settings of the Past

A writer who uses a setting familiar to his or her readers can count on the readers to fill in any details that are not specifically mentioned. For example, if a scene is set in a modern-day amusement park, the writer doesn't need to describe every ride, booth, and eating place to create a picture of the park. Readers already have an idea of what the park may look like, how the rides feel, and how the park sounds and smells. The writer, then, can focus on the few characteristics about the park that are important to the story.

In a novel set in an unfamiliar time and place, however, the writer must present a great deal of background information. The information must be presented in small enough pieces that it does not slow down the plot. Yet it must be specific enough to bring out differences between our own world and that of the unfamiliar time period. Notice how the following passage gives information about Roman times. It tells about the Romans' food, furniture, and eating habits, and even their casual acceptance of slavery.

> "Listen," I said. "I'll do what I can. On one condition. I must see you safe somewhere first."
>
> "We can't talk in the street, Paul—" That was true. It was hard even to walk two abreast, what with the narrowness and the crowds and the goods pushed out in front of the shops. "Anyway, I'm hungry, and you must be, too." That was also true.
>
> We turned into an eating house which looked slightly less scruffy than most. I did not like taking a girl into such a place, but we both needed a cooked meal after all we had gone through. We sat down at a big three-legged table, and a slave girl, eyeing us with curious glances, brought us some kind of porridge and then a dish of pork, strongly flavored with garlic. At this early hour we were the only customers.

"I'll pay," said Tonia, "since I've still got money."

"Right. Now, first, what's to be done about you?"

This description of a lunch composed of porridge and garlic-flavored pork—and of diners satisfied by it—is enough to convince readers that the story happens in a time other than the present day. In addition, readers learn that in at least certain neighborhoods of Rome the narrow streets were crowded with shops and shoppers, and that well-brought-up girls were not expected to eat in public eating houses.

## Exercise 1

Read the following passage, in which the chariot race is about to begin. Then use what you have learned in this lesson to answer the questions that follow the passage.

> Further conversation was impossible—which was perhaps as well. The presiding magistrate was on his feet, splendid in a scarlet tunic with a purple toga draped over it. On his head was a wreath of gold, in one hand he held an ivory scepter, in the other a white cloth with which to give the starting signal.
>
> The stable doors were open. The teams were lining up, the horses bedecked with lucky charms and their stable colors. There was Manlius, a proud, erect figure in his chariot, helmeted and whip in hand. The reins were tied around his blue tunic at the waist, and I caught there the glint of a dagger, ready to cut himself free if he were thrown out.
>
> The restless horses edged at last into a reasonable line. The white cloth fluttered down to the sand below, the trumpet blared—and they were off!
>
> About two hundred thousand people promptly took leave of their senses. Or so it seemed.

1. Who is the official starter of the race, and how does he dress for the occasion? What signal does he use to start the race?

2. How do the chariot drivers dress? What clues tell you that chariot racing is dangerous and can easily cause injuries?

3. How does the size of the audience at the race compare with a major-league sporting event of today? How does the behavior of the audiences compare?

Now check your answers with your teacher. Review this part of the lesson if you don't understand why an answer was incorrect.

## Writing on Your Own 1

In this exercise you will use what you have learned in this lesson as a guide to researching the past. Then you will write a short description of a place in the past. Follow these steps:

- Choose one of the historical periods that you jotted down for Developing an Account of an Event of the Past on pages 221–222. Do enough research to discover an athletic activity in which men, women, or children competed.

- List several questions about the place where the competition was held. For example, what were the stands, the refreshments, and the rest areas like? What about this location made it a good place to hold such a competition?

- Continue your research into this sporting event. (If you can't find enough information, you should probably start over with a different period or a different sport.) Write at least two paragraphs describing the place where the competition was held and what it looked like during the competition.

## 2 • Conflicts of the Past

In a crime story set in modern times, the criminals might steal from a bank by doing computer hacking. They could change computer files or digital images to create false papers and records. The conflict in this story would focus on how police or private investigators hunt for electronic clues to the crime. The criminals would most likely be caught by someone sitting at a computer, rather than someone chasing them in a car.

The problems faced by the characters in any setting must be related to the conditions of that setting. For example, a sheriff in the Wild West would practice his shooting skills, not his computer-programming abilities. A cave man would watch out for thrown rocks, not bullets. In the best historical novels, the problems grow out of the conditions of the setting.

In *Message to Hadrian* the main problem, Severus's exile, is one that could not happen in modern America. Under our laws, Severus would have been free to voice an attack on the government. The forgery would have hurt his reputation as a poet, but he would not have been punished for it. Furthermore, since poetry is not held in as high regard in our society as it was in Roman times, Calvus would not have feared an attack by a poet. Had he been irritated by Severus's poem, he would have taken more direct action to stop him. The basic conflict in the novel, therefore, arises from conditions that were special to ancient Rome.

The way Calvus frames Severus is also appropriate to Roman times. It was common for wealthy Romans to own educated slaves who did such tasks as keeping financial records, translating messages from other languages, and taking dictation. Since Severus trusted Theodore, he gave him all his original manuscript on wax tablets—poetry dictated to the slave for later copying. Without his original notes, Severus could not prove that Theodore had changed the poem.

Read this passage, in which Tonia is questioning Theodore. See how important the tablets are as proof of a deception:

"What did you do with my father's notes?"
"Vettius took them."
"Vettius? Not Calvus?"
"No. Calvus thought they had been destroyed—"
"And they weren't destroyed?" I broke in, unable to keep silent any longer.

No, Theodore explained. Vettius had quietly retained the tablets. Why? That was easy. It was a chance for Vettius to get something on Calvus. There was no love lost between them. In that company no one trusted anyone else. The day might come when Calvus tried to tighten his screw too far— or when Vettius saw the chance to break his chain. Vettius, the proud aristocrat, did not enjoy being at the beck and call of a hopped-up adventurer like Calvus.

So Theodore had picked up a useful extra bribe by handing over the tablets to Vettius and telling Calvus he had burned them. Vettius had hidden them in his library overlooking the sea. He had put them behind a painted panel, the one which showed the wooden horse at Troy—

"Did he let you see him?" Tonia interrupted, amazed.

"Oh, no, Miss Tonia! . . . Vettius thought he was alone. But I watched. So that now I can tell you, Miss Tonia—"

Calvus knows he is not safe as long as the tablets show Severus's original words, so he orders them destroyed. Vettius willingly pays Theodore to disobey the orders. And Theodore, hoping to sell information about the tablets, spies on Vettius to see where he hides them.

## Exercise 2

Read the passage below, in which Paul agrees with Tonia that they must both go to Baiae to look for evidence. Use what you have learned in the lesson to answer the questions that follow the passage.

"You win," I said reluctantly. "But how are we going to get to Baiae?"

"Easy. It's a very good road—you see, all the best people go to Baiae—the Emperor, everyone. It's like Tibur, only more so, being seaside. Lots of carriages for hire on that road."

"But it's over a hundred miles! What about money?"

"H'm . . . we may need a lot. We may have to bribe servants at the villa, too."

"And you have no friends or relatives in Rome!"

"I know—couldn't you borrow from that friend of yours, Manlius? Charioteers make loads and loads of money."

1.  In Roman times, travelers needed cash to pay carriage drivers, just as we would need cash for a bus or a cab. After thinking of the carriages, Tonia immediately thinks of a second reason she and Paul need money. What is that reason? Why do you suppose it was natural for a Roman to consider this problem?

2.  From whom do Tonia and Paul decide to borrow money? Why do they choose this person? If this story were happening today, would this person be anyone's first choice? Why or why not?

Now check your answers with your teacher. Review this part of the lesson if you don't understand why an answer was incorrect.

## Writing on Your Own 2

In this exercise you will focus on the problems that either athletes or audiences faced because of the conditions of their time. For example, in Ancient Greece, what difficulties did women face in attending the Olympic competitions? How did the politics or transportation of the time make it difficult for men to take part? Review your previous research or continue it as needed. Follow these steps:

- Write a sentence or more describing each of the problems you discovered that relate to the sporting event you are researching. Make it clear whether the problem is one that a contestant would face or one that a fan would face.

- Then choose one specific problem. Write several paragraphs explaining how you would face—and possibly solve—the problem if you were a contestant or a fan. Make sure your solution, like the problem, fits the time period.

## 3 • Characters of the Past

Throughout history, people have reacted to the world in different ways, depending on the society and time in which they lived. For example, few people today believe that humans make pacts with the devil and become witches. A little more than 300 years ago, however, whole towns voted to execute citizens accused of doing just that.

In a realistic novel set in a particular time, the characters accept and live according to the beliefs of that time. In *Message to Hadrian*, one of Paul's persistent concerns arises from his society's rules about how respectable girls should behave. At the beginning of this passage, he is more intent on getting Tonia back to her family than on solving his own predicament:

> "Do you mean you have no friends or relations in Rome at all? Nowhere to go?"
>
> The bowed head nodded. I was appalled. It looked as though we should have to go on to her mother at Terni. Heaven knows how far that was—and I had spent nearly all my money.
>
> "I don't understand," I said sharply. "Why did you tell me a lie?"
>
> She flung up her head. She was pink and defiant. "There wasn't time to argue and explain. If I hadn't, we shouldn't *be* in Rome now."
>
> "True enough." I retorted. Nobody likes being tricked. I felt sure now that, if she had been honest with me, I could have taken her to someplace of safety nearer to her own home. Instead, I was back in the city with a girl on my hands. The responsibility was alarming.

Then, when Tonia points out to Paul that she should talk to Theodore, she must first convince Paul that her social standing is not a barrier.

> "The Subura's a low part of town. No place for you."
>
> "Remember, I know him. He may talk to me."
>
> "All right, but it isn't a district for a respectable young girl—"
>
> "Do I *look* respectable?"
>
> I had to laugh. She did not, after the night's adventures. I must have looked a pretty sight myself. But we could not do much about it. We had nothing but the clothes we stood up in.

Even when Tonia's safety is not a concern, Paul is worried that her actions will affect her reputation. He is very much a man of his time.

## Exercise 3

Read the following passage from the verbal exchange between Tonia and Theodore. Then use what you have learned in this lesson to answer the questions that follow the passage.

"The game's up, Theodore. If you value your skin—" She paused significantly.

"You can't frighten me," said the slave, licking his lips—it was only too obvious that she could. "I was promised protection—"

"Do you call this protection?" She laughed, and glanced over her shoulder toward me. I played up to the part. I looked as grim as I could, as though only waiting for the word to tear him apart. "Calvus has finished with you. You've served your purpose. You're safer dead that alive, so far as *he's* concerned. You don't deserve any consideration from us," she went on scornfully, "but you *were* once our slave—still are, indeed. So I've come to warn you."

"Warn me?"

"To expect a visit from the Killer, very soon."

. . . He dropped to his knees, babbling, excusing himself, begging forgiveness for the past, promising deathless fidelity for the future. He was a sickening sight.

1. Theodore has betrayed his master and run away. Yet he believes Tonia when she says that, because he once belonged to her family, she has come to warn him of danger. From this fact, what can you conclude about the attitude of some Romans, like Tonia's family, toward their slaves?

2. Faced with the news of his danger from Calvus, Theodore chooses to make amends with his owners. He even promises to return to the life of a slave. What does this suggest about the

conditions Theodore expects in slavery, compared to the situation he would be in as a free man?

3. Do you think Tonia is a dishonorable character because she accepts the attitudes of her time toward slavery? How would the believability of the novel be affected if Tonia were to state that slavery is wrong?

Now check your answers with your teacher. Review this part of the lesson if you don't understand why an answer was incorrect.

## Writing on Your Own 3

In this exercise you will use what you have learned in this lesson to write a short paper on your chosen sporting event. Follow these steps:

- Review your answers to the directions for Writing on Your Own 2. Look over what you have learned about your chosen sporting event to see if people of today might react differently to it than people of the past did. For example, would your city government allow jousting, in which men use long poles to try to knock each other off their horses? Or would warring countries call a truce to a war just to hold a sports competition?

- Write a short paper on one of these topics: 1) Compare a sports fan of your chosen period with a sports fan of today. Point out ways in which they are alike and different. Give special attention to their attitudes toward matters related to the sporting event, or 2) Write a dialogue between a sports fan of your chosen period and a sports fan of today. Have them compare—or argue about—their favorite sport.

## Discussion Guides

1. Imagine that you and your classmates are citizens of Rome who want to see the Subura cleaned up. With a small group, develop a campaign—complete with posters, speeches, and petitions—to demand political action against that slum area. Keep your protest in the setting of ancient Rome, and address your complaints to the Emperor. Hold a rally in your classroom to arouse public interest.

2. Imagine the conversation between Theodore and Calvus, in which the slave tells Calvus about his master's plan to attack him in a poem. Use what you know about Theodore and Calvus to guess what they say and how they say it. Then work with a partner to write a dialogue between these two characters. Present your dialogue to the rest of the class.

3. Although things work out well for her, Tonia decides that betting is an unpleasant experience. She joins her father and Paul in objecting to it. How do your friends and classmates feel about legalized gambling, including state lotteries and gambling boats? With a group of at least five classmates, survey several dozen people to find out how many of them approve of betting, and how many would disapprove. Ask for their reasons for or against. Then use your own ideas, as well as responses from those surveyed, as ammunition in a debate. Three of your group should support betting and three should oppose it. Hold the debate in front of your classmates. Take a vote both before and after the debate to determine whether your debate changed anyone's mind.

# Write an Account of a Sporting Event of the Past

You have done research on a past era and on a sports competition typical of that era. You have written about the scene of a sports event, problems related to it, and a typical person involved in it. Now it is time to put the pieces together and write an account of such a competition.

If you have questions about the writing process, refer to Using the Writing Process on page 295.

- Assemble the notes you took and the writing you did for all the exercises in this unit. Review and compare these assignments: *a*) your scene for a sporting event, *b*) your explanation of problems relating to that event that are special to the period, *c*) your comparison or dialogue between sports fans of the past and today. Also review all your research notes.

- Write a realistic account of the sporting event you have researched. You can present it as a news report—using the third-person point of view—or as an eyewitness account, using the first-person point of view. Include enough detail about the setting, conflict or conflicts, and individuals' attitudes to make it clear that the event is happening in a different time and place.

- Read your account to one or more classmates who can point out passages that should be improved. Make any revisions you agree with.

- Proofread your account to find spelling, grammar, punctuation, and capitalization errors. Make a final copy and save it in your writing portfolio.

# Unit 8 Fantasy

# A Wrinkle in Time
by Madeleine L'Engle

## About the Illustration

Study this scene from the chapter you are about to read. What do you think is happening? Use details from the illustration to support your answer. Then answer the following questions. They will help you begin to think about the selection.

- Where do you think this scene could be taking place? What are the children about to do?

- How might these characters all know each other?

- What details in this scene are especially unusual?

# Unit 8

## Introduction

## About the Novel

Meg Murry is a member of a somewhat unusual family. Her father is a physicist who has been missing for more than a year. Her mother is a scientist who has been experimenting with a new concept called a *tesseract*. Her five-year-old brother Charles Wallace has extraordinary intelligence and can read other people's thoughts and feelings. Meg herself is considered a bit odd, probably because she is smarter than most of her classmates. Her ten-year-old twin brothers, Sandy and Dennys, are the only "normal" ones in the family. Meg's friend Calvin is not a member of the family but feels like one, since he is more comfortable with the Murrys than with his own unhappy family.

Meg and Charles Wallace are very worried about their father. Before his disappearance, he had been doing top secret work for the government. His last letter home arrived about a year ago, and since then there has been no word of him. The family is afraid that something terrible has happened to him, but they are trying to stay optimistic.

Just recently, three kind but mysterious old women have come into the children's lives. Charles Wallace, who has a special understanding of these women, trusts them to help him and Meg find and rescue their father. Just before this chapter begins, Charles Wallace announces to Meg and Calvin that it is time to go rescue Father. Mrs. Whatsit, Mrs. Who, and Mrs. Which appear, and the story really takes off.

Where has Father gone, and what has happened to him? Will the children be able to rescue him? How will the three old women be able to help? To answer all these questions, you will need to read the entire novel.

## About the Author

Madeleine L'Engle was born in New York City in 1918. Growing up, she worked in the theater and was also a teacher and a librarian for several years. She also taught at the University of Indiana, lectured at Wheaton College in Illinois, and was the writer-in-residence at the Ohio State University and the University of Rochester. In addition to her award-winning novels for young adults, L'Engle has written fiction for adults and young children, plays, poetry, and nonfiction.

L'Engle's books are popular with young adults because they are creative, original, and optimistic. They are often fantasies that let readers visit strange places and meet extraordinary characters. Her characters successfully face frightening situations that require courage and cleverness, proving that everyone's life has meaning and that each of us can make a difference in the world.

*A Wrinkle in Time* has won numerous awards, including the Newbery Medal, the Hans Christian Andersen runner-up award, and the Lewis Carroll Shelf Award. The Murrys and Calvin O'Keefe are featured again in a few of L'Engle's other books, such as *A Wind in the Door* and *A Swiftly Tilting Planet*. L'Engle has won awards for some of her other novels, including *A Ring of Endless Light* and *The Young Unicorns*.

# About the Lessons

The lessons that follow this chapter from *A Wrinkle in Time* focus on the kind of writing called *fantasy*. Fantasy stories usually contain events that couldn't happen and creatures that don't exist in the real world. Some fantasies take place in realistic settings, but others take place in settings where the normal rules of life don't apply. For example, characters may find themselves in places where people can fly, or where instead of aging, people get younger with each passing day. To get the most enjoyment out of a fantasy, readers must forget for a while what is real and open themselves up to a whole new world of possibilities.

# Writing: Picturing Another World

To write a fantasy story, you have to leave the normal world behind and picture a new world with its own rules. Fantasy writers must be able to use their imaginations, but they also must be able to use their understanding of people in order to make their fantasy characters believable. In this unit, you will write your own fantasy story. As you learn more about the techniques a writer uses to create a fantasy, you will have a chance to try them for yourself. The suggestions below will help you get started:

- Think about the fantasy stories you have enjoyed in the past. They may be ones you have read or seen on television or at the movies. List the titles of several kinds of fantasies, such as tales about time travel, life on other planets, or characters who can transform themselves into different shapes at will.

- Choose two or three of the fantasies on your list. Draw a cluster map about each one. Surrounding each title or kind of fantasy, write some of the things you like best about it. Focus on its characters, its setting, the fantastic machines or creatures that inhabit its world, and the magic that the story includes.

- Save your list and cluster maps in your writing portfolio. You will use them for ideas later on in the unit.

# Before Reading

The questions below will help you see how author Madeleine L'Engle has developed the setting, characters, and conflicts in the fantasy *A Wrinkle in Time*. As you read the selection, think about the answers to these questions:

- How is the setting of this story different from the real world? What feeling does the setting give you?

- How does the author make the characters believable, even when they are facing incredible events?

- What conflicts do the characters face? Which of those conflicts probably couldn't happen in the real world?

# Vocabulary Tips

This selection uses some words that may be unfamiliar to you but that are important for understanding the story. Below, you will find some of the more difficult words and their definitions, as well as sentences that show how the words are used. Look them over before you begin reading the selection.

**corporeal**     of the body. The Ghost of Christmas Past was a spirit, not a <u>corporeal</u> being.

**ineffable**     impossible to be described in words. He couldn't explain why, but the song had an <u>ineffable</u> sadness that made him start to cry.

**ephemeral**     lasting for a very short time. The rainbow's appearance was <u>ephemeral</u>, so we enjoyed it while we could.

**shimmer**     flicker; shine off and on. The gold threads in her dress <u>shimmered</u> in the candlelight.

**metamorphose**     change from one form to another. In the coming weeks, we will watch the tadpole <u>metamorphose</u> into a frog.

**verbalize**     put into words. The gifted speaker is able to <u>verbalize</u> the hopes and dreams of his fellow citizens.

**incomprehensible**     not able to be understood. It is <u>incomprehensible</u> to me how you can eat two pieces of pie after that huge meal.

**bliss**     joy; peaceful happiness. Many religions teach that after death we will find eternal <u>bliss</u>.

**obscure**     hide from view. The famous actor put up a tall fence to <u>obscure</u> his yard from tourists and photographers.

# A Wrinkle in Time

Madeleine L'Engle

## The Black Thing

The trees were lashed into a violent frenzy. Meg screamed and clutched at Calvin, and Mrs. Which's authoritative voice called out, "Qquiett, chilldd!"

Did a shadow fall across the moon or did the moon simply go out, extinguished as abruptly and completely as a candle? There was still the sound of leaves, a terrified, terrifying rushing. All light was gone. Darkness was complete. Suddenly the wind was gone, and all sound. Meg felt that Calvin was being torn from her. When she reached for him her fingers touched nothing.

She screamed out, "Charles!" and whether it was to help him or for him to help her, she did not know. The word was flung back down her throat, and she choked on it.

She was completely alone.

She had lost the protection of Calvin's hand. Charles was nowhere, either to save or to turn to. She was alone in a fragment of nothingness. No light, no sound, no feeling. Where was her body? She tried to move in her panic, but there was nothing to move. Just as light and sound had vanished, she was gone too. The corporeal Meg simply was not.

Then she felt her limbs again. Her legs and arms were tingling faintly, as though they had been asleep. She blinked her eyes rapidly, but though she herself was somehow back, nothing else was. It was not as simple as darkness or absence of light. Darkness has a tangible quality; it can be moved through and felt; in darkness you can bark your shins. The world of things still exists around you. She was lost in a horrifying void.

It was the same way with the silence. This was more than silence. A deaf person can feel vibrations. Here there was nothing to feel.

Suddenly she was aware of her heart beating rapidly within the cage of her ribs. Had it stopped before? What had made it start again? The tingling in her arms and legs grew stronger, and suddenly she felt movement. This movement, she felt, must be the turning of the earth, rotating on its axis, traveling its elliptic course about the sun. And this feeling of moving with the earth was somewhat like the feeling of being in the ocean, out in the ocean beyond this rising and falling of the breakers, lying on the moving water, pulsing gently with the swells, and feeling the gentle, inexorable tug of the moon.

I am asleep. I am dreaming, she thought. I'm having a nightmare. I want to wake up. Let me wake up.

"Well!" Charles Wallace's voice said. "That was quite a trip! I do think you might have warned us."

Light began to pulse and quiver. Meg blinked and shoved shakily at her glasses, and there was Charles Wallace standing indignantly in front of her, his hands on his hips. "Meg!" he shouted. "Calvin! Where are you?"

She saw Charles, she heard him, but she could not go to him. She could not shove through the strange, trembling light to meet him.

Calvin's voice came as though it were pushing through a cloud. "Well, just give me time, will you? I'm older than you are."

Meg gasped. It wasn't that Calvin wasn't there and then that he was. It wasn't that part of him came first and then the rest of him followed, like a hand, and then an arm, an eye, and then a nose. It was a sort of shimmering, a looking at Calvin through water, through smoke, through fire, and then there he was, solid and reassuring.

"Meg!" Charles Wallace's voice came. "Meg! Calvin, where's Meg?"

"I'm right here," she tried to say, but her voice seemed to be caught at its source.

"Meg!" Calvin cried and he turned around, looking about wildly.

"Mrs. Which, you haven't left Meg be*hind*, have you?" Charles Wallace shouted.

"If you've hurt Meg, any of you—" Calvin started, but suddenly Meg felt a violent push and a shattering as though she had been thrust through a wall of glass.

"Oh, *there* you are!" Charles Wallace said and rushed over to her and hugged her.

"But *where* am I?" Meg asked breathlessly, relieved to hear that her voice was now coming out of her in more or less a normal way.

She looked around rather wildly. They were standing in a sunlit field, and the air about them was moving with the delicious fragrance that comes only on the rarest of spring days when the sun's touch is gentle, and the apple blossoms are just beginning to unfold. She pushed her glasses up on her nose to reassure herself that what she was seeing was real.

They had left the silver glint of a biting autumn evening, and now around them everything was golden with light. The grasses of the field were a tender new green and scattered about were tiny, multicolored flowers. Meg turned slowly to face a mountain reaching so high into the sky that its peak was lost in a crown of puffy white clouds. From the trees at the base of the mountain came a sudden singing of birds. There was an air of such ineffable peace and joy all around her that her heart's wild thumping slowed.

*When shall we three meet again,*
*In thunder, lightning, or in rain,*

came Mrs. Who's voice. Suddenly the three of them were there: Mrs. Whatsit with her pink stole askew; Mrs. Who with her spectacles gleaming; and Mrs. Which still little more than a shimmer. Delicate, multicolored butterflies were fluttering about them, as though in greeting.

Mrs. Whatsit and Mrs. Who began to giggle and they giggled until it seemed that, whatever their private joke was, they would fall down with the wild fun of it. The shimmer seemed to be laughing too. It became vaguely darker and more solid, and then there appeared a figure in a black robe and a black peaked hat, beady eyes, a beaked nose, and long gray hair. One bony claw clutched a broomstick.

"Wwell, jusstt ttoo kkeepp yyou girrlls happpy," the strange voice said, and Mrs. Whatsit and Mrs. Who fell into each other's arms in gales of laughter.

"If you ladies have had your fun, I think you should tell Calvin and Meg a little more about all this," Charles Wallace said coldly. "You scared Meg half out of her wits, whisking her off this way without any warning."

"*Finxerunt animi, raro et perpauca loquentis,*" Mrs. Who intoned. "Horace. *To action little, less to words inclined.*"

"Mrs. Who, I wish you'd stop quoting!" Charles Wallace sounded very annoyed.

Mrs. Whatsit adjusted her stole. "But she finds it so difficult to verbalize, Charles dear. It helps her if she can quote instead of working out words of her own."

"Anndd wee mussttn'tt looose ourr sensses of hummorr," Mrs. Which said. "Thee onnlly wway ttoo ccope withh ssometthingg ddeadly sseriouss iss ttoo ttry ttoo trreatt itt a llittlle lligghtly."

"But that's going to be hard for Meg," Mrs. Whatsit said. "It's going to be hard for her to realize that we *are* serious."

"What about me?" Calvin asked.

"The life of your father isn't at stake," Mrs. Whatsit told him.

"What about Charles Wallace then?"

Mrs. Whatsit's unoiled-door-hinge voice was warm with affection and pride. "Charles Wallace knows. Charles Wallace knows that it's far more than just the life of his father. Charles Wallace knows what's at stake."

"Remember," Mrs. Who said "Αεηπου οὐδὲν, πὰντα δ' εηπίζειν χρεωτ. .Euripides. *Nothing is hopeless; we must hope for everything.*"

"Where are we now, and how did we get here?" Calvin asked.

"Uriel, the third planet of the star Malak in the spiral nebula Messier 101."

"This I'm supposed to believe?" Calvin asked indignantly.

"Aas yyou llike," Mrs. Which said coldly.

For some reason Meg felt that Mrs. Which, despite her looks and ephemeral broomstick, was someone in whom one could put complete trust. "It doesn't seem any more peculiar than anything else that's happened."

"Well, then, someone just tell me how we got here!" Calvin's voice was still angry and his freckles seemed to stand out on his face. "Even traveling at the speed of light, it would take us years and years to get here."

"Oh, we don't travel at the speed of *anything*," Mrs. Whatsit explained earnestly. "We *tesser*. Or you might say, we *wrinkle*."

"Clear as mud," Calvin said.

Tesser, Meg thought. Could that have anything to do with Mother's tesseract?

She was about to ask when Mrs. Which started to speak, and one did not interrupt when Mrs. Which was speaking. "Mrs. Whatsitt iss yyoungg andd nnaïve."

"She keeps thinking she can explain things in words," Mrs. Who said. "*Qui plus sali, plus se tait.* French, you know. *The more a man knows, the less he talks.*"

"But she has to use words for Meg and Calvin," Charles reminded Mrs. Who. "If you brought them along, they have a right to know what's going on."

Meg went up to Mrs. Which. In the intensity of her question she had forgotten all about the tesseract. "Is my father here?"

Mrs. Which shook her head. "Nnott heeere, Megg. Llett Mrs. Whatsitt expllainn. Shee isss yyoungg annd thee llanguage of worrds iss ccasierr fforr hherr thann itt iss fforr Mrs. Whoo andd mee."

"We stopped here," Mrs. Whatsit explained, "more or less to catch our breaths. And to give you a chance to know what you're up against."

"But what about Father?" Meg asked. "Is he all right?"

"For the moment, love, yes. He's one of the reasons we're here. But you see, he's only one."

"Well, where is he? Please take me to him!"

"We can't, not yet." Charles said. "You have to be patient, Meg."

"But I'm *not* patient!" Meg cried passionately. "I've never been patient!"

Mrs. Who's glasses shone at her gently. "If you want to help your father then you must learn patience. *Vitam impendere vero. To stake one's life for the truth.* That is what we must do."

"That is what your father is doing." Mrs. Whatsit nodded, her voice, like Mrs. Who's, very serious, very solemn. Then she smiled her radiant smile. "Now! Why don't you three children wander around, and Charles can explain things a little. You're perfectly safe on Uriel. That's why we stopped here to rest."

"But aren't you coming with us?" Meg asked fearfully.

There was silence for a moment. Then Mrs. Which raised her authoritative hand. "Sshoww themm," she said to Mrs. Whatsit, and at something in her voice Meg felt prickles of apprehension.

"*Now?*" Mrs. Whatsit asked, her creaky voice rising to a squeak. Whatever it was Mrs. Which wanted them to see, it was something that made Mrs. Whatsit uncomfortable too.

"Nnoww," Mrs. Which said. "Tthey mmay aas welll knoww."

"Should—should I *change?*" Mrs. Whatsit asked.

"Bbetter."

"I hope it won't upset the children too much," Mrs. Whatsit murmured, as though to herself.

"Should I change too?" Mrs. Who asked. "Oh, but I've had *fun* in these clothes. But I'll have to admit Mrs. Whatsit is the best at it. *Das Werk lobt den Meister.* German. *The work proves the craftsman.* Shall I transform now too?"

Mrs. Which shook her head. "Nnott yett. Nnott heere. Yyou mmay wwaitt."

"Now, don't be frightened, loves," Mrs. Whatsit said. Her plump little body began to shimmer, to quiver, to shift. The wild colors of her clothes became muted, whitened. The pudding-bag shape stretched, lengthened, merged. And suddenly before the children was a creature more beautiful than any Meg had even imagined, and the beauty lay in far more than the outward description. Outwardly Mrs. Whatsit was surely no longer a Mrs. Whatsit. She was a marble white body with powerful flanks, something like a horse but at the same time completely unlike a horse, for from the magnificently modeled back sprang a nobly formed torso, arms, and a head resembling a man's, but a man with a perfection of dignity and virtue, an exaltation of joy such as Meg had never before seen. No, she thought, it's not like a Greek centaur. Not in the least.

From the shoulders, slowly a pair of wings unfolded, wings made of rainbows, of light upon water, of poetry.

Calvin fell to his knees.

"No," Mrs. Whatsit said, though her voice was not Mrs. Whatsit's voice. "Not to me, Calvin. Never to me. Stand up."

"'Ccarrry themm," Mrs. Which commanded.

With a gesture both delicate and strong, Mrs. Whatsit knelt in front of the children, stretching her wings wide and holding them steady, but quivering. "Onto my back, now," the new voice said.

The children took hesitant steps toward the beautiful creature.

"But what do we call you now?" Calvin asked.

"Oh, my dears," came the new voice, a rich voice with the warmth of a woodwind, the clarity of a trumpet, the mystery of an English horn. "You can't go on changing my name each time I metamorphose. And I've had such pleasure being Mrs. Whatsit, I think you'd better keep to that." She? he? it? smiled at them, and the radiance of the smile was as tangible as a soft breeze, as directly warming as the rays of the sun.

"Come." Charles Wallace clambered up.

Meg and Calvin followed him, Meg sitting between the two boys. A tremor went through the great wings, and then Mrs. Whatsit lifted, and they were moving through the air.

Meg soon found that there was no need to cling to Charles Wallace or Calvin. The great creature's flight was serenely smooth. The boys were eagerly looking around the landscape.

"Look." Charles Wallace pointed. "The mountains are so tall that you can't see where they end."

Meg looked upwards and indeed the mountains seemed to be reaching into infinity.

They left the fertile fields and flew across a great plateau of granitelike rock shaped into enormous monoliths. These had a definite, rhythmic form, but they were not statues; they were like nothing Meg had ever seen before, and she wondered if they had been made by wind and weather, by the formation of this earth, or if they were a creation of beings like the one on which she rode.

They left the great granite plain and flew over a garden even more beautiful than anything in a dream. In it were gathered many of the creatures like the one Mrs. Whatsit had become, some lying among the flowers, some swimming in a broad, crystal river that flowed through the garden, some flying in what Meg was sure must be a kind of dance, moving in and out above the trees. They were making music, music that came not only from their throats but from the movement of their great wings as well.

"What are they singing?" Meg asked excitedly.

Mrs. Whatsit shook her beautiful head. "It won't go into your words. I can't possibly transfer it to your words. Are you getting any of it, Charles?"

Charles Wallace sat very still on the broad back, on his face an intently listening look, the look he had when he delved into Meg or his mother. "A little. Just a very little. But I think I could get more in time."

"Yes. You could learn it, Charles. But there isn't time. We can only stay here long enough to rest up and make a few preparations."

Meg hardly listened to her. "I want to know what they're saying! I want to know what it means."

"Try, Charles," Mrs. Whatsit urged. "Try to translate. You can let yourself go, now. You don't have to hold back."

"But I can't!" Charles Wallace cried in an anguished voice. "I don't know enough! Not yet!"

"Then try to work with me, and I'll see if I can't verbalize it a little for them."

Charles Wallace got his look of probing, of listening.

*I* know that look! Meg thought suddenly. Now I think I know what it means! Because I've had it myself, sometimes, doing math with Father, when a problem is just about to come clear—

Mrs. Whatsit seemed to be listening to Charles' thoughts. "Well, yes, that's an idea. I can try. Too bad you don't really know it so you can give it to me direct, Charles. It's much more work this way."

"Don't be lazy," Charles said.

Mrs. Whatsit did not take offense. She explained, "Oh, it's my favorite kind of work, Charles. That's why they chose me to go along, even though I'm so much younger. It's my one real talent. But it takes a tremendous amount of energy, and we're going to need every ounce of energy for what's ahead of us. But I'll try. For Calvin and Meg I'll try." She was silent; the great wings almost stopped moving; only a delicate stirring seemed to keep them aloft. "Listen, then," Mrs. Whatsit said. The resonant voice rose and the words seemed to be all around them so that Meg felt that she could almost reach out and touch them:

> *Sing unto the Lord a new song,*
> *and his praise from the end of the earth,*
> *ye that go down to the sea,*
> *and all that is therein;*
> *the isles, and the inhabitants thereof.*
> *Let the wilderness and the cities*
>    *thereof lift their voice;*

*let the inhabitants of the rock sing,*
*let them shout from the top of the mountains.*
*Let them give glory unto the Lord!*

Throughout her entire body, Meg felt a pulse of joy such as she had never known before. Calvin's hand reached out; he did not clasp her hand in his; he moved his fingers so that they were barely touching hers, but joy flowed through them, back and forth between them, around them and about them and inside them.

When Mrs. Whatsit sighed, it seemed completely incomprehensible that through this bliss could come the faintest whisper of doubt.

"We must go now, children." Mrs. Whatsit's voice was deep with sadness, and Meg could not understand. Raising her head, Mrs. Whatsit gave a call that seemed to be a command, and one of the creatures flying above the trees nearest them raised its head to listen, and then flew off and picked three flowers from a tree growing near the river and brought them over. "Each of you take one," Mrs. Whatsit said. "I'll tell you how to use them later."

As Meg took her flower she realized that it was not a single blossom, but hundreds of tiny flowerets forming a kind of hollow bell.

"Where are we going?" Calvin asked.

"Up."

The wings moved steadily, swiftly. The garden was left behind, the stretch of granite, the mighty shapes, and then Mrs. Whatsit was flying upward, climbing steadily up, up. Below them the trees of the mountain dwindled, became sparse, were replaced by bushes and then small, dry grasses, and then vegetation ceased entirely, and there were only rocks, points and peaks of rock, sharp and dangerous. "Hold on tight," Mrs. Whatsit said. "Don't slip."

Meg felt Calvin's arm circle her waist in a secure hold. Still they moved upward.

Now they were in clouds. They could see nothing but drifting whiteness, and the moisture clung to them and condensed in icy droplets. As Meg shivered, Calvin's grip tightened. In front of her, Charles Wallace sat quietly. Once he turned just long enough to give her a swift glance of tenderness and concern. But Meg felt as each moment passed that he was growing farther and farther away, that he was becoming less and less her adored baby brother and more and more one with whatever kind of being Mrs. Whatsit, Mrs. Who, and Mrs. Which in actuality were.

Abruptly they burst out of the clouds into a shaft of light. Below them there were still rocks; above them the rocks continued to reach up into the sky, but now, though it seemed miles upward, Meg could see where the mountain at last came to an end.

Mrs. Whatsit continued to climb, her wings straining a little. Meg felt her heart racing; cold sweat began to gather on her face, and her lips felt as though they were turning blue. She began to gasp.

"All right, children, use your flowers now," Mrs. Whatsit said. "The atmosphere will continue to get thinner from now on. Hold the flowers up to your face and breathe through them, and they will give you enough oxygen. It won't be as much as you're used to, but it will be enough."

Meg had almost forgotten the flowers and was grateful to realize that she was still clasping them, that she hadn't let them fall from her fingers. She pressed her face into the blossoms and breathed deeply.

Calvin still held her with one arm, but he too held the flowers to his face.

Charles Wallace moved the hand with the flowers slowly, almost as though he were in a dream.

Mrs. Whatsit's wings strained against the thinness of the atmosphere. The summit was only a little way above them, and then they were there. Mrs. Whatsit came to rest on a small plateau of smooth silvery rock. There ahead of them was a great white disk.

"One of Uriel's moons," Mrs. Whatsit told them, her mighty voice faintly breathless.

"Oh, it's beautiful!" Meg cried. "It's beautiful!"

The silver light from the enormous moon poured over them, blending with the golden quality of the day, flowing over the children, over Mrs. Whatsit, over the mountain peak.

"Now we will turn around," Mrs. Whatsit said, and at the quality of her voice, Meg was afraid again.

But when they turned she saw nothing. Ahead of them was the thin clear blue of sky; below them the rocks thrusting out of the shifting sea of white clouds.

"Now we will wait," Mrs. Whatsit said, "for sunset and moonset."

Almost as she spoke the light began to deepen, to darken.

"I want to watch the moon set," Charles Wallace said.

"No, child. Do not turn around, any of you. Face out toward the dark. What I have to show you will be more visible then. Look ahead, straight ahead, as far as you can possibly look."

Meg's eyes ached from the strain of looking and seeing nothing. Then, above the clouds that encircled the mountain, she seemed to see a shadow, a faint thing of darkness so far off that she was scarcely sure she was really seeing it.

Charles Wallace said, "What's that?"

"That sort of shadow out there," Calvin gestured. "What is it? I don't like it."

"Watch," Mrs. Whatsit commanded.

It was a shadow, nothing but a shadow. It was not even as tangible as a cloud. Was it cast by something? Or was it a Thing in itself?

The sky darkened. The gold left the light and they were surrounded by blue, blue deepening until where there had been nothing but the evening sky, there was now a faint pulse of star, and then another and another and another. There were more stars than Meg had ever seen before.

"The atmosphere is so thin here," Mrs. Whatsit said as though in answer to her unasked question, "that it does not obscure your vision as it would at home. Now look. Look straight ahead."

Meg looked. The dark shadow was still there. It had not lessened or dispersed with the coming of night. And where the shadow was the stars were not visible.

What could there be about a shadow that was so terrible that she knew that there had never been before or ever would be again, anything that would chill her with a fear that was beyond shuddering, beyond crying or screaming, beyond the possibility of comfort?

Meg's hand holding the blossoms slowly dropped, and it seemed as though a knife gashed through her lungs. She gasped, but there was no air for her to breathe. Darkness glazed her eyes and mind, but as she started to fall into unconsciousness her head dropped down into the flowers, which she was still clutching; and as she inhaled the fragrance of their purity her mind and body revived, and she sat up again.

The shadow was still there, dark and dreadful.

Calvin held her hand strongly in his, but she felt neither strength nor reassurance in his touch. Beside her a tremor went through Charles Wallace, but he sat very still.

He shouldn't be seeing this, Meg thought. This is too

much for so little a boy, no matter how different and extraordinary a little boy.

Calvin turned, rejecting the dark Thing that blotted out the light of the stars. "Make it go away, Mrs. Whatsit," he whispered. "Make it go away. It's evil."

Slowly the great creature turned around so that the shadow was behind them, so that they saw only the stars unobscured, the soft throb of starlight on the mountain, the descending circle of the great moon swiftly slipping over the horizon. Then, without a word from Mrs. Whatsit, they were traveling downward, down, down. When they reached the corona of clouds Mrs. Whatsit said, "You can breathe without the flowers now, my children."

Silence again. Not a word. It was as though the shadow had somehow reached out with its dark power and touched them so that they were incapable of speech. When they got back to the flowery field, bathed now in starlight, and moonlight from another, smaller, yellower, rising moon, a little of the tenseness went out of their bodies, and they realized that the body of the beautiful creature on which they rode had been as rigid as theirs.

With a graceful gesture it dropped to the ground and folded its great wings. Charles Wallace was the first to slide off. "Mrs. Who! Mrs. Which!" he called, and there was an immediate quivering of the air. Mrs. Who's familiar glasses gleamed at them. Mrs. Which appeared too; but as she had told the children, it was difficult for her to materialize completely, and though there was the robe and peaked hat, Meg could look through them to mountain and stars. She slid off Mrs. Whatsit's back and walked, rather unsteadily after the long ride, over to Mrs. Which.

"That dark Thing we saw," she said. "Is that what my father is fighting?"

# Reviewing and Interpreting the Selection

Record your answers to these questions in your personal literature notebook. Follow the directions for each part.

**Reviewing**   Try to complete each of the following sentences without looking back at the selection.

Identifying
Cause and Effect

1. At first, Charles Wallace is angry with Mrs. Whatsit, Mrs. Who, and Mrs. Which because

    a. they have frightened his sister.

    b. they giggle too much.

    c. he is always in a bad mood.

    d. he thinks they are wasting time.

Recognizing
Literary
Elements
(Character)

2. Readers see what is happening in this novel through the eyes of

    a. Mrs. Whatsit.

    b. Meg.

    c. Calvin.

    d. Charles Wallace.

Identifying
Sequence

3. The children first see the shadow, or Thing,

    a. just before sunset.

    b. in the middle of the night.

    c. at sunrise.

    d. just after sunrise.

4. The reason the children have traveled through space and time is

   a. to prove to scientists that it can be done.
   b. because their parents want them to be scientists.
   c. because they are experimenting with time travel.
   d. to find and rescue their father.

5. The children have been taken to the third planet of the star Malak in order to

   a. amuse the three women.
   b. learn how to tesser.
   c. catch their breath and see what they are up against.
   d. become better acquainted with the three women.

**Interpreting** To complete these sentences, you may look back at the story if you'd like.

6. Now that Mrs. Whatsit has shown the children the Thing, she probably will

   a. help them defeat it.
   b. let them figure out how to fight it by themselves.
   c. ask them what to do next.
   d. fly off, never to return.

7. The person who seems to be in charge of
the three women is

   a. Calvin.

   b. Mrs. Whatsit.

   c. Mrs. Who.

   d. Mrs. Which.

8. The mood of this selection can best be
described as

   a. realistic and factual.

   b. strange and magical.

   c. giddy and funny.

   d. sad and lonely.

9. Mrs. Whatsit, Mrs. Who, and Mrs. Which
probably don't show their true forms to the
children while they are still on Earth
because

   a. they don't have the power to change
   while in Earth's atmosphere.

   b. they don't have space enough to spread
   their wings.

   c. their true forms would shock and
   frighten the children if they changed
   there.

   d. they need other, similar creatures
   around to make the change.

10. The three women give the children a
    chance to look at the Thing that they must
    fight because they believe that

    a. "Children should be seen and not heard."

    b. "A long journey begins with a single step."

    c. "The shortest distance between two
       points is a straight line."

    d. "If at first you don't succeed, you should
       try, try again."

Now check your answers with your teacher. Study the questions
you answered incorrectly. What types of questions were they? Talk
with your teacher about ways to work on those skills.

# Fantasy

A fantasy is a story about an impossible set of events that take place in an unbelievable place and involve characters who can do things they could never do in the real world. Probably some of the first stories you were ever read were fantasies. You may remember stories about Peter Rabbit or Ananzi the Spider or the Little Engine That Could. All of those stories contain elements of fantasy.

Fantasies are fun to write and read. The authors of fantasies can let their imaginations run free. They can make the impossible suddenly possible. They can create places that couldn't possibly exist, and they can make them as real as your school or neighborhood. They can make you believe in characters who have incredible powers and abilities.

Readers of fantasies can leave the everyday world behind. If you have had a bad day, you can pick up a fantasy and join a character who is facing even worse problems than yours. And you can be pretty sure that he or she will conquer the problem before the story ends.

In these lessons, you will look at these ways in which author Madeleine L'Engle creates a new world in *A Wrinkle in Time*:

1. She creates a fantastic setting and a special mood.

2. She makes characters and their reactions to impossible events seem realistic and believable.

3. She makes the conflict a battle between the forces of good and evil.

## 1 • Fantasy, Setting, and Mood

When you read a realistic story that is set in a familiar setting, you probably can guess what is likely to happen. Most realistic fiction takes place in settings with which you are at least a little familiar. When you read a fantasy set in an imaginary setting, however, just about anything can happen. In fantasy, even a seemingly normal backyard can become a meeting place for talking frogs or creatures from Mars. In fact, some fantasy writers use familiar settings to emphasize how strange the events of a story really are.

Other fantasies are set in places you will never find on a map. They can be found only in a writer's imagination. The author must describe these strange settings very carefully so you can picture them clearly. In addition to painting a visual picture of the setting, the author must create a feeling or mood to help explain the setting even further. Reading about a place, you may feel tense or peaceful, rushed or lazy, depending on the words the author uses to describe it.

Read the following description of the place where Meg, Charles Wallace, and Calvin are taken at the beginning of the selection. Look for specific words that L'Engle uses to paint a picture of the place in your mind. As you read the passage, also pay attention to the way her description makes you—and the characters—feel.

> They had left the silver glint of a biting autumn evening, and now around them everything was golden with light. The grasses of the field were a tender new green and scattered about were tiny, multicolored flowers. Meg turned slowly to face a mountain reaching so high into the sky that its peak was lost in a crown of puffy white clouds. From the trees at the base of the mountain came a sudden singing of birds. There was an air of such ineffable peace and joy all around her that her heart's wild thumping slowed.

The place the children have been taken to is somewhat like Earth but different from it too. Instead of the cold, fading light of autumn, it is filled with warm, golden light. The flowers all around are multicolored and lovely. The mountain is enormous and the birds are singing joyfully. The mood that this setting creates in the children, and probably in you the reader, is one of happiness and peace, as well as wonder that any place could be so perfect.

## Exercise 1

Read this passage in which Mrs. Whatsit guides the children upward into the desolate and dangerous environment of the Thing. Then use what you have learned in this lesson to answer the questions that follow the passage.

The wings moved steadily, swiftly. The garden was left behind, the stretch of granite, the mighty shapes, and then Mrs. Whatsit was flying upward, climbing steadily up, up. Below them the trees of the mountain dwindled, became sparse, were replaced by bushes and then small, dry grasses, and then vegetation ceased entirely, and there were only rocks, points and peaks of rock, sharp and dangerous. "Hold on tight," Mrs. Whatsit said. "Don't slip."

Meg felt Calvin's arm circle her waist in a secure hold.

Still they moved upward.

Now they were in clouds. They could see nothing but drifting whiteness, and the moisture clung to them and condensed in icy droplets. As Meg shivered, Calvin's grip tightened. . . .

Abruptly they burst out of the clouds into a shaft of light. Below them there were still rocks; above them the rocks continued to reach up into the sky, but now, though it seemed miles upward, Meg could see where the mountain at last came to an end.

1. How is this setting different from the setting described earlier in this lesson? Which details help create the mood?

2. Describe the reaction of the characters to this new situation. What would your feelings be if you found yourself in this setting?

Now check your answers with your teacher. Review this part of the lesson if you don't understand why an answer was incorrect.

## Writing on Your Own 1

In this exercise you will use what you have learned in this lesson to write a setting that creates a particular mood. Follow these steps:

- Review your notes for Picturing Another World on page 261. Choose a setting that you feel you could describe well. Just as the author of *A Wrinkle in Time* did, make the setting similar to Earth in some ways but different in other ways. Make some notes about what you could see, hear, smell, taste, and feel in your chosen setting.

- Think about the mood that your chosen setting would create in someone who was there. Decide on the mood you want to create in your readers. Do you want them to be frightened? Do you want them to feel peaceful or angry? Circle the details in your notes that would help you create the mood. Add more details as you think of them.

- Now write a description of the setting, using the notes you have made. Reread it a few times and add any details that you feel would make the mood clearer. Be sure that the setting is different in at least one way from normal, everyday places that you might see on Earth.

## 2 • Fantasy and Characters

As people get older, it becomes harder and harder for some of them to free their imaginations. They begin to say, "That's just silly. It couldn't really happen." They start to lose their ability to have fun with ideas that are not logical and sensible.

Writers of fantasy understand that readers must be pulled into the magic slowly. To help readers enter a fantasy world, they provide guides in the form of the story's characters. Like us, the characters often can't believe what is happening to them. They sometimes feel frightened, angry, or helpless in the face of such strange happenings.

Read the following passage from *A Wrinkle in Time* to see how Calvin reacts to the sudden change of location from Earth to an unknown land. Do you think you would react in the same way Calvin does?

"Where are we now, and how did we get here?" Calvin asked.

"Uriel, the third planet of the star Malak in the spiral nebula Messier 101."

"This I'm supposed to believe?" Calvin asked indignantly.

"Aas yyou llike," Mrs. Which said coldly.

For some reason Meg felt that Mrs. Which, despite her looks and ephemeral broomstick, was someone in whom one could put complete trust. "It doesn't seem any more peculiar than anything else that's happened."

"Well, then, someone just tell me how we got here!" Calvin's voice was still angry and his freckles seemed to stand out on his face. "Even traveling at the speed of light, it would take us years and years to get here."

"Oh, we don't travel at the speed of *anything*," Mrs. Whatsit explained earnestly. "We *tesser*. Or you might say, we *wrinkle*."

"Clear as mud," Calvin said.

Calvin speaks for most readers when he expresses his confusion, frustration, and anger. By showing us Calvin's feelings, the author helps readers identify with him and feel what he is feeling. Readers agree with Calvin and are waiting to have someone persuade them to go further into the story. Only if the author is successful in winning over the doubting Calvin can we readers be won over too. Luckily, the author has complete control over Calvin's reaction, and soon he will understand his situation, helping us all become believers.

## Exercise 2

Read the following passage, which details how frightened Meg becomes. Then use what you have learned in this lesson to answer the questions that follow the passage.

She screamed out, "Charles!" and whether it was to help him or for him to help her, she did not know. The word was flung back down her throat, and she choked on it.

She was completely alone.

She had lost the protection of Calvin's hand. Charles was nowhere, either to save or to turn to. She was alone in a fragment of nothingness. No light, no sound, no feeling. Where was her body? She tried to move in her panic, but there was nothing to move. Just as light and sound had vanished, she was gone too. The corporeal Meg simply was not. . . .

Suddenly she was aware of her heart beating rapidly within the cage of her ribs. Had it stopped before? What had made it start again? The tingling in her arms and legs grew stronger, and suddenly she felt movement. This movement, she felt, must be the turning of the earth, rotating on its axis, traveling its elliptic course about the sun. And this feeling of moving with the earth was somewhat like the feeling of being in the ocean, out in the ocean beyond this rising and falling of the breakers, lying on the moving water, pulsing gently with the swells, and feeling the gentle, inexorable tug of the moon.

I am asleep. I am dreaming, she thought. I'm having a nightmare. I want to wake up. Let me wake up.

1. What details show that the experience is upsetting to Meg? How is her body reacting to the excitement? Is that a believable reaction?

2. Meg decides that she must be dreaming, and she wants desperately to wake up from her nightmare. Which of the experiences that Meg goes through remind you of a nightmare? Which would you personally find hardest to take? How might your reactions compare with Meg's?

Now check your answers with your teacher. Review this part of the lesson if you don't understand why an answer was incorrect.

## Writing on Your Own 2

In this exercise you will use what you have learned in the lesson to describe a character and his or her reaction to a problem. Follow these steps:

• Review the description of a setting that you wrote for the previous writing exercise. Try to picture a character who might find himself or herself in that place. Write a few notes about the character's age, appearance, and personality.

- Think about the kinds of problems that the main character might encounter in your chosen setting. For example, if the setting is another planet, could there be a conflict between the creatures who live there and the character who has just arrived? Jot down ideas about a conflict that the character might face.

- Now write a paragraph in which your character reacts to his or her problems. Is the character nervous or frightened? Is he or she excited and happy? Write the paragraph from the first-person point of view, using the pronouns *I* and *me*. Make the character's reactions realistic and believable.

## 3 • Fantasy and Good vs. Evil

Think back to some of the best fantasies you have ever read or seen. In many of them, characters who are ordinary people are presented with huge and unusual tasks. For example, in the movie *Star Wars,* a few brave but ordinary characters must fight an evil empire determined to rule the universe. In *The Wizard of Oz,* four simple characters must outwit a wicked witch who wants to destroy them and maintain control over innocent creatures. Even in fantasy computer games, it is often the player's job to make sure the world isn't destroyed by evil invaders.

It is common for the characters in fantasies to take on seemingly impossible tasks. They often find themselves on the side of good, protecting the world from evil forces. Read the following passage from *A Wrinkle in Time* to see how the author introduces this classic confrontation.

"Anndd wee mussttn'tt looose ourr sensses of hummorr," Mrs. Which said. "Thee onnlly wway ttoo ccope withh ssometthingg ddeadly sseriouss iss ttoo ttry ttoo trreatt itt a llittllee lligghtly."

"But that's going to be hard for Meg," Mrs. Whatsit said. "It's going to be hard for her to realize that we *are* serious."

"What about me?" Calvin asked.

"The life of your father isn't at stake," Mrs. Whatsit told him.

"What about Charles Wallace, then?"

Mrs. Whatsit's unoiled-door-hinge voice was warm with affection and pride. "Charles Wallace knows. Charles Wallace knows that it's far more than just the life of his father. Charles Wallace knows what's at stake."

Although she doesn't explain exactly why, Mrs. Whatsit suggests that the fate of Meg and Charles Wallace's father is linked to a much more dangerous and terrifying problem. That problem will affect many more people than just the Murry family. Readers get the feeling in this passage that they need to know more about why Mrs. Whatsit, Mrs. Who, and Mrs. Which have become involved in rescuing Dr. Murry. What evil force must be conquered? What force is so strong that it can kidnap a man and hold him away from his family? What force is so dangerous that supernatural beings must ask ordinary humans for help in fighting it?

Up until this point, we readers have been concerned about the Murry family, but now we are concerned about everyone on Earth. Finding a solution to the problem has become absolutely necessary.

## Exercise 3

Read this passage, which describes the children's reactions to the dark Thing. Then use what you have learned in this lesson to answer the questions that follow the passage.

Meg looked. The dark shadow was still there. It had not lessened or dispersed with the coming of night. And where the shadow was the stars were not visible.

What could there be about a shadow that was so terrible that she knew that there had never been before or ever would be again, anything that would chill her with a fear that was beyond shuddering, beyond crying or screaming, beyond the possibility of comfort? . . .

Calvin turned, rejecting the dark Thing that blotted out the light of the stars. "Make it go away, Mrs. Whatsit," he whispered. "Make it go away. It's evil."

Slowly the great creature turned around so that the shadow was behind them, so that they saw only the stars unobscured, the soft throb of starlight on the mountain, the descending circle of the great moon swiftly slipping over the horizon.

1. How does Meg feel about the dark Thing? At this point, who do you think Meg believes would win the fight if she had to battle the Thing? Find evidence for your answer.

2. Does Calvin seem eager to confront the Thing? If later in the novel Calvin does find the courage to face it, what does that tell you about Calvin's personality and the importance of winning the battle?

Now check your answers with your teacher. Review this part of the lesson if you don't understand why an answer was incorrect.

## Writing on Your Own 3

In this exercise you will write a paragraph explaining why your characters must face a conflict between good and evil. Follow these steps:

- Review the conflict you wrote about in Writing on Your Own 2. How can you change or add to the conflict to make it into a battle between good and evil? For example, if the creatures on another planet are warlike, must they be stopped before they attack Earth? Write a paragraph explaining why the conflict your characters must face is between the forces of good and evil. Explain why it is important that the good forces win, that is, tell what would happen if evil forces won.

- Reread your paragraph. Have you shown why the outcome of the conflict is crucial? Have you shown who will suffer if the evil forces win? Add more details if you need to.

# Discussion Guides

1. Imagine that you could read the mind of the Black Thing. What thoughts might fill its evil mind? Work with a partner to write what it is saying to itself as it stares at Meg, Charles Wallace, Calvin, and Mrs. Whatsit. Practice your speech and then present it to the class.

2. Do you enjoy reading fantasy stories? With a small group of classmates, talk about what you like and don't like about this kind of writing. Have one person in the group make two lists: one that gives everyone's reasons for liking fantasy and one that gives everyone's reasons for disliking it. Share your lists with the entire class, and then take a vote on which type of writing everyone likes better—fantasy or realistic fiction.

3. Throughout the chapter, Mrs. Who quotes several famous sayings from around the world. With a partner, do some research on Horace and Euripedes, the two writers she mentions. Have they given us any other memorable quotes? Summarize what you find out, and present it to the rest of the class.

# Write a Fantasy

You have been working on a fantasy throughout this unit. Now is the time to write the entire story.

If you have any questions about the writing process, refer to Using the Writing Process, beginning on page 295.

- Review the list and cluster maps that you made for Picturing Another World at the beginning of the unit. These notes will remind you of what you particularly like about fantasies, so you can include some of those ideas in your own writing.

- Assemble the writing you did for each Writing on Your Own exercise. You should have three pieces of writing: *a*) a description of a fantastic setting that creates a particular mood; *b*) a description of a character and a paragraph showing how the character reacts to conflict, and *c*) a paragraph explaining how a particular conflict can be thought of as a battle between the forces of good and evil. Reread these pieces now to get ideas for the story you are about to write.

- Decide how you will narrate your fantasy story. Will you tell it in the first person, using the pronouns *I* and *me*? Will you tell it in the third person, using the pronouns *he, she,* and *they*?

- Make a list of the events in your story. Arrange them in the correct time order. Refer to this list as you write your story.

- Write your fantasy, using your previous writing exercises for ideas. Be sure that the setting, the characters, and the conflict all set this story apart as a fantasy.

- Proofread your story for errors in grammar, spelling, capitalization, and punctuation. Read your story aloud to a small group of classmates. Listen while the others read their stories aloud too. Then make a clean, final copy to share in a class book or to keep in your writing portfolio.

# Using the Writing Process

*This reference section explains the major steps in the writing process. It will help you complete the writing exercises in this book. Read the information carefully so you can understand the process thoroughly. Whenever you need a quick review of important things to think about when you write, refer to the handy checklist on page 301.*

Most tasks worth doing have several steps. For example, houses can be built only after the builder follows a number of complicated, logical steps. Moviemakers must go through a series of steps before releasing a film. Even a task as simple as making a peanut butter and jelly sandwich requires that the sandwich maker perform specific steps in order. So it should be no surprise that anyone who wants to write a good story, play, poem, report, or article must follow certain steps too. Taken together, the steps a writer follows are called the *writing process*.

The writing process is divided into three main stages: prewriting, writing, and revising. Each stage is important for good writing.

## Stage 1: Prewriting

Prewriting consists of all the preparation you do before you put a single word down on paper. There are many decisions that you must make in order to make your writing as interesting, logical, and easy to read as possible. Here are the steps you should take before you begin to write:

1. **Decide on your audience**. Who will read your writing? Will your audience be your teacher? Will it be readers of the school newspaper? Or will your audience be yourself or your friends? Your writing will change, depending on who you think your audience will be.

2. **Decide on your purpose**. Why are you writing? Do you want to teach your audience something? Do you want to entertain? Do you want to change someone's mind about an issue? Think about your purpose before you begin to write.

3. **Think about possible topics.** What are some topics that interest you? Make a list of topics that you are familiar with and might like to write about. Make another list of topics that interest you and that you want to learn about.

   One technique that helps some writers at this stage is *brainstorming*. When you brainstorm, you let your mind wander freely. Without judging your ideas first, scribble them down as they come to you—even if they seem silly or far-fetched. Good ideas often develop from unusual thoughts.

   If you're having trouble coming up with ideas by yourself, brainstorm with a partner or a group of classmates. Jot down everyone's ideas as they say them. Brainstorming alone or with others should give you a long list of possible writing topics.

4. **Choose and narrow your topic**. Once you have chosen a topic, it is impossible to cover every aspect of that topic in one piece of writing. Say, for example, you have chosen to write about the possibility of life on other planets. In a single piece of writing, you could not possibly include everything that has been researched about extraterrestrial life. Therefore you must choose one or two aspects to focus on, such as alleged sightings in the United States or worldwide organizations that study extraterrestrial life. Otherwise you might overload your writing with too many ideas. Concentrate on telling about a few things thoroughly and well.

5. **Research your topic**. You probably have had experience using an encyclopedia, the library, or the Internet to look up information for factual reports. But even when you write fictional stories, you often need to do some research. In a story set

during the Civil War, for example, your characters wouldn't use pocket cameras or wear suits of armor. In order to make your story as accurate and believable as possible, you would have to research how Americans lived and dressed during the years of the Civil War.

To conduct your research, you may want to use books, magazines, newspapers, encyclopedias, or electronic sources such as the Internet. Some topics may require you to interview knowledgeable people. For realistic stories set in the present time, you may find that the best research is simple observation of everyday life. Thorough research will help ensure that your facts and details are accurate.

6. **Organize your research.** Now you have the facts, ideas, and details you need to write. How will you arrange them? Which order will you choose? No matter what you are writing, it is always helpful to begin with a written plan. If you are writing a story, you probably will tell it in time order. Make a list of the major story events, arranged from first to last.

Arranging details in time order is not the only way to organize information, however. Some writers start by making *lists* (informal outlines) of the facts and ideas they have gathered. Then they rearrange the items on their lists until they have the order that will work well in their writing.

Other writers make formal *outlines*, designating the most important ideas with roman numerals (I, II, III, IV, and so on) and related details with letters and numerals (A, B, C; 1, 2, 3; a, b, c; and so on). An outline is a more formal version of a list, and like a list, the items in an outline can be rearranged until you decide on a logical order. Both outlines and lists help you organize and group your ideas.

*Mapping* or *clustering* is another helpful technique used by many writers. With this method, you write your main idea in the center and then surround it with facts and ideas connected to that idea. Here is an example of a cluster map:

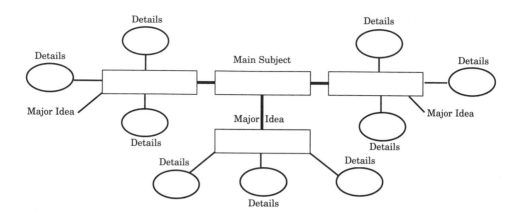

## Stage 2: Writing

1. **Get started.** Begin your writing with an introductory sentence or paragraph. A good introduction can become a guide for the rest of your piece. For ideas on good opening sentences, take a look at some of your favorite stories or magazine articles.

   Your introduction should give your audience a hint about what is coming next. If you are writing a story, your introduction should set the tone and mood. It should reveal the narrator's point of view; and it may introduce the main characters, the setting, and your purpose for writing. Do the best you can with your introduction, but remember that if you wish to, you can always change it later.

2. **Keep writing.** Get your thoughts down as quickly as possible, referring to your prewriting notes to keep you on track. Later, when you are done with this *rough draft*, you will have a chance to revise and polish your work to make it as clear and accurate as possible. For right now, however, don't stop for spelling, grammar, or exact wording problems. Come as close as you can to what you want to say, but don't let yourself get bogged down in details.

## Stage 3: Revising

Now you're ready to revise your work. Careful revision includes editing and reorganizing that can make a big difference in the final product. You may wish to get feedback from your classmates or your teacher about how to revise your work.

1. **Revise and edit your work**. When you are revising and editing, ask yourself these questions:
   - **Did I follow my prewriting plan?** Reread your entire first draft. Compare it to your original plan. Did you skip anything important? If you added an idea, did it work logically with the rest of your plan? Even if you decide that your prewriting plan is no longer what you want, it may include ideas you don't want to lose.
   - **Is my writing clear and logical?** Does one idea follow the other in a sensible order? Do you want to change the order or add ideas to make the organization clearer?
   - **Is my language clear and interesting?** Have you chosen exact verbs, nouns, and adjectives? For example, have you used forms of the verb *to be* (*is, are, being, become*) more often than you should? If so, replace them, or change your sentence to make them unnecessary. Include precise action words such as *raced, hiked, zoomed,* and *hurried* in place of the overused verb *went.* Instead of using vague nouns such as *water* and *green,* choose exact ones such as *pond* or *cascade* and *lime.* Replace common adjectives such as *beautiful* and *nice* with precise ones such as *elegant, gorgeous,* and *lovely.*
   - **Is my writing clear and to the point?** Take out words that repeat the same ideas. For example, don't use both *liberty* and *freedom.* These words are synonyms. Choose one word or the other.

2. **Proofread for errors in spelling, grammar, capitalization, and punctuation**. Anyone reading your writing will notice such errors immediately. These errors can confuse your readers or make them lose interest in what they are reading.

   If you are in doubt about the spelling of a word, look it up or ask someone for help. If you are unsure about your grammar, read your writing aloud and listen carefully. Does anything sound wrong? Check with a friend or classmate if you need a second opinion, or refer to a grammar handbook.

Make sure every group of words is a complete sentence. Are any of your sentences run-ons? Do proper nouns begin with capital letters? Is the first word of every sentence capitalized? Do all your sentences have the correct end marks? Should you add any other punctuation to your writing to make your ideas even clearer? If your writing includes dialogue, have you used quotation marks correctly?

3. **Make a clean final draft to share.** After you are satisfied with your writing, it is time to share it with your audience. If you are lucky enough to be composing on a computer, you can print out a final copy easily, after running a spell-check. If you are writing your final draft by hand, make sure your handwriting is clear and easy to read. Leave margins on either side of the page. You may want to skip every other line. Make your writing look inviting to your readers. After all, you put a lot of work into this piece. It's important that someone read and enjoy it.

# A Writing Checklist

*Ask yourself these questions before beginning a writing assignment:*

- Have I chosen a topic that is both interesting and manageable? Should I narrow it so I can cover it in the space that I have?

- Do I have a clear prewriting plan?

- What should I do to gather my facts and ideas? Read? Interview? Observe?

- How will I organize my ideas? A list? An outline? A cluster map?

- Do I have an opening sentence or paragraph that will pull my readers in?

- Do I need to add more information? Switch the order of paragraphs? Take out unnecessary information?

*Ask yourself these questions after completing a writing assignment:*

- Did I use my prewriting plan?

- Is the organization of my writing clear? Should I move, add, or delete any paragraphs or sentences to make the ideas flow more logically?

- Do all the sentences in one paragraph relate to one idea?

- Have I used active, precise words? Is my language interesting? Do the words say what I mean to say?

- Is the spelling correct?

- Have I used correct grammar, capitalization, and punctuation?

- Is my final draft legible, clean, and attractive?